SingaporeCinema

The publisher acknowledges the generous support of the
Singapore Film Commission without which the publication
of this book would not have been possible.

First published in 2006 by Editions Didier Millet Pte Ltd
121 Telok Ayer Street #03-01
Singapore 068590

www.edmbooks.com

Editorial Director: **Timothy Auger**
Editors: **Christopher Khoo, Carol Kraal, Ong Suet Yen**
Designer: **Pascal Chan**
Production Manager: **Sin Kam Cheong**
Colour separation by Pica Digital, Singapore

Printed and bound by Star Standard, Singapore.

ISBN: 981-4155-42-X

SingaporeCinema

Raphaël Millet

Editions Didier Millet

Singapore • Paris • Kuala Lumpur • Bali

CONTENTS

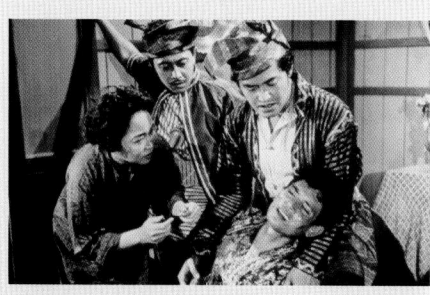

Inconsistencies in the spelling of names and titles may be the result of regional spelling differences, transliterations, language reforms or simply typographical errors in the original reference material.

FOREWORD

In 1902, Singapore had its first public film screening. Organised by a travelling showman, an open area in the city was turned into an outdoor theatre. Such was the humble beginning of the Singapore film industry. A century has since passed, and it is timely to capture the significant milestones in our film history.

Singapore Cinema is therefore a worthy effort and it should serve as an important chronicle of the history and development of our film industry. It is my hope to see Singapore's new generation of filmmakers draw strength and inspiration from our heritage of filmmaking and the industry's recent successes in international markets and film festivals.

2005 has been a remarkable year for the Singapore film industry. Local films like *Be With Me* and *The Maid* were not only box-office successes; these films were also screened globally, picking up international accolades, and touring the global film festival circuit.

These achievements are both inspiring and heartening for my colleagues and I at the Singapore Film Commission (SFC). We will continue to help develop the vibrant film industry in Singapore and profile Singapore in the international film arena.

The big screen and the medium of moving images remain one of the most powerful tools to tell a story. I am confident *Singapore Cinema* will be able to bring to life the compelling and colourful history of our nation's show business.

Jennie Chua
Chairman
Singapore Film Commission
April 2006

ACKNOWLEDGEMENTS

I would like to express my gratitude to all who have, in one way or other, helped me to produce this book, from providing me with information, sharing their views on the topic, opening up their archives, to giving me moral or financial support.

First of all, Shirlene Noordin, for being my partner (in crime), and in watching many Malay movies. And also my good friends Yvonne and Jan Uhde, who wrote the first comprehensive book on Singapore cinema, *Latent Images*, which I am deeply indebted to; Tony Yeow, whose passion for filmmaking still burns bright even though he has undergone much hardship because of it; Peter Chong, for lending me some of his personal photos and for being my favourite Singaporean cult movie icon; Choo Meileen, for granting me access to Cathay's archives, and Lui Oi Leng, for her great help; Seow Sher Yen and Chu Chi Wang; Tania Sng, for her kindness; Dato L. Krishnan, for his massive contribution to the Singapore film industry; Maria Menado, for her availability and everlasting elegance.

I would also like to thank Philip Cheah and Teo Swee Leng for sharing their numerous contacts and materials as well as their belief in cinema; Richard Lim, who put me in touch with Tony Yeow, and has been a good friend right from the beginning of my sojourn in Singapore; Gerrie Lim, whose books are more fun than mine; Ben Slater, Stephen Cremin and Lorenzo Codelli, for sharing my passion for films; Bertrand Lee, for believing so strongly in cinema and life; Djinn, for his youthful energy against all odds; Wee Li Lin; Zilah Abdullah; Zaedi Zolkafli, who is so passionate about P. Ramlee; Ho Tzu Nyen, for knowing more about Michel Foucault than I will ever do; Wong Han Min; Ow Yong Mun; Daniel Yun, for his courtesy; Jeremy Segay, for helping me to screen Singapore films in Paris; Rosnani and Jamil Sulong, for making me drive so far, all the way to Pahang to find them; Christopher Shaw, for generously opening up the Shaw family archives; Clarence Anthony, for showing me his amazing collection of movie magazines; Doris Young, for granting me access to the secret life of "Cleopatra Wong" and being my favourite booted queen.

Raphaël Millet

PRE**FACE**

Sang Nila Utama saw a lion when he arrived in Singapore. I saw a movie.

Before stepping foot on the island, all I knew of cinema in the city was limited to one or two movies seen at festival screenings. I had also seen *They Call Her... Cleopatra Wong* ages ago, but never knew it was partly a Singaporean production.

For a film buff who is also a film critic-cum-film teacher like me with a strong interest in movies from all over the world, this was a very limited acquaintance with Singapore cinema. Far too limited for my own taste.

So when I arrived in Singapore in March 2002, one of the first things I did was to watch a local movie. Jack Neo's *I Not Stupid* was still playing in cinemas, and I managed to catch one of the last few screenings. The movie was rather funny, although surely half the jokes went over my head. It was also very moving. I saw it as an excellent introduction to Singapore culture, as movies often say something about local situations and times. And, contrary to what most of my Singaporean friends presumed, I did not find the movie so local as to be incomprehensible.

It also had me thinking that there must be more to the Singapore film industry. With my insatiable curiosity for films, I began researching the Singapore film industry. Did I have to dig deep and hard!

Delving into the past, I learnt about the "pontianak" and "oily man", and encountered many interesting people, including old movie directors believed by quite a few to be long dead. I drove all the way to Kuala Lumpur and other parts of Malaysia many times, visiting some of the forgotten movie stars of yesteryear.

I survived coffee with an intimidating martial arts master, afternoon tea with a retired action lady, and monologues from a famously infamous local film critic-cum-director. All in all, I viewed more than 180 feature films, dating from the early days of Singapore's film industry right up to the revival era. I also watched many of the short films made by the young filmmakers of the 1990s.

The effort was well worth it. The movies, even the not-so-good ones, were enjoyable. And I learnt much about Singapore. They gave me a clearer idea of what Singapore was like in the past, in the 1940s, the 1950s, and in fact every decade up to the 1990s.

I have seen Beach Road when it was actually by the beach, Clementi when it was just a *kampong* or village, Pasir Ris when it was still mostly mangrove, and Shenton Way under construction.

I now have a better understanding of the Singaporean psyche and identity (or, at least, that is what my friends would have me believe). The films painted a fairly comprehensive portrait of Singapore and helped me to a greater appreciation of this nation. Somehow.

My research yielded a treasure trove of cinematic gems, both old and new. Believe me, there are not many such lost film treasures in the world. Singapore's heritage first of all includes

Huang Po Ju, Shawn Lee and Joshua Ang in *I Not Stupid* by Jack Neo, 2002.

the almost-forgotten Studio Era of Shaw and Cathay when numerous Malay movies were made. Yet there are some even more unknown Chinese movies from the 1950s to the 1970s which are even more difficult to unearth. As for the emerging new generation of post-1990 filmmakers, there is still a need for it to achieve greater international exposure.

It has been my impression that many in Singapore are not fully aware of this valuable legacy. I hope that this book can serve as a starting point for those wishing to explore Singapore cinema, and that they may discover its real cultural and historical value, as well as realise its unique contribution to the growth of a Singaporean identity and world film history. I also hope it will help foreigners, like myself, discover a whole new side to Singapore.

I had already written a book on Singapore cinema in French and, initially, did not intend to write another one for publication in Singapore. I believed that there was a need for it, but felt that a Singaporean should do it. And I dare say there are a few people who can, and maybe should, do it, because they know more than I do. But none seemed ready to do so. Realising that there was a gap to be filled, and that some of the last witnesses, vintage materials and rare documents of the past may soon be gone forever, I decided to go ahead and write this book. My intention was to produce an accessible and enjoyable reference book which would give Singapore cinema more visibility and generate greater interest in watching it.

This work is not an academic dissertation. Nor is it loaded with gender, postcolonial, post-structuralist or modernist analyses, although these

Marrie Lee in *They Call Her... Cleopatra Wong* by George Richardson, 1978.

were at the back of my mind as I was writing it. For those eager to read up on the available literature, they are most welcome to take a look at the references section of this book.

Singapore Cinema merely aims to provide a coherent picture of the film history of Singapore — lining up the facts, putting them into historical perspective, and highlighting the changes in the local industry. It looks at important movies and talks about key figures in the industry, including those usually forgotten and overlooked.

It is definitely my hope that some will use this book as a springboard to further research, as there is currently a lack of criticism and academic analyses on cinema in Singapore.

Films that are never shown or seen, never talked and written about, are films that will sooner or later die. This book, in its own limited way, hopes to help keep these movies alive. At least in our memories.

Raphaël Millet

INTRODUCTION

RAIDERS OF THE LOST ART Filmmaking in Singapore developed within a unique geographical, historical and cultural context. It is both a product as well as a reflection of a richly multiethnic and multicultural society. From its early years, Singapore filmmaking has been impacted by Malay, Indian, Chinese, British, as well as Middle-Eastern and Japanese influences. It has also been affected by social and political events in the 20th century, such as colonisation, the Japanese occupation, autonomy from colonial rule, the shortlived integration into the Federation of Malaysia, independence, the 1997 financial crisis, etc. All these give Singapore cinema its distinct identity.

Peter Chong at the time of *Ring of Fury* by Tony Yeow and James Sebastian, 1973.

Singapore filmmaking began in the mid-1920s to mid-1930s, reaching what is commonly regarded as the golden age in the years spanning 1947 to 1972, a period known as the Studio Era due to the dominance of the Shaw and Cathay studios.

From the early 1930s to the early 1970s, the cultural reference or root was almost always Malay, apart from a handful of movies shot in Chinese Mandarin or various Chinese dialects. Thus, local movies were mainly in Malay, using Malay actors. This was even though the producers were always Chinese and the first directors were from India.

The predominant Malayness of Singapore cinema was simply due to the fact that the island was, at that time, still very much part of a larger cultural and geographical entity known as Nusantara, the Malay world of Southeast Asia dating back to the days of the early Malay kingdoms which ruled over parts of the territories known today as Malaysia, Singapore, the Philippines, Indonesia and Brunei.

The former British colony was made autonomous in 1959, and subsequently joined the Federation of Malaysia in 1963. In 1965, Singapore finally gained independence. The making of Malay movies in pre-independence Singapore was, in a sense, part of that integration process into the Federation and somehow a legacy from that period. Singapore kept Malay as its national language, and used Malay for its national anthem and all its state symbols (and, in fact, it still retains the same national language and symbols today).

Yet, by the 1950s, the island's population was predominantly Chinese, with Malays and Indians constituting the larger minority groups. Thus, it was only natural that there were also a few attempts in the 1950s and 1960s at making Chinese movies to serve the growing market. These movies were generally filmed in a local variant of Mandarin (also known as Malayan Mandarin), or in a Chinese dialect such as Hokkien or Cantonese.

Singapore, after independence in 1965, experienced numerous changes, and the films of that time reflected them. The content and style of Malay movies changed. There were fewer historical period dramas, and more contemporary social dramas dealing with issues faced by a new country undergoing rapid modernisation.

Even the music used in post-1965 movies was different. Studios moved away from using in-house orchestras. Instead, they began to showcase *pop yeh yeh*, a type of music influenced by Western pop songs which was very popular in Malaysia and Singapore at that time. Rock 'n' roll had also reached Singapore, and made its presence felt, even on celluloid.

The landscape in newly independent Singapore was also changing, with the construction of highrise buildings, bridges and shopping centres, as could be seen in many movies of that era.

 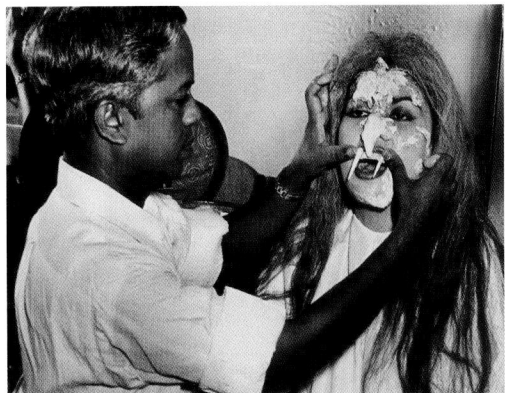 

Left to right: Noordin Ahmad in *Hang Jebat* by Hussain Haniff, 1961; Maria Menado being transformed into a pontianak for *Sumpah Pontianak* by B. N. Rao, 1958; P. Ramlee in his own movie, *Tiga Abdul*, 1964.

However, the major change in the film industry came between 1967 and 1972. Shaw and Cathay, due to a series of shifts in their movie production strategies, abruptly stopped the production of Malay films, never to resume.

In the years immediately following the Studio Era in the 1970s, Singapore became more Chinese-focused, and filmmaking shifted away from Malay movies and the heritage of the Malay archipelago. A handful of more independently produced movies were shot in Chinese or even in English during this period.

Even though the film industry would come to a halt in the 1980s, these first attempts to produce Chinese movies in the 1970s paved the way for an industry that would, from the 1990s onwards, produce movies mainly in Chinese (featuring the various Chinese dialects) and English.

Malay language, culture and society were relegated to a few isolated short movies, no Singaporean features having been shot in Malay or by a Malay between 1995 and 2005. This shift was also reflected in the fact that prior to 1972, the actors were mostly Malay. After 1972, the actors were mainly Chinese, and there was little representation of the minority races in film.

The blockbuster movies of the late 1990s and early 2000s were almost entirely made by Chinese producers and directors, and featured Chinese casts. For a cinema viewer who would know Singapore only through its movies, it would have seemed that the country's population changed from Malay to Chinese overnight.

Singapore cinema had also completely disappeared by the late 1970s and was nonexistent through the 1980s. Such a situation is unheard of in the history of cinema. Even countries that suffered major civil wars, such as Lebanon and Sri Lanka, or large-scale international wars in their territory, such as Germany or Japan, or major financial crises, such as the USA in 1929, never had a 12-to-15-year shutdown of their film industry. It was almost like a coma, a rather long one. This happened even though, in the 1980s, Singapore was enjoying peace, stability and double-digit economic growth.

This long stoppage of production erased Singapore from the map of world cinema, at exactly the time that other neighbouring film industries were growing. Mainland China saw the rise of its Fifth Generation filmmakers. Hong Kong was riding high on its New Wave cinema. Taiwanese movies were flooding the international scene. Malaysia's film production was steadily increasing in quantity and quality.

Once off the map, it would prove to be an uphill task to get back on it, as filmmakers in Singapore attempting to do so from the mid-1990s onwards found out. Only a few directors have been able to gain international recognition, Jack Neo's success being largely local, and only occasionally regional.

Such a hiatus in movie production seems even more amazing when you consider that the Singapore film industry once ranked among the top in Asia. And that it was in fact the leader in Southeast Asia from the late 1940s to the early 1960s.

By 1955, Singapore had already produced about 100 movies, and this was 10 years before its independence. By 1960, almost 200 feature films had been

Megan Zheng in *Homerun* by Jack Neo, 2003.

produced in Singapore, mostly by Shaw and Cathay. By 1972, the end of the Studio Era, Singapore had produced around 300 to 325 films. However, after 1972, things went downhill. From 1973 to 1978, fewer than 10 independently made features were made.

In its heydays, the Shaw and Cathay studios produced about 20 films a year, making the Singapore film industry as prolific as the ones in Indonesia or the Philippines, if not more. Furthermore, Singapore's influence grew when both Cathay and Shaw expanded their businesses in Hong Kong in the second half of the 1950s. Shaw and Cathay became the driving forces behind the revitalised film industry there, where they made hundreds of Chinese language movies.

Thus, by controlling the bulk of both the Malay and Hong Kong movie industries, Singapore dominated, for a very few years, quite a large part of the Asian film industry (with the exception of the Japanese and Indian movie industries and markets which, being so particular and self-sufficient, remained inaccessible).

Ironically enough, Singapore was the one which laid some of the foundations for the Hong Kong film industry, an industry which would later be one of its main competitors. The few attempts by Singapore to counter the rise of Hong Kong by trying to beat it at its own game, such as *Ring of Fury* in 1973, or *They Call Her... Cleopatra Wong* in 1978, were less than successful.

Today, we find that the early history of the Singapore film industry has been consigned to near oblivion. Some movie prints have been destroyed or disposed of. Movies from the 1920s or 1930s are missing. Even some major films from the heydays of the Studio Era have disappeared and cannot be traced. These include the first colour movie, *Buloh Perindu* (a.k.a. *Magic Flute*), which was made in 1953, and *Pontianak*, the first of the eponymous series, which was filmed in 1957. Some of the films in Cantonese, Hokkien or other Chinese dialects shot around the same time are also missing, and very little is remembered of these movies.

Ivy Cheng and Lim Kay Tong in *Perth* by Djinn, 2004.

However, Singapore is not alone in losing parts of its cinematic heritage. Of some 500 features made in Hong Kong before 1941, only four are said to exist in print today. In the USA, 40% of the movies produced prior to 1960 are gone forever.

Ironically, while much of Singapore's film heritage has been lost or forgotten, with the situation compounded by a long hiatus in movie production, Singaporeans have ranked among the world's most avid cinemagoers over the last 50 to 60 years and still remain so.

Although film production seemed all but dead in the late 1970s to early 1980s, filmmaking still continued in a small way through video clubs and amateur home movies. These activities paved the way for the revival of filmmaking in Singapore in the mid-1990s with directors such as Lim Suat Yen, Glen Goei, Jack Neo, Cheek, Djinn and others.

This revival was not the work of the historical studios. Shaw did not produce any movies, and Cathay produced only two movies in the 1990s. It was also not the work of past directors, Tony Yeow being the only 'survivor'.

Instead, this revival was the work of a totally new generation of filmmakers and producers, who gave a totally new face to Singapore cinema, revealing to the world a nation which had undergone many changes since its independence.

Indeed, there is hardly any medium better than cinema to portray the fabric of an entire nation. Even though the case of Singapore, due to the peculiarities of colonisation and its intricate aftermath, raises many interesting questions as to what actually constitutes 'national cinema', it is still possible to identify a Singaporean cinema that spans the pre- and post-independence eras.

Singapore cinema captures the numerous ethnicities and languages spoken in the country, including Singlish, the local variety of English which draws from different languages and dialects. It also documents the everchanging landscape, the varied fashions and lifestyles of the different generations, as well as contributes to the representation of a people and a nation.

Street theatre near Ellenborough market c. 1890, before cinema arrived in Singapore.

EARLY DAYS
1902–1945

CINEMA IN SINGAPORE BEGAN very much like anywhere else in the world. The first documentary filmmakers from the West came to shoot a few vistas and newsreels in the 1900s, and with them, came the first cinema exhibitors.

THE CINEMATOGRAPH ARRIVES A first private screening of Queen Victoria's funeral was apparently held at the City Hall in 1901. Singapore's inaugural public screening is said to have taken place in April 1902. A travelling Parsi exhibitor named Basrai had set up a tent in an open space at the junction of River Valley Road and Hill Street, most likely near where Singapore's Ministry of Information, Communications and the Arts (MICA) is now located. Electricity being still largely unavailable in Singapore at that time, the reels were projected onto the screen using limelight. The reels were, according to some accounts, mostly French, such as the famous *Miroir de Cagliostro* (a.k.a. *Cagliostro's Mirror*) and *Le rêve d'un astronome* (a.k.a. *Astronomer's Dream*) by Georges Méliès, with a few American and British ones like *Photographing a Ghost* by George Albert Smith eventually being introduced. These reels, totalling 25 movies, were the property of the exhibitor.

The first truly imported movies can be traced to 1904, and were brought in by the Levy Hermanos brothers (but *hermanos* already meaning

Hill Street in the early 1900s.

"brothers" in Spanish, they might just have been the Levy brothers, perhaps a Jewish family of Spanish descent), who owned a diamond trading firm. Most of the movies were French, from the Gaumont and Pathé production houses which then dominated the international film market, a few years ahead of Hollywood's inception.

The Levy (Hermanos) brothers screened their movies in a picture-showing building at 320 Victoria Street, which gradually started resembling a real cinema, with proper seats and a projection cabin. Managed by Paul Picard, it was named the Paris Cinema, Singapore's first real cinema hall.

The Paris Cinema was later passed on to one Mohamed Kassim, who developed the business further. Within a short time, a movie exhibition network had spread all over the island, slowly taking over theatres and music halls (purpose-built cinemas coming onto the scene only later on). Going to the movies became a favourite Singaporean pastime, and so it remains to this day.

Along with the Paris Cinema, a Japanese cinema, named the Matsuo Cinema, opened on North Bridge Road. It was later renamed Harima, after its eponymous Japanese owner, and moved to Beach Road, not too far from where Shaw Tower now stands. Some early Pathé newsreels, shot in the late 1900s, show the existence of the Harima cinema.

Movie screenings having proven to be popular, a third cinema opened at the junction of Hill Street and River Valley, on the very same spot that Basrai, the Parsi exhibitor, had once shown his films. It was named The Royal, and its owner, Lim Eng Seng, had set it up by ordering some Gaumont screening material. A fourth cinema opened its doors in 1906 under the name French Cinema, but lasted only two years.

Until 1906, local exhibitors directly imported the movies they wanted to screen. But in 1907, Fernand Dreyfus, of French descent, opened the first film distribution agency in Singapore specialising in Pathé movies. He was Pathé's accredited agent in Singapore for a few years, and continued to dominate the movie market even when competition became fierce. F. Dreyfus also started the Alhambra cinema at the end of 1907, and he ran it until 1914. The Levy (Hermanos) brothers were still in the business and continued importing Gaumont films. In 1907, they brought in for the first time British movies produced by Charles Urban Trading Co. There were also newcomers, such as a firm named Weill & Zerner, which imported movies by French cinema pioneer, Georges Méliès, who was still actively producing at that time.

By 1920, just prior to the arrival of the Shaw brothers, some of the key players in the film distribution business in Singapore were Australasian Films Ltd (which specialised in showing Paramount, Universal and Vitagraph features, as well as some "Houdini specials", as they were known then, and who also brought in David W. Griffith's *Intolerance* in 1920), Middle East Films Ltd (which advertised itself as "the house of serials and super features", no less), Far Eastern Film Service Ltd and Pathé Frères-Singapore. These companies were mostly Western.

Only in the period 1922 to 1924 did some new players enter the scene. They were Chinese immigrants starting their own movie businesses, specialising in importing films generally produced in Shanghai. In a sense, they paved the way for the Shaw brothers, who would soon take over the market.

THE SHAW BROTHERS
The Shaw brothers, Runje, Runde, Runme, Run Run and Runfun were the sons of Shaw Yuh Hsuen, who hailed from Zhejiang, China. Shaw Yuh Hsuen was a successful businessman who made his fortune trading pigments. Four years after his death in 1924, his eldest son, Runje, decided to enter the movie industry in Shanghai.

The brothers formed a company called Tian Yi Film Co. (a.k.a. Unique Film Company and Unique Film Productions) and soon started making silent

Shaw Run Run.

movies such as *Li Di Cheng Fo* (lit. New Leaf), *Niuxia Li Fei Fei* (lit. Heroine Li Fei Fei), *Liang Zhu Tong Shi* (lit. The Eternal Love), etc., which Shaw Runje is sometimes said to have directed himself (he apparently directed movies until 1939, a little known fact).

The movie market being still rather small in China, the brothers sent Runme to explore new territories for the expansion of their business. Those were the days of silent movies, which made language barriers a non-issue, and the brothers felt that their movies could thus appeal to all Chinese, whether they spoke Mandarin, Cantonese, Hokkien or Teochew.

Shaw Runme.

Runme, who was in charge of film distribution, travelled to Singapore, in 1924 according to some accounts, in 1925 according to others. By then, Singapore was already predominantly Chinese. He settled down in the city and started distributing silent movies produced by his family in Shanghai.

In 1927, his younger brother, Run Run, came to Singapore to help him expand the business. Both of them formed the Hai Seng Company, which would later make way for Shaw Brothers Pte Ltd. It was really Runme and Run Run who made a success of their family's venture into Singapore, starting a branch that would eventually be a key player in the Shaw empire, and contributing immensely to the history of cinema in Singapore (and, incidentally, Hong Kong).

Even though the story of the Shaw movie business in Singapore would later prove to be an impressive one, it is nevertheless typical of what was happening in Asia at that time, both in terms of migration and burgeoning movie industries. In fact, at about the same time, the Wong brothers, also originally from Shanghai, established their own movie business in Jakarta, Indonesia. Like the Shaws in Singapore, they would play a major role in building up the local film industry in Indonesia.

Under the Hai Seng Company, Runme and Run Run developed their distribution business, at first screening their movies in cinemas owned by other entrepreneurs, who were mostly Chinese of Hokkien or Teochew origin. However, these cinema owners refused at times to screen Shaw movies, preferring to exhibit films they imported directly themselves.

As competition was fierce, the Shaws swiftly decided to add exhibition to their business, even though distribution initially remained their forte. To do so, they teamed up with other local players throughout the whole of Malaya, all the way up to the north where Runme worked for a while with Ho Ah Loke

(who would a few decades later become one of the most influential producers in Singapore) in the Penang and Ipoh area. With some screening material brought from Shanghai, the brothers opened their first Singapore cinema in Tanjong Pagar in 1927, just as the silent movie era was coming to an end.

However, the first sound film had actually arrived in Singapore as early as 1910. It was the experimental Edison Talking Picture made by Edison Electric Co., which, as in almost everywhere else in the world, proved to be a technical and financial failure. Indeed, in the first years of the 20th century, many colour and sound experiments were conducted, and eventually tested on the market.

Almost two decades later, in 1927, 1928 and 1929, the real talkies as we know them today slowly appeared, gradually replacing silent movies. These made their way to Singapore with the premiere of *The Rainbow Man*, starring Eddie Dowling, at the Alhambra cinema, and the screening of the world-famous *The Jazz Singer*, starring Al Jolson, at the Victoria Theatre.

In 1931, the Shaw studio in Shanghai produced one of the very first Chinese talkies, *Gechang Chunse* (a.k.a. *The Nightclub Colours*), which is said to have been a huge success in China and all over Chinese-speaking Asia. For Runme and Run Run, having a supply of good movies benefited their Southeast Asian distribution and exhibition businesses tremendously. In 1934, they even bought over Ho Ah Loke's exhibition circuit in northern Malaya, as well as a few independent cinema halls in the south.

At the end of the 1930s, just before the start of World War II, the Shaw exhibition arm, Malayan Theatres Ltd, owned no less than 139 cinemas in Malaya, Singapore, Thailand and parts of Indochina. To manage this growing empire, Runme took charge of the north while Run Run took charge of the south, including Singapore.

In the island-city, like everywhere else in Malaya, the Shaws expanded their business either by building new venues, or by taking over existing ones, like the old, famous and established Alhambra, of which they became the lessees in 1938. They renovated it, and turned it into the first air-conditioned cinema in Singapore and Malaya, thus gaining what was going to be a very useful competitive advantage for a short while.

FIRST LOCALLY MADE MOVIES
When it comes to cinema, "birth certificates" are generally always a problem. Even the invention of cinema itself remains open to debate, as it lies somewhere among pe ople like Eadweard Muybridge, Thomas Edison and the Lumière brothers. Trying to put one's finger on the very first Singapore-made movie is not easy either, though it has long been claimed that *Leila Majnun*, shot entirely in Singapore in 1933, by Indian film director B. S. Rajhans, was the first local production. It would be too easy to adhere to this official version even though, as will be shown, there are many reasons to regard this 1933 movie as a major landmark in the history of film production in Singapore.

The Alhambra and Marlborough cinemas in the 1920s.

The earliest films made in Singapore were probably by film exhibitors who shot footage of the places they were travelling through so they could exhibit it elsewhere. However, nothing much of this material seems to have remained, apart from a Pathé newsreel filmed in the 1900s.

Félix Mesguich, one of the most famous operators hired by the Lumière brothers, is said to have done a world tour in the years 1909 to 1910 which took him to places like India, Burma, Cambodia and... Singapore. Yet, it is not known whether or not he shot reels during his stay in the island-city.

Traces exist as well of a 1913 Georges Méliès production, titled *A Day at Singapore*, yet it remains unclear who directed it, and whether it was produced under Méliès' American company or under his French company. The poster presented it as "a most interesting little trip around the show places of Singapore, Straits Settlements, one of the largest seaports in the world".

Another account of "picture-making in Singapore" (as it was termed then) is from 1920, when the newly incorporated Oriental Film Company made plans to produce two-reel comedies and dramas for a Western audience, using Eastern settings. They had also hoped to attract local moviegoers. The material apparently was to be provided by Pathé Cinema, while the production was to be handled by Charles Kits (also, on occasion, spelled Kitts), formerly of the London Film Company and later of South African Films. In the end, it seems likely that not much came of it and shooting was cancelled, since nothing more is known about the release or even completion of this movie.

Soon after, in 1922, Merian C. Cooper, who was to become famous ten years later for codirecting with Ernst Schoedsack the first *King Kong*,

travelled through Singapore on his boat Wisdom II. It was one of his first explorations of a region which would inspire him to make numerous movies, documentaries and novels.

XIN KE The first movie with a known title (aside from some early documentary-type films) said to have been shot in Singapore seems to be *Xin Ke* (lit. The Immigrant), produced in 1926 by a Chinese named Liu Peh Jing, according to some accounts. It premiered in November 1926 at the Marlborough Theatre, and was later exhibited at the Empire and Palacegay. This silent movie most certainly targeted the newly arrived Chinese on the island. Such an appropriate title obviously endowed this movie with great symbolic value.

The production came at the same time as the general growth of domestic filmmaking in the region. The first movie made in Indonesia, *Loetoeng Kasaroeng* (a.k.a. *The Monkey Kasaroeng*), was also in 1926, and it was followed in 1928 by a film about upper-class Chinese called *Lily van Java* (a.k.a. *Lily from Java*). However, many other details about *Xin Ke*, including the name of the director, remain unclear, and there does not seem to be any print remaining.

What makes *Xin Ke* even more interesting from a historical perspective is the fact that, as a movie about the Chinese in Singapore, it was to remain a rare exception for two to three decades. The local movie industry that grew from the 1930s to 1950s was largely a Malay phenomenon, at least culturally and visually. The movies were in Malay and acted by Malays, directed first by Indians and Filipinos and then by Malays. The Chinese were working mainly behind-the-scenes as producers.

Following one or two Chinese features immediately after the end of World War II, there were a few movies shot in Teochew, Cantonese or Hokkien in the mid 1950s, and a few Malay movies dubbed in Chinese (such as the first Cathay-Keris' *Pontianak* in 1957, or Shaw's *Anak Pontianak* in 1958) so as to make them accessible to Chinese Singaporeans.

However, the next truly Chinese Singaporean movie, *Shi Zi Cheng* (a.k.a. *Lion City*) by Yi Sui (a.k.a. Tang Pak Chee), entirely shot in Singapore with Singaporeans, in Malayan Mandarin, would not be made until 1960, a gap of 35 years after *Xin Ke*.

Needless to say then, that *Xin Ke*, while technically the first Singapore-made movie, is far from being a seminal work, not having left a significant legacy. Yet, very interestingly, it softens a little the usual and official version of the strictly Malay foundations of the Singapore movie industry.

SINGAPORE AS EXOTIC BACKDROP

With the growth of the international film industry, Singapore also began to be featured in some movies by foreign filmmakers. In 1928, at least three movies made reference to Singapore, although they were not necessarily shot on the island, the Lion City being quite a distance from Hollywood. It was a time when the West was interested in featuring exotic locations, and Singapore, a typical East-of-Suez destination, appeared to have caught the eye of these filmmakers, after having been actively promoted by writers such as Somerset Maugham.

The very name of Singapore thus seemed to attract a lot of attention and carry great power of suggestion. Two American movies made in 1928 even had the island's name in their titles, *Across to Singapore*, an MGM production starring a young Joan Crawford, and *Sal of Singapore*, shot by the then famous and highly productive but now long-forgotten Howard Higgin. The third movie, *The Crimson City*, which could have referred to Singapore at sunset, was also known under its Italian title, *La Schiava di Singapore*, and starred the so erotic Hollywood Asian vamp, Anna May Wong, who was born in Los Angeles and might have never set her foot (and a very pretty one she had too) in Singapore.

With the end of the silent era came the first talkies. In 1931, *The Road to Singapore* (not to be confused with the similarly titled movie starring Bob Hope and Bing Crosby 10 years later) was shot by Alfred E. Green. Set mainly on a steamer, this movie had nothing to do with Singapore, the island's name apparently being used as a form of exotic attraction to lure potential viewers.

In 1932 and 1933, no less than six American and British movies made reference to Singapore. These included *Out of Singapore*, about Malay pirates, directed by Charles Hutchinson and reissued as *Gangsters of the Sea*. Like many of its predecessors, it hardly used any local actors, the Caucasian actors being made up to look as Asian as possible. *Shadows of Singapore* (a.k.a. *Malay Nights*) also portrayed the exotic East from a Western perspective, and showed how little Hollywood cared about accurately representing local cultures.

WHITE PEARL AND *SAMARANG*

Bucking the trend were two movies on Singapore directed by Westerners in 1932. *White Pearl* was believed to be a project by an Englishman called Russell, to be filmed entirely in Singapore with numerous outdoor shots. Significantly, it was also known under a local Malay title, *Mutiara Putih* (an exact translation of the English title). Unfortunately, very little is known about the movie, and both its release and even its completion remain uncertain.

The other movie, American Ward Wing's *Samarang* (a.k.a. *Out of the Sea*, a.k.a. *Shark Woman*), is about pearl divers, bathing beauties, and huge, dangerous fish. Shot at the end of 1932, it premiered in the USA in 1933. It was released in Singapore, at the Roxy cinema, in early 1934, and advertised

Ad for *Samarang* by Ward Wing, 1932.

as "Malaya's first sensational thriller, filmed entirely in Singapore, with local artists". *Samarang* (now more commonly known under the spelling of Semarang) also happens to be the name of a port city in northern Java, Indonesia, that Joseph Conrad mentions in *The Mirror of the Sea*.

Indeed, both movies were shot on location, and most important of all, used local actors, some of whom were *bangsawan* or Malay opera performers. *Samarang's* cast included local actors such as Ahmang, Chang Fu and Mamounah. It is believed that *White Pearl* starred Shariff Medan, making his first appearance on screen. He would later go on to act in more than 30 Malay Singaporean movies of the 1940s, 1950s and 1960s.

It does seem that *White Pearl* and *Samarang* left more of a cinematic legacy than *Xin Ke*. They hinted at what the Singapore movie industry would be like over the next 40 years — the production of films using Malay-based stories (such as those featuring pearl divers and fishermen), a Malay cast (such as Shariff Medan and his peers), and directed for half of its total production by foreigners.

LEILA MAJNUN

Shot in 1933, and released in 1934 just two days after Ward Wing's *Samarang*, B. S. Rajhans' *Leila Majnun* would enjoy greater success with the local audience. And it would have a far greater impact on the history of film in Singapore, introducing elements which would constitute the core identity of the local movie industry for 40 years.

Balden Singh Rajhans, the director, was not Singaporean. He came from Calcutta, India, where he had already gained experience and recognition in the movie industry with at least two films, *Krishnabarna Tirandaz* (a.k.a. *Black Archer*) in 1930 and *Gupta Ratna* (a.k.a. *Hidden Treasure*) in 1931.

Ads for the Urdu film, *Leila Majnu*, by Kanjibhai Rathob, 1931 (left) and the Singapore-made *Leila Majnun* by B. S. Rajhans, 1933 (right).

He came to Singapore to work on *Leila Majnun*, a movie project driven by Rai Bahadur Seth and Hurdutroy Motilall Chamria.

Seth and Chamria were from the Motilall Chemical Company, which had its head office in Bombay. Far from being a real film production house, its main business was in distributing screening materials such as lamp carbons in Malaya and Singapore. However, in the early 1930s, it had started bringing Indian films to Singapore, including, in 1932, an Urdu movie titled *Leila Majnu*. This movie met with enough success in Singapore that the distributors decided to turn themselves into producers and do a local remake. Therefore, neither the director nor the producers were of Singaporean origin, nor permanently based in Singapore, which is of note since this movie is usually cited as the founding movie of the local industry.

The *Leila Majnun* story itself is not really Malay as it was mainly inspired by Arabian folklore, specifically *One Thousand and One Nights*, and also partly by Shakespeare's *Romeo and Juliet*. It is the story of a young woman and a young man who are deeply in love, but unable to fulfill their desire because of social conventions. "Leila" is the name of the woman, while *majnun* is an Arabic word meaning "crazy" or "crazy about". Typically, the *majnun* lover cannot get the girl he loves.

There were to be hordes of *majnun* lovers, many played by P. Ramlee or S. Roomai Noor, in the 1950s and 1960s, during the Malay cinema era dominated by the Shaw and Cathay studios. The Middle-Eastern influence on Singapore cinema was to be long-lasting and should not be overlooked. One newspaper advertisement appeared to anticipate this when it described the movie as having "numerous beautiful Arabian and Egyptian dances".

Yet, very interestingly, the movie was also promoted as being rooted in local Malay culture, "with songs and dialogue in classical Malay", thus making it "the first spectacular colonial Malay talkie". The movie starred many *bangsawan* actors, such as "Miss Fatima Benti Jasman of HMV Record's fame" or "Mr Syed Ali Bin Mansoor, the renowned artiste of the Malay stage". The use of many famous Malay stage actors undoubtedly contributed to the film's success, even though none of them appeared to have furthered their film careers much after *Leila Majnun*.

With its mix of Middle-Eastern, Western, Indian and Malay influences, and its numerous dance and song numbers, *Leila Majnun* set the tone for what was to be the golden age of Singapore cinema in the next four decades. A remake of it would even be filmed by B. N. Rao almost 40 years later in 1962 (under the same title, but spelt with an "a", i.e. *Laila Majnun*).

FOUNDING FATHER, B. S. RAJHANS Had B. S. Rajhans returned to India for good after the release of *Leila Majnun*, this movie might never have gained such a prominent place in Singapore film history. It would have remained one more foreign-produced and directed movie of the early 1930s, long before any real local film production started. But, with this movie, Rajhans set a major trend for cinema in Singapore, which he himself would reinforce with his later movies.

After directing yet another movie in India in 1939, Rajhans returned to Singapore in the 1940s, and made his next Malay movie, *Menantu Derhaka* (lit. The Rebellious Daughter-in-law), in 1942. Once again he used a local cast (including S. Kadarisman, who would turn out to have a long-lasting career as an actor and director), and this time he worked with a locally based Chinese production company, Tan & Wong Film (a.k.a. Tan Weng Film).

B. S. Rajhans.

Rajhans had, with his two films made in Singapore in 1933 and 1942, opened and closed the first decade of Malay cinema here. This would not have been sufficient to earn him the honour of being a founding father of Singapore cinema had he not resumed his moviemaking career here after the war, thus spanning over two generations of filmmaking, and paving the way for the Studio Era.

CATHAY ENTERS THE INDUSTRY

In 1932, just before local film production started, the Singapore movie exhibition industry comprised no less than nine main cinemas: the Alhambra (the oldest, established in 1907), the Capitol (the largest, with a 1,700-seat capacity), the Marlborough, the Pavilion, the Roxy, the Wembley, the Tivoli, the Empire and the Gaiety. Movies were occasionally shown at the Victoria Theatre, as well as in temporary installations for itinerant screenings in the *kampong* (villages). The average number of cinemagoers in Singapore was then estimated at 2,500 per day, i.e. slightly more than 910,000 a year. The market was large and stable enough to nurture local movie production. It was ripe for new entrepreneurs to come in.

Ten years after the Shaw brothers set foot in Singapore, another family, the Lokes, entered the cinema industry. The father, Loke Yew, was born in China in 1845. He came to Singapore at the age of 13, and succeeded in his rubber, coconut and tin businesses. After his death, which occurred when his son, Wan Tho, was only two, the Loke family, under his widow's initiative, considered venturing into the movie business which was then thriving in Southeast Asia. By the time he was 13, and while still in school, Wan Tho was already, through his trustees, head of the Loke family.

Due to his delicate health, he left the region in the early 1930s to study at Chillon College, an English school in Montreux, Switzerland. His health obviously took a turn for the better in the cool mountain climate for he became Chillon's *Victor Ludorum* (Latin for "winner of the games") and captain of the school's soccer eleven. He was also the 1932 long-jump champion of the Swiss county of Vaud. His jump record stood for at least 30 years. Dr Harold Abrahams, the 1924 Olympic sprinter featured in the 1981 Hollywood movie *Chariots of Fire*, was so impressed with Wan Tho that he urged him to take up athletics, believing he could make a name for himself in the athletics world. Wan Tho had made the Vaud athletics team when a broken ankle forced him to retire from the sport for good.

Meanwhile, back in Kuala Lumpur, Malaysia, his mother was going into the movie business. It was just after the Shaw brothers had fully expanded their business by buying over Ho Ah Loke's exhibition circuit in northern Malaya. Entering the competition, Mrs Loke decided in 1935 to incorporate a new company, Associated Theatres Ltd, which would operate under the name Cathay Organisation after 1959. She registered Wan Tho as an absentee fourth founding partner along with her and two others — a British associate, Max Baker, and a relative, Khoo Teik Ee.

In young Wan Tho's absence, it was Khoo Teik Ee who, under Mrs Loke's supervision, managed Associated Theatres Ltd during its first few years of existence before World War II, and laid the foundations for what was to become the Cathay movie empire. Like what the Shaw brothers had done 10 years before, Khoo Teik Ee first ventured into the distribution and exhibition businesses.

Khoo managed the construction of the 1,200-seat Pavilion cinema in Kuala Lumpur, which opened in 1936 just as Wan Tho graduated with an Honours degree in English Literature and History. Khoo then coordinated the construction between 1937 and 1939

Loke Wan Tho.

The Cathay building pictured here in 1958.

of the Cathay Building, which was to be the first cinema complex as well as the tallest building in Singapore then. Even though it has undergone many renovations and modifications, the Cathay Building is still a major Singapore landmark today.

Singapore's first 16-storey skyscraper soon became such an important symbol for the whole company that it was part of its official logo for many years. All Cathay-Keris movies made between 1953 and 1972, that is, over a period of exactly 20 years, opened with a picture of the Cathay Building. Most

filmmakers working for one of the Cathay studios, be it the Malay studio (Cathay-Keris) or the Hong Kong studio (MP&GI), included, whenever they could, one or two shots of the building in their movies.

Within the Cathay Building was the the 1,300-seat Cathay Cinema, offering spacious seats and air-conditioning, which opened shortly after Wan Tho's return to Malaya on October 3rd, 1939. However, not long after that, Wan Tho found himself an evacuee on a ship fleeing the city, just before Singapore was bombed by the Japanese.

SHAW GOES INTO PRODUCTION The Shaws, Runme and Run Run, after having, in just a decade, established a cinema empire based on movie distribution and exhibition, decided to diversify their activities. They added production to their business and became a major player in the cinema scene with a fully integrated movie business, just like the French studios Gaumont and Pathé and the American studios Paramount and MGM. With the support of their brothers' studio back in mainland China, they had everything they needed to be a major regional player.

The Singapore-based Shaw brothers, instead of trying to make Chinese movies for the Chinese audience (since all they needed to do was to bring in movies produced in Shanghai or Hong Kong), sought to win over the Malay audience. Seeing the success of B. S. Rajhans' seminal movie, *Leila Majnun*, they not only started to import Indonesian films such as *Asmara Moerni* (lit. Pure Love) or *Bajar Dengan Djiwa* (possibly meaning Paying With The Soul), but also started producing their own Malay movies, shot in Malay with Malay actors.

At least eight features were filmed between 1938 and 1941. The first was *Mutiara* (lit. Pearl), followed by *Bermadu* (lit. Polygamy), *Toping Shaitan* (lit. The Devil's Mask), *Hanchor Hati* (lit. A Crushed Heart), *Terang Bulan di Malaya* (lit. Full Moon over Malaya), *Ibu Tiri* (lit. Stepmother), *Tiga Kekasih* (lit. Three Lovers) and *Mata Hantu* (lit. Ghost Eyes).

Produced in the brand new Shaw studios at Jalan Ampas in the heart of Singapore, each movie often featured the same set of actors, familiar names like Habsah, Roekiah, Yem, Haji Gong and Puteh Lawak, some of whom would resume their acting careers with the Shaw brothers after World War II. These early Shaw Malay language feature films had love, adventure and horror themes, which were to be some of the key themes of the Malay film industry in the decades to come. Unfortunately, no footage of these films from the 1930s seems to have survived.

Unlike the producer of *Leila Majnun*, the Shaw brothers did not engage an Indian filmmaker, who would be culturally closer to the Malay world, to direct their movies. Instead, they turned to mainland China, employing Hau Yaw (a.k.a. Hou Yao) and Wan Hai Ling (a.k.a. Wan Hoi Ling) as codirectors.

The Shaws may have chosen these Chinese filmmakers because, around that time, Run Run and Runme had turned their eyes towards China again, and in particular towards Hong Kong. There, Run Run and Runme had started, with their brothers who had remained in mainland China, the Nan Hua Film Company in 1936, which apparently produced a very limited number of movies that the brothers are sometimes said to have directed themselves. This was followed by the setting up, shortly after, of the Nanyang Film Company in 1937, which would remain active until the early 1950s and churn out close to 90 features (the bulk of it being, for roughly 70 titles, produced between 1937 and 1941).

Run Run, following the example of his elder brother Runje, had apparently tried his hand at directing one of the company's first movies (which may also be the one and only movie for which he is credited as director), *Xiangxialao Ta Qinjia* (a.k.a. *The Country Bumpkin Visits His In-laws*) in 1937, produced by Runme and acted by Lam Kwun Shan and Tong Suet Hing. Forty years later, in 1976, after settling down for good in Hong Kong, Run Run would produce a movie called *Crazy Bumpkin in Singapore*. What goes around, comes around.

Both Hau Yaw and Wan Hai Ling had started working for Shaw's Nanyang Film Company, for which they codirected and cowrote at least three Cantonese movies: *Xiao Zi Luan Jing Tang* (a.k.a. *The Filial Son* and *The Unworthy Mother*), *Gui Zhi Gao Zhuang* (a.k.a. *Daughter against Stepmother*) and *Zhong Guo Yeren Wang* (a.k.a. *The Chinese Tarzan*). Hau Yaw, on his own, directed six more movies for the same company.

The early Malay movies which they also made for the Shaw brothers in Singapore were very much inspired by their previous works in Hong Kong. Therefore, they were not directly based on Malay stories, but on Chinese ones. These ended up being a rather confusing cultural mix, appealing neither to the Malays, who were the main target, nor to the Chinese, and were not that well-received at the box office. Malay viewers rejected what was presented as ostensibly Malay, but which was clearly adapted from earlier Chinese films, with many elements foreign to Malay art and culture. Nevertheless, this was a useful experience for the Shaw brothers and helped them to remain committed to local film production after World War II.

Meanwhile, they could rely on imported Indonesian talkies, which were more immediately profitable. Also, the bulk of the Shaw business was actually in exhibiting American films. In the late 1930s, Hollywood movies (brought to cinema screens by the Shaw family with their Malayan Theatres Ltd branch, and the Loke family with their Associated Theatres Ltd, as well as other local distributors and exhibitors such as Amalgamated Theatres Ltd) held 70 per cent of the market. Another 16 per cent of ticket sales were from British movies (Britain being the ruling colonial power then and there was a large British population in Singapore) and 13 per cent from Chinese movies. Malay movies enjoyed only one per cent of ticket sales.

THE JAPANESE OCCUPATION World War II soon spread across the globe with the Japanese attacking Pearl Harbor in December 1941 and then invading Southeast Asia, including Singapore. A large part of the movie industry very quickly collapsed. Some cinemas managed to carry on their activities, and were sometimes compelled to open their doors to Japanese troops. Apart from B. S. Rajhans' 1942 Malay movie, *Menantu Derhaka* (lit. The Rebellious Daughter-in-law), produced by the locally based Chinese firm, Tan & Wong Film, there was hardly any movie production in Singapore and Malaya.

In November 1943, the Japanese decided to forbid the screening of Western movies, and allow only the screening of Japanese films, in an effort to abolish all Western influences, and nipponise the island-city. The Japanese broadcasting department, the military propaganda department and the military information bureau were housed in the Cathay Building. Cathay Cinema had its name changed to Dai Toa Gekkyo and showed Japanese propaganda films to promote the "Southeast Asia Co-Prosperity Sphere", as the Japanese called it.

Chinese ad for a Japanese propaganda movie c. 1943.

There were plenty of newsreels featuring the victory of the Japanese over the Allied armies, as well as film clippings encouraging locals to adopt elements of Japanese culture such as bushido, the code of honour and morals of the Japanese samurai. Amidst the propaganda movies, whether documentaries, or edifying dramas such as Shochiku's *Obasan* and Toho's *Ai No Ikka*, local viewers were exposed to some of the best Japanese films made around that time, by Mizoguchi and Ozu, as well as Kurosawa's early features.

Ad for *Obasan* at the Alhambra Theatre.

Japanese movies released in Singapore during the war were subtitled either in English or Malay, and sometimes in both languages. They were also advertised in both languages to reach out to local audiences. The Chinese, who were distrusted by the Japanese due to a longer history of conflict, were most of the time purposely left out.

Some of the later Malay filmmakers claimed to have learnt much from watching the movies of great Japanese directors during the war days, especially in the areas of photography and editing. P. Ramlee himself is said to have been inspired by Kurosawa and his peers, and this was seen as early as his second feature, *Semerah Padi*, made in 1956, with its contrasted photography, tracking shots, and the use of low-angle shots with the camera close to the ground. He even deliberately did a remake of Kurosawa's famous 1943 *Sanshiro Sugata* (a.k.a. *Judo Saga*) with his 1969 *Kancan Tirana*, after he had left Singapore and settled down in Kuala Lumpur.

When the British returned, the first movie they brought in was a propaganda film, *Desert Victory*, about British success in the North African desert campaign, in order to counter Japanese propaganda and restore British prestige. Significantly, it was screened at the Cathay Cinema complex, which also served as headquarters for Admiral Lord Mountbatten, Southeast Asia Supreme Allied Commander until 1946.

The various cinema chains in Singapore slowly resumed their activities, very quickly toning down on propaganda films, and showing more and more entertaining movies from Hollywood, Bollywood as well as the Middle-East. These would strongly influence the Malay film industry that would soon bloom and know its golden age.

Hang Jebat by Hussain Haniff, 1961.

THE STUDIO ERA
1947–1972

IN THE LATE 1940s AND EARLY 1950s, Malayans in general, and Singaporeans in particular, became some of the world's most avid moviegoers. That was also when they began to have access to an increasing number of locally made movies.

THE GOLDEN AGE There was undoubtedly a market for homegrown productions, pioneered by the Shaw brothers and a few independent entrepreneurs, as the record-breaking year 1952 would soon prove. That year alone, around 23 feature films were churned out by one studio, Shaw's Malay Film Productions, and a handful of independent production houses.

The next year, Loke Wan Tho made his move and, with the help of Ho Ah Loke, created Cathay-Keris, signalling the beginning of what was going to be the heyday of the studios. Singapore cinema thus saw a golden age that was to last 25 years, during which the films which were locally produced would be predominantly in Malay.

POST-WORLD WAR II RECOVERY Once again, the first signs that the local film industry was alive came from Indian director B. S. Rajhans, who began filming in 1946 the Malay movie *Seruan Merdeka* (lit. The Call for Freedom), starring Salleh Ghani, Rokiah Hanafi, Johar and Siti Tanjung Perak. Two of these actors, Salleh Ghani and Siti Tanjung

Perak, would go on to pursue very successful careers in the film industry that would develop in the coming years. Salleh Ghani even directed his own movies from 1961 onwards.

Besides the fact that it was the first post-World War Malay movie, *Seruan Merdeka* would remain outstanding in Singapore film history for two reasons. Firstly, it was a totally independent production by Malayan Arts Productions based in Singapore's Istana Kampung Glam, and headed by a Mr Chisty, an Indian businessman who had hardly any link with any distribution-exhibition group such as Shaw or Cathay. Secondly, the movie was about how young Malay and Chinese Singaporeans came together under a united front to resist the Japanese. Seeing both Malay and Chinese actors on screen at the same time was very unusual and would remain so until the late 1950s.

Unfortunately, *Seruan Merdeka* was a commercial failure, not because no one wanted to watch it, but because hardly anyone was even able to. The main exhibition circuits apparently boycotted it, refusing to screen it in their theatres. It was a very efficient way to kill off any independent initiative in the film industry, at a time when the two major groups were about to expand their businesses, vigorously pursuing vertical integration of all segments of their industry, from production to distribution and exhibition.

In 1946 as well, another movie featured the recently ended World War II. This was *Hua Jiao Shue Liu* (lit. The Overseas Chinese Blood Story), produced by Zhong Hua Film Company. Shaw apparently also ventured into production with a little remembered Mandarin film titled *Xin Jia Po Ze Ge* (lit. Song of Singapore), which addressed the overseas Chinese resistance to the Japanese occupation in the island-city. Yet, these two Chinese productions did not spark a tradition of local Chinese filmmaking.

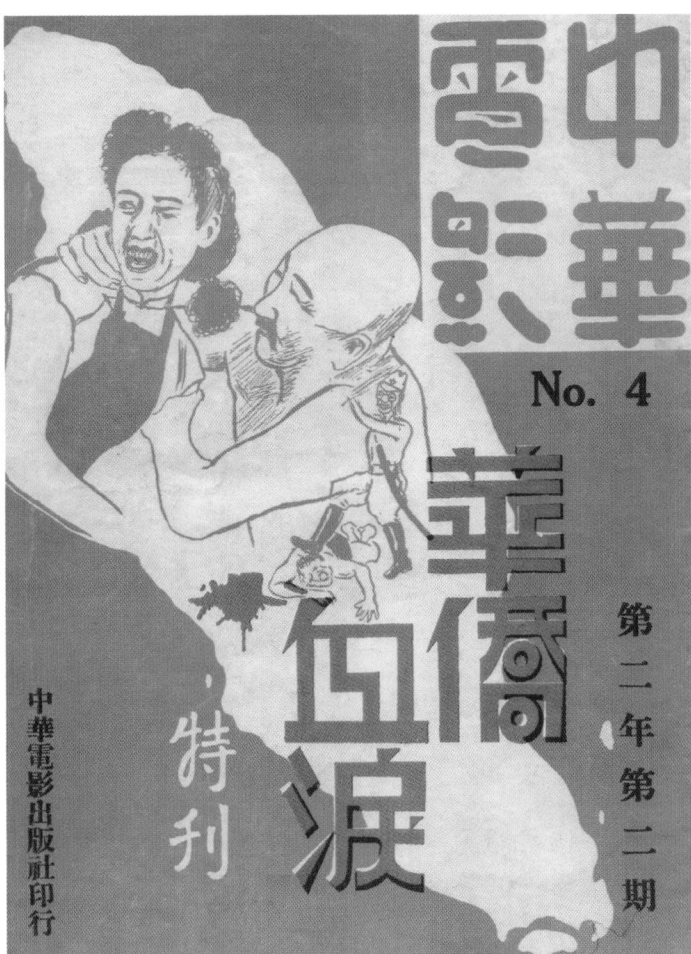

Cover of "China Screen" magazine featuring *Hua Jiao Shue Liu* (lit. The Overseas Chinese Blood Story).

Testing the potential of the Malay market, Shaw also slowly reissued its prewar Malay titles, like *Bermadu* (lit. Polygamy) and *Mutiara* (lit. Pearl), some of which had been completed right before the Japanese assault and, as such, might never have been properly shown. The success of these releases prompted Shaw to venture again into the production of Malay films. They made the simpler choice, employing B. S. Rajhans, the seminal director of the 1933 *Leila Majnun* and 1946 *Seruan Merdeka*. In a sense, it was *Seruan Merdeka*, that unsuccessful independent movie, that was the real starting point for what would turn out to be a 25-year golden age of film for Singapore.

SHAW'S MALAY FILM PRODUCTIONS Some of the installations and equipment owned by Shaw studios had remained at their original location on Jalan Ampas through the war. The Shaw brothers decided to reopen these studios in 1947. They still saw the need to produce films, and to cater to the local Malay audience, not only in Singapore, but also in Malaya, which was then the fastest expanding market in the region, albeit a predominantly Malay one.

Screenlogo of Shaw's Malay Film Productions.

They incorporated a new company named Malay Film Productions while retaining Malayan Theatres Ltd as their exhibition arm. This decision was what really kicked off the Studio Era in Singapore. Until its closure in 1967 (some of its last productions being shown until 1968), Malay Film Productions generated around 160 movies out of its Singapore-based studios, making it the most prolific production unit ever in the history of Singapore.

With Malay Film Productions, the Shaw brothers followed the successful example of Hollywood studios like MGM and Paramount, in which everything was integrated, and the producer had final control over every film. The Shaw brothers started signing a number of actors and technicians. These were going to be their fulltime employees for many years, without having the possibility of going to a competitor (since there was going to be hardly any until the very early 1950s).

The Shaw brothers, enjoying a quasi-monopoly in production in its first few years, were the rulers of the Malay film industry, with a total output

Omar Rojik (2nd row, 6th from left) and his crew in Shaw's studio while shooting *Singapura Dilanggar Todak* in September, 1961.

of 37 features between 1947 and 1952. This was right before the other main studio, Cathay-Keris, would go into production. Production had to be fast and profitable; and even though artistic quality was not the main concern, the creativity shown in some of their Malay productions would be a source of inspiration for Shaw Run Run in his Hong Kong years, after he moved there in 1958. More significantly, the Shaw way got the Malay film industry off the ground. Others that would come into the business later were only going to be followers.

SINGAPURA DI WAKTU MALAM
B. S. Rajhans remained Shaw's only active director until 1950. He was thus responsible for the first seven films made under Shaw's Malay Film Productions, in which almost all the seeds of the Malay film industry of the 1950s were sown.

His first Shaw movie, *Singapura di Waktu Malam* (lit. Singapore by Night) is, as may be discerned by its title alone, a Malay film that firmly belongs in Singapore film history. Outdoor scenes were shot in Singapore, Muar and Segamat. Even though the Malay film industry from the 1940s to the mid-1960s was a shared entity, claimed by both Singapore and Malaya (as Malaysia was then called), Malay film would more often than not be a Singapore affair (at least until the Malaysian Merdeka Studio opened its doors in Kuala Lumpur in 1960). *Singapura di Waktu Malam* captured the tone of the island-city, soon to be a city-state, by portraying local themes and shooting on location in Singapore itself.

In the following years, two other local films would carry the name of Singapore in their titles: *Berbahagia di Singapura* (lit. Happy in Singapore) by Jaafar Wiryo in 1953 and *Singapura Dilanggar Todak* (a.k.a. *Swordfish*

Attack on Singapore) by Omar Rojik in 1962. And many more would address rather directly Singaporean issues such as cultural identity, social structure and nation-building.

Backed by their chain of theatres, of which they were either the owners or the lessees, the Shaw brothers were able to bring *Singapura di Waktu Malam* to local audiences. The film enjoyed good response, proving that the movie business could be profitable.

SHAW PRODUCTION EXPANDS

The Shaw brothers thus proceeded to produce more films. They introduced new faces to the screen, one of them being Sumatran-born Kasma Booty, a Eurasian (of half Dutch parentage) who had started as a *sandiwara* or Malay theatre actress. She was given the starring role in their next film, *Chempaka* (lit. Magnolia Tree), which revolved around the life of a native island girl.

Kasma Booty.

The Shaw studio, capitalising on these early successes, went on to produce two more films in 1948, and then slowly but steadily increased its production to three movies in 1949, seven in 1950, and eight in 1951. It suddenly peaked at 15 features in 1952, one of its most prolific years in terms of production output, Shaw being motivated both by the growing audience and profits, and by the increasing competition from new, independent production houses like Nusantara, Rimau and Keris.

The year 1952 was also to be the most productive in moviemaking for the Singapore film industry as a whole, with a total of 23 films. This was the result of a highly competitive environment, at a time when the industry was rapidly expanding with unprecedented freedom, a freedom soon to be lost with the coming of the duopolistic studio system of Shaw and Cathay.

NUSANTARA FILM

The Shaw brothers did not remain the only player in the burgeoning film industry for very long. A few independent producers decided to try their luck in the lucrative film business, and soon two small production houses appeared on the scene. They came with partners who were not necessarily Singaporean; some were from Indonesia, others from northern Malaya. Yet, they were all looking at Singapore with desire and envy, as it seemed the place to be.

The first of these two independent production houses was Nusantara Film, located at 4 Keramat Road. It was started by Hsu Chiu Meng (also spelled Hsu Chio Meng). And its production line was headed by Ong Keng Huat, apparently from Penang and connected to Ho Ah Loke. The company's name itself indicated an intention to reach across borders and cover the whole Malay archipelago (*nusantara* meaning "Malay archipelago").

As they had to find new talent, Nusantara Film brought in Indonesian and Malayan directors and actors, some with experience, some without. As early as 1950, it produced two movies. *Pelangi* (lit. Rainbow) was directed by Indonesian Naz Achnas, and *Sesal Tak Sudah* (lit. Neverending Regret) by Malayan A. R. Tompel.

Tompel, whose real name was Aman Ramli bin Jaafa, began his film career as assistant director on Shaw's *Aloha* directed by B. S. Rajhans in 1950, after having been the top dancer at the Kris Opera from 1938 onwards. Both films also cast a different set of actors from the ones signed and used by Shaw. New talent came on screen, with Ismail Kasim, Nona Asiah, Saloma, Eloni Hayat, Mustarjo, S. Naning, Ratna Si, R. Suriani. Some of them would eventually go on to work for Shaw or Cathay-Keris.

In 1951 and 1952, Nusantara Film produced a few more movies, including *Dian* (lit. Candle), directed by Naz Achnas, this time with actors more established on the Singapore scene, like S. Kadarisman, Normadiah, Osman Gumanti or Daeng Idris. Another movie was *Norma* by A. R. Tompel, featuring almost the same cast, who, following the practice started by Shaw, had been signed to a few films.

Some of Nusantara's last titles were *Pacar Putih* (lit. White Lover) by Naz Achnas, and *Seniyati* (lit. Film Star), interestingly codirected by A. R. Tompel and Chow Wing Kok, thus bringing together both Malay and Chinese references and influences.

It is also said that Nusantara Film produced two more movies, one titled *Perkahwinan Rahsia* (lit. Secret Wedding), and the other said to be directed by Hsu Chiu Meng himself — but under the name M. Widjaya (even

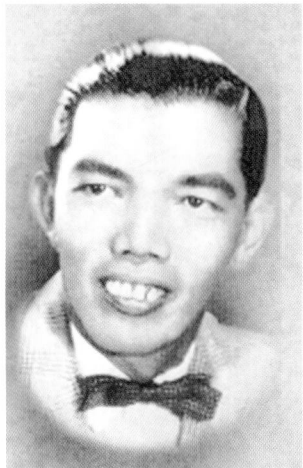

A. R. Tompel.

though it is sometimes said that this was also a pseudonym for Tompel) — and titled *Mencari Jodoh* (lit. Waiting for the Perfect Match). Little is known about those films in particular, and about Nusantara Film in general.

Nusantara Film produced a rather limited number of films, six to seven known productions over a period of less than three years (though some sources attribute up to 12 movies to them). Nevertheless, it made a significant contribution to the history of Singapore cinema by introducing diversity, not only in the choice of actors, but more importantly, in the choice of directors. For the first time, film direction was not assigned only to Indian filmmakers (which was Shaw's policy up to that point), but to Malays. However, Nusantara Film's two main directors, A. R. Tompel and Naz Achnas, had rather shortlived careers as filmmakers in Singapore.

A. R. Tompel acted in a few Shaw movies directed by B. S. Rajhans, L. Krishnan and S. Ramanathan in the early 1950s. He then stopped for a period, and resumed acting in Malaysian movies produced by the Kuala Lumpur-based Merdeka Studio in the mid- to late-1960s. He was often seen playing the villain. He also wrote the lyrics of numerous P. Ramlee songs in the 1950s and 1960s.

In the 1960s and 1970s, he even started directing his own movies again, mostly for Merdeka Film Productions in Kuala Lumpur. He continued until his death in 1973, the same year as his long-time friend P. Ramlee. Their last movie together was *Laksmana Do Re Mi*, filmed just the year before, in 1972.

Beyond movies, A. R. Tompel was famous as well for having, some say, no fewer than seven wives. This may have been trivia, except for the fact that his greatest legacy is perhaps his children, some of whom have gone on to acting or directing careers. One of his sons, Adlin Aman Ramlee, was recently cast as Sultan Mahmud Shah in Malaysia's big-budget *Puteri Gunung Ledang* (lit. Princess of Mount Ledang) made in 2003.

Achnas quickly disappeared from the Singapore film industry, except for a short comeback in 1959 when he directed *Rahsia Hatiku* (lit. The Secret of My Heart) for Shaw's Malay Film Productions. He remained active in Indonesia and Malaysia, where he was still directing movies in the 1970s, making *Dosa Remaja* (lit. Sins of Youth) in 1971 and *Mastura* in 1974, both for Merdeka Film Productions, and *Loceng Maut* (lit. The Death Knell) as late as 1976.

As for Nusantara Film, it depended heavily on independent theatres to screen its productions. These were rapidly decreasing in number since both Malayan Theatres Ltd for the Shaw brothers and Associated Theatres Ltd for Loke Wan Tho were slowly taking control of most of the Malay exhibition market. Eventually, in 1954, Nusantara Film had to cease operations.

HO AH LOKE'S RIMAU AND KERIS
Ho Ah Loke is the undeservedly forgotten figure in most written historical accounts of the local film industry. Born in 1901 in British Guinea, Abraham Ho Ah Loke, popularly known either as Ah Loke or as Abe, was educated in Edinburgh and Penang, before going to university in Hong Kong to further his engineering studies. During his university days, he was named champion athlete of Hong Kong University three years in a row.

After returning to Penang in 1925, Ho, now in his mid-20s, ventured into the film exhibition business, at about the same time that the Shaw brothers, Runme and Run Run, moved to Singapore. Whereas the Shaws expanded their business first in Singapore and South Malaya, Ho developed his exhibition network in northern Malaya and even southern Thailand. Equipped with a simple projector, he started roaming the countryside, introducing

Ho Ah Loke.

cinema to small-town inhabitants. When the Shaws also moved North under the initiative of Shaw Runme, Ho eventually teamed up with them, running what they called their "mosquito lorry", hopping from small town to village, screening Charlie Chaplin movies and other American slapsticks.

Business being good, Ho was soon able to buy The Union cinema hall in Ipoh as early as 1926, then the Oriental in 1930, followed by more and more acquisitions in Taiping, Telok Anson, Kampar and Klang. He suddenly sold off his theatre hall network to Shaw in 1934, but quickly resumed business with his Odeon chain in Kuala Lumpur, Ipoh and Penang. By the beginning of World War II, he was a major force in the film exhibition business, and was duly known as North Malaya's movie tycoon.

To avoid the Japanese, Ho went to Thailand where he remained until the end of the war, returning to Malaya only in late 1945. He resumed his movie activities while looking out for new ventures. In 1948, instead of teaming up with the Shaws, he approached Loke Wan Tho and formed a new company with him called Associated, International and Loke Theatres, of which he became director, as well as head of the Film Booking department. Ho was not only older than Loke Wan Tho, he was also far more experienced, having gone into the movie business 20 years before Loke started running Cathay.

Eager to finally explore movie production, Ho opened a two-set studio, named Keris Film Studio, on Tampines Road, Singapore, in 1951. He also started a production company named Rimau Film Productions, a joint venture between Cathay and an Indian partner said to be called Hardial Singh. After producing his first two films, *Bunga Percintaan* (lit. Love Flower) and *Untuk Sesuap Nasi* (lit. For a Mouthful of Rice), both directed by L. Krishnan, he changed its name to Keris Film Productions, and under that label went on to produce some of the most interesting movies of the 1950s.

Ho was in fact becoming more involved in the making of films locally, leaving the running of his earlier film exhibition business to Loke. As his homegrown productions expanded and proved to be increasingly successful, he was able to convince Loke to become a full partner as well. Together, they formed Cathay-Keris, a new major studio.

Ho Ah Loke's venture into production took Singapore cinema to new levels. In just a few years, he would achieve many firsts. He would be the man partly responsible for breaking away from the *bangsawan* influence with *Setia* (lit. Faithful) in 1952, followed by a series of other titles.

Loke Wan Tho and Ho Ah Loke (standing, both wearing glasses) with S. Roomai Noor (standing, centre) and the tribal cast of *Chinta Gadis Rimba* by L. Krishnan, 1958.

He would also be responsible for the first two local films shot in colour, *Perwira Lautan Teduh* (lit. Warrior of the Calm Seas) in 1952, of which little is known and no print seems to remain, and *Buloh Perindu* (a.k.a. *Magic Flute*) in 1953. While not a box-office hit, *Buloh Perindu* was an important step forward for local moviemaking.

Ho was also the man behind the first adaptation of the then famous local novel, *Chinta Gadis Rimba* (a.k.a. *The Virgin of Borneo*, lit. Love of the Jungle Girl), written by Harun Hamid Rashid, and made into a movie by L. Krishnan. Filmed in 1958, it was also one of the rare local movies shot in colour then.

Ho's trust in local talent boosted the industry and instilled creativity in a manner unknown at that time. He was a great supporter of actors like S. Roomai Noor, Mat Sentol and Wahid Satay. His views on cinema also tremendously benefited Cathay, which he led into the Malay moviemaking business, and for which he initiated the ultimate Singapore-made cult movie, the first *Pontianak* in 1957.

At the turn of the 1960s, after heading south to Singapore, Ho made one last move. He left Cathay-Keris, taking with him the rights and prints of roughly 20 movies (those in which he had had significant production involvement, such as *Buloh Perindu* or *Pontianak*), and returned north, to a newly-independent Malaysia. There, he was one of the founding fathers of the Merdeka Studio in Kuala Lumpur. He made the very first Malaysian (and not only Malay anymore) movies, shot once again by his old partner L. Krishnan.

He also apparently ventured into producing a local movie filmed entirely in Cantonese, *You Kow Pik Ying* (a.k.a. *Ask and It Shall be Given*) in 1962. Much remains unknown about it, and it is not even clear whether it was still a Cathay-Keris movie, or already a Merdeka Film Productions one, or a totally independent venture.

Things were always a bit vague with Ho, who worked spontaneously, following sudden impulses, ceaselessly digging up new ideas, and never waiting for things to be settled or done the conventional way. He is said to have always had cash on him, and was known to go almost everywhere carrying large amounts of money in a paper bag. He would then be able to hire someone on the spot, without a contract or formal agreement. Perhaps that is how he got so much done, and also perhaps why he got into so much trouble.

Having worked with the Shaw brothers in their early days in Singapore and Malaya, having given them the opportunity to vastly expand their empire in the mid-1930s by selling them his exhibition circuit, having worked with Cathay first in the exhibition then in the production lines, but having also always remained independent, carrying on projects of his own in his own indecipherable manner, Ho undeniably exerted a major influence on the history of film in Singapore and Malaysia.

Not always on the frontline, he acted more as the brains behind all the groundbreaking projects, slowly growing into a godfather-like figure within the industry. A close look at the title credits on the film prints reveal that he was the driving force behind most of the movies he was deeply involved in, even during his Cathay-Keris days. It was Keris Film Productions which was credited as the producer, while Cathay Organisation was the presenter. This was true for the first pontianak movies, no less. This was true even for *Chinta Gadis Rimba* (a.k.a. The *Virgin of Borneo*). For this movie, Ho was also credited for the screenplay along with L. Krishnan.

Cathay-Keris' screenlogo featuring the Malay *keris*.

Yet, total independence exacted its price. After Ho gave up on Merdeka Studio in the mid-1960s (and it passed into Shaw's hands), he was unable to find new partners and other projects. He became a lonely figure, and he died in 1982 — more or less forgotten by all except a few faithful friends — exactly 30 years after he had been largely responsible for the birth of the golden age of Singapore cinema. Unfortunately, most of his legacy has been lost, since one day, on an impulse, he himself dumped the prints of the movies he had taken with him when he left Cathay.

CATHAY-KERIS Initially, Cathay did not screen local Malay movies, for the simple reason that Shaw, the major producer of Malay movies did not distribute them into Cathay's exhibition circuit, but rather kept them for its own cinemas. Cathay thus distributed mostly Chinese and Western movies. To secure its supplies, Loke Wan Tho struck an exclusive deal with UK-based Rank Organisation to distribute and exhibit its productions in Singapore, Malaya, Thailand and Hong Kong. He also introduced the first colour movies to Singapore and screened them to a thrilled audience from 1950 onwards.

Loke Wan Tho.

Nevertheless, Loke, like the Shaws a few years before, made the observation that the Malayan market, as it was known at that time, was fast expanding, and had the highest potential for growth. In 1951, Malaya's takings for Cathay's International Associated Theatres was double Singapore's takings.

Therefore, in 1953, Loke became fully involved in production with Ho Ah Loke (whom he had already partnered with in the film distribution and exhibition businesses since 1948, and also in coproduction since Rimau and Keris). Together, they formed Cathay-Keris, which was going to be Cathay's famous production branch and, historically, Singapore's second film studio, one of only two studios in Singapore for the next 20 years.

The new company had its facilities on East Coast Road. Supported by its own theatre chain throughout Malaya and Singapore, Cathay-Keris was the first competitor to pose a serious challenge to the Shaw empire. Its entry into the moviemaking business took the Studio Era to a new stage, which would last until the closure of the Cathay-Keris studios in 1972.

A very organised and passionate man, Loke took great care of his new venture. He visited studios in India to learn first-hand how movies were made, and invited Hollywood personalities to coach his newly hired stars. In his studio system, he encouraged everyone to compete with one another — director with director, producer with producer, actor with actor — so as to bring out the best in everyone. Like Ho, he had great belief in talent, and was ready to give his best directors, actors and technicians whatever they needed to make the dream movie. Loke's naturally more artistic approach differed substantially from Shaw Run Run's originally more strictly profit-driven one. Yet, they both established a very structured studio system, producing 15 to 20 movies annually for the next 15 years.

THE SHAW AND CATHAY STUDIOS Both the Shaw and Cathay studios had their own facilities: sets, laboratories, recording and editing rooms. The people who made the movies, whether actors or

Cathay-Keris studios on East Coast Road in 1950s (top) and a cameraman working at that studio (bottom).

contributed specialised skills, mostly as technicians involved in lab processing. The Indians provided the know-how as directors and cinematography technicians, and the Malays provided screen talent as actors, singers, dancers, and, on very rare occasions, actors-turned-directors (it was only after 1959 that the employment of Malays as directors would really expand).

The directors, actors, artists and technicians generally signed contracts for three to five years with the studio, and thus became fulltime salaried employees. Everyone focused only on the movies to be made. The pay was

Life at Shaw's studio on Jalan Ampas (top) and its lab processing facilities (bottom) in the early 1960s.

technicians, generally lived together in nearby housing estates provided by each company. Accommodation was free, with tenants only having to pay for water and electricity. Shaw's Malay Film Productions was on Jalan Ampas, with accommodation within walking distance on Boon Teck Road. Cathay-Keris had a similar set-up at its Jalan Keris studio on East Coast Road. It was like living on a campus, or in a *kampong*. Everything was done in-house.

One particular movie, *Seniman Bujang Lapok* (a.k.a. *The Nit-wit Movie Stars*) directed by P. Ramlee in 1961, captured life at the Shaw studio very well. Besides being an excellent comedy, the film is now also an invaluable "documentary" on a long-gone era.

In the first years of the studio system, up to 1958, the Chinese provided the money as distributors, exhibitors and producers. Eventually, they also

Noordin Ahmad signing autographs for some visitors at the Cathay-Keris studio in the late 1950s.

not high, but at least there was regular work, and making a living was no longer something they had to worry about. Salaries rose when Cathay came in as a competitor to Shaw, and tried to attract talent. The studio employees were eventually paid bonuses based on the success of the films they worked on.

Most of the actors were typecast. Villain roles regularly went to Mahmud June, A. R. Tompel, Siput Sarawak or Ahmad Nesfu (a.k.a. Nisfu), while the innocent girl was played by Latiffah Omar, Saadiah or Rose Yatimah.

The studios also had their in-house orchestras, such as Shaw's famous MFP Orkes, which was also known as MFP Orchestra. They worked a lot with local composers as well, mostly P. Ramlee himself for Shaw, and Yusoff B., Rahim Hamid and Zubir Said (who, in 1959, also happened to write Singapore's national anthem, *Majulah Singapura*, significantly sung in Malay) for Cathay.

The studios sometimes used outside groups, like The Fabulous Flamingos in Ramon Estella's 1964 movie, *Melanchong ke Tokyo* (lit. Going to Tokyo). After 1965, both studios, and particularly Cathay-Keris, increasingly engaged local groups playing rock 'n' roll and *pop yeh yeh* music. The Swallows performed in Ramon Estella's *Pusaka Pontianak* (a.k.a. *The Accursed Heritage*, a.k.a. *The Pontianak Legacy*), in 1965, and The O.K. Boys in M. Amin's *Dua Kali Lima* (lit. Two Times Five) in 1966. Les Feontones was in Noordin Ahmad's *Playboy*, The Pretenders in Mat Sentol's *Mat Bond*, and The Rhythm Boys in M. Amin's *Dosa Wanita* (lit. A Woman's Sin), all in 1967.

During these studio years, the overwhelming majority of the films were in black-and-white. Only six colour movies were produced by the studios, three each by Cathay-Keris and Shaw; very few considering that about 280 movies were produced by the two studios. Cathay-Keris was the pioneer with

Buloh Perindu (a.k.a. *Magic Flute*) in 1953; then *Chinta Gadis Rimba* (a.k.a. *The Virgin of Borneo*) and *Mahsuri*, both in 1958. Shaw's first colour movies were *Ribut* (lit. Storm) in 1955, *Hang Tuah* in 1956 and *Raja Bersiong* (a.k.a. *King with The Fangs*) in 1967. As for sound, direct sound recording was the practice from the beginning. The 1960s saw the advent of postsynchronizing and dubbing systems.

Scripts were mostly based on folk tales and legends, and fictional and real historical heroes like *Hang Tuah*, *Hang Jebat* and *Tun Fatimah*, and were rarely adapted from contemporary stage plays or novels.

Most importantly, both Shaw and Cathay were real studios. They vertically integrated the whole industry, from production to distribution and then to exhibition. Their movie theatre chains were their most profitable sources of revenue. From the mid-1940s to the early 1970s, they consistently and continually expanded their exhibition circuits, revamping cinema halls and building new ones.

Shaw took over Capitol Theatre from the Namazie brothers in 1946. They built the Odeon in 1953, which would operate for 30 years until its closure in 1983. In 1959, the Shaw brothers opened their flagship theatre, the Lido, on Orchard Road. It was renovated in the early 1990s.

As for Cathay, it started operating the Coliseum Theatre in

Hang Tuah by Phani Majumdar, 1956, one of Shaw's first colour movies.

Kuala Lumpur in 1947, and renovated it in 1962, and once again in 1979. Loke Wan Tho also bought the Queen's theatre, previously owned by Shaw. This was strategically located in the heart of Singapore's Chinatown, an ideal venue for the release of all the MP&GI productions that were to flood the market for the next 15 years. In 1965, The Orchard, a brand new Cathay cinema opened in downtown Singapore. And in 1971, just when it was about to close its production line and focus only on its exhibition business, Cathay opened its famous Jurong drive-in cinema.

THE FOCUS ON MALAYNESS   Even though the studios eventually ventured into a few non-Malay experiments (for instance, Cathay-Keris' Chinese movie shot in Mandarin in 1960, *Shi Zi Cheng*, a.k.a. *Lion City*), their main focus was making Malay movies portraying authentic Malayness.

As a matter of fact, and very symbolically, cinema in Singapore and Malaya in the 1950s was still frequently called by its Malay name, *panggung*

Left to right: famous Malay film stars, Siput Sarawak, S. Roomai Noor, Jins Shamsudin and Rokiah.

wayang. More precisely, *panggung* traditionally referred to a theatre hall, that is theatre as a place, comprising the stage and the audience. As for *wayang*, it traditionally referred to shadow puppetry. Combining these two words was highly appropriate since it linked cinema in Singapore and Malaya to two pre- or proto-cinematic forms directly originating form the Malay world. Furthermore, cinema in its early days had greatly borrowed some of its inspiration as well as most of its cast from *sandiwara* (Malay theatre) and *bangsawan* (Malay opera).

The influence of *bangsawan* seemed to have been the strongest, both in terms of cast and repertoire. When it came to casting its first Malay movies, in the late 1930s and early 1940s, it was clear that Shaw recruited from among *bangsawan* actors: Tina, Habsah, Puteh Lawak, Aman Belon, Adi Teruna, and others. In terms of repertoire, *bangsawan* was based on, firstly, local historical stories, secondly, local folktales, and thirdly, a mixture of Arabian, Indian, Chinese, Indian and even European classics. If Hang Tuah was a familiar figure on the *bangsawan* stage, so was Hamlet. But it was an integrated and adapted version of Hamlet, Malay culture having always been able to absorb and adapt varied influences and sources of inspiration, due to its natural syncretic attitude.

However, the main source of inspiration was the history and folklore of the Malay archipelago. For instance, *Bawang Puteh Bawang Merah* (names meaning lit. Garlic and Onion) or *Batu Belah Batu Bertangkup* (lit. Stone Splits Stone Closes) were folk tales that found expression first in *bangsawan*, before being turned into movies in 1959, by S. Roomai Noor and Jamil Sulong respectively, two Malay directors who were particularly keen on instilling more and more Malayness in local films.

Significantly, during the first decade of the golden age of the studios when Singapore was a multiracial community with a strong Chinese base, most of the actors on screen were Malay. Hardly any Chinese was featured, or they appeared only in caricature: laughing coolies, shrewd businessmen, and the like. Indian characters were even more rare, ironic considering that the majority of these movies were directed by Indians.

The Shaw studio was aptly named "Malay" Film Productions; and the Cathay studio appropriated one of the most significant Malay symbols inherited from the Nusantara days, the *keris* (also spelled *kris*) which is the traditional Malay dagger. Other production houses, such as Keris, Rimau or Nusantara, were also obviously named to appeal to the wider Malay world.

As a matter of fact, the Malay world embraced by the then growing film industry was definitely not limited to the Malay peninsula, but offered far more diversity. This is clearly shown not only by the involvement of Chinese, Indians and Filipinos, as we shall see later, but by the varied origins of the Malay artists themselves.

If a high number of them were born in Singapore, such as Mariam, S. Shamsuddin, Neng Yatimah, Yusoff Latiff, Zaiton, Hashimah Yon, Saadiah, Saloma or Rose Yatimah, many others, like P. Ramlee, Mohamed Zain, Noordin Ahmad or Ahmad Nesfu came from Penang; or from Kuala Lumpur like Ibrahim Din or Latiffah Omar. Ahmad Mahmud, Rokiah and Haji Mahadi were from Negeri Sembilan; Ibrahim Pendek and Jins Shamsudin from Perak; Jamil Sulong from Johor; S. Roomai Noor (whose real name was Mohamed Taid bin Salleh) and Sarimah from Pahang. A massive contingent came from Indonesia: Kasma Booty, one of the earliest movie actresses, as well as Ahmad Ja'afar, Rosnani, Rubiah and Osman Gumanti were from Sumatra; Aziz Sattar, S. Sudarmadji and Malik Sutan Muda from Java; Maria Menado, Siti Tanjung Perak, Normadiah and Daeng Harris from Sulawesi. As for Siput Sarawak, born Ramlah binti Abdullah, she was from... Sarawak.

Like *bangsawan* artists before them, it was the trend in the early days of Malay cinema for actors to adopt a screen name which would carry the trace of a geographical origin. This was particularly true for the women. Following the example of Siput Sarawak, Maria Menado took as her surname the name of her hometown. Malay cinema, even in the name of its artists, was definitely rooted in the geography of the Malay archipelago itself.

Another unique characteristic of Malay cinema in those early days was the language. Quite a few of the actors were previously trained in *bangsawan* so they were used to improvisation, and often incorporated their own personal traits into their roles. As they were from all over the Malay archipelago, it was common for these actors to play their roles in their own dialects, or at least, use their own regional accents. This did not seem to bother the filmmakers and producers, or anyone else for that matter. The end result was that the language used in some films was not necessarily representative of the character being portrayed, but rather of the actor playing the part.

Emphasis was often placed on the fact that the movie had been "locally filmed", shot "in Malay", sometimes even in "classical Malay" (even if these descriptions did not accurately reflect the content of the movie), thus telling us that language was undeniably a main source of identity and authenticity. The movies were often not subtitled in Chinese or English. And if there were subtitles, the reviews in the newspapers would make special mention: "There are English subtitles too, so that those of us who have been too lazy to strengthen our Malay vocabulary will enjoy it to the full". In those days, Singapore was still part of a larger entity, the Malay world, that encompassed neighbouring Malaya, which would soon to become the Federation of Malaysia, and which the island-city would try to be a part of.

Furthermore, when the movie happened to be a period drama, great attention was given to an accurate portrayal of the old days of Nusantara, where the Malay world had some of its roots. Explicit mention would be made that teams of specialists advised on "Malay etiquette and customs", as could be seen in the title credits of the famous *Hang Tuah* directed by Phani Majumdar for Shaw. Very often as well, the opening of the film would be a frontal shot of either a Malay palace or a Malay village, easily identifiable to the local audience.

DIVERSITY OF INFLUENCES

Focusing on Malayness and giving it priority did not mean local cinema was not influenced by other cultures, particularly the dominant film culture of the time. While Malay on the face of it, Singapore cinema was in fact characterised by great internal cultural heterogeneity. Its development and growth was the result of a wide set of influences from far beyond Nusantara.

Indian culture in general, and Indian cinema in particular, played a major role, to the extent that, as we shall see later, the Indian connection exerted what could be considered an overwhelming influence. Filipino film culture also played a significant role in the growth of Singapore Malay film, and an entire group of Filipino directors who shot movies either for Shaw or for Cathay deserve to be fully included in the history of Singapore cinema.

Less direct and internalised, but nevertheless undeniable and observable, was the influence of culturally and geographically more distant film cultures and industries such as American, Egyptian and Japanese cinemas. In the case of Hollywood, one cannot ignore the fact that in the 1940s, 1950s and 1960s, Singapore was flooded with American movies, distributed and exhibited by Cathay and Shaw themselves. The moviegoing audience was definitely familiar with genres such as Westerns and film noir. So were local filmmakers.

The P. Ramlee movie, *Labu dan Labi* (lit. Labu and Labi), even makes explicit references to this familiarity, through a series of sketches in which the actors take on different identities and parody different genres. Mohamed Zain

Jefri Zain — Gerak Kilat by Jamil Sulong, 1966 featuring Jins Shamsudin as "Singapore's own Bond".

(Labu) becomes "Jesse Labu" while P. Ramlee (Labi) turns into "the Sheriff" and pretends to be Nat King Cole's brother (which has got nothing to do with a Western, but, hey, what does it matter...). In another scene, Labu and Labi (who then introduces himself as "the Magistrate") meet in a nightclub directly borrowed from a typical film noir. A very farfetched fantasy even turns Labu into Tarzan and Labi into Harimau (which means tiger in Malay), a scene in which, happily mixing all references without deference, Harimau (who can speak) asks, "Does Tarzan wear a *kris*?", and Tarzan replies, "Ah ah! This is a Malayan Tarzan!" Silly, yes, but ultimately exemplifying the fact that the Singapore movie industry was totally aware of who and what it was influenced by.

The direct influence of movies from the West on locally produced films can be seen in the impact made by James Bond in the 1960s, which was as huge in Singapore as it was in the rest of the world. As early as 1966, Malay director Jamil Sulong came up with a rip-off of the Bond movies. *Gerak Kilat* (lit. Moves in a Flash) introduced "S'pore's own Bond", secret agent Jefri Zain, played by the dashing Jins Shamsudin. This was going to be the first of a series of Jefri Zain movies, in the manner of the Bond series, taking that Singaporean hero around Asia.

It is worth noting that the sequels, *Bayangan Ajal* (lit. Overshadowed by Doom) and *Jurang Bahaya* (lit. Caught in between Two Dangers), shot largely in Hong Kong, were directed by Lo Wei, a young filmmaker recruited by the Shaw brothers in Hong Kong. Lo Wei would later direct some of the very first Bruce Lee movies, no less. Jefri Zain was in good company. And, needless to

Shooting of *Ali Baba Bujang Lapok* by P. Ramlee, 1961.

say, the Singapore film industry was amazingly connected to many film industries throughout the world, though it would be for a rather short period.

As for Arabic cinema, the audience had been familiar with it since the mid-1930s. This was particularly so for films from Egypt, the most active place for filmmaking in the Middle-East at that time. Here again, local film distributors were the first ones to actively propagate Arabic movies. These films were, in many ways, perfectly suited to the Malay audience, who not only shared the Muslim cultural background of such movies, but was also very familiar with old Arabian tales and traditions. Moreover, the Malays used *jawi*, a script adapted from Arabic and used for writing the Malay language until the late 1950s when the Roman script, called *rumi*, took over.

The Middle-Eastern influence is obvious in the narrative themselves, with Malay films adapting *Ali Baba* or *Sinbad the Sailor* in many different ways, and in the numerous Arabian dances profusely advertised on posters and flyers announcing a new local movie. Such was blatantly the case for *Nilam* (lit. Sapphire), shot as early as 1949 by B. S. Rajhans, in which a young Malay,

played by S. Roomai Noor, travelled all the way to the Middle-East, where he encountered hordes of belly-dancers. On a more serious tone, Cathay-Keris' 1960 *Noor Islam* (lit. The Light of Islam) by K. M. Basker directly addressed the coming of Islam to the Malay world.

However, once again, the best synthesis was provided by P. Ramlee who, with his usual wit and genius, spotted this influence and used it as a source of parody in his 1961 comedy *Ali Baba Bujang Lapok* (lit. Ali Baba Confirmed Bachelor).

THE INDIAN CONNECTION

While Western or Middle-Eastern influences were undeniable, Indian culture was to have the most impact on Malay cinema. Initially, there was no experienced local director in Singapore. Producers who ventured into Malay films had to rely on foreign filmmakers (ironically, they would be called "foreign talents" in today's Singapore), either from China or India, where structured movie industries existed.

The Shaws discovered that their Indian director B. S. Rajhans was far more skilled at making local Malay films than the Chinese film directors Hau Yaw and Wan Hai Ling. This was partly because Rajhans, due to his

Indian origins, was more in tune with Malay culture. It is a historical fact that Malay culture had been strongly influenced by Indian tradition. Stories in old Malay culture, and particularly *bangsawan*, very often drew on influences predating the arrival of Islam, from as far back as the early Indian culture of the region.

In order to increase production, the Shaw brothers brought in a host of directors from India. They chose the first of these directors based on their talent but also, more pragmatically, their familiarity with

S. Ramanathan.

Malay culture and language. L. Krishnan and S. Ramanathan were both hired in 1949, and the former, although born in Madras, had spent many years of his youth in Penang and Singapore, while the latter was born and raised in Kuala Lumpur (before going back with his family to India).

They were followed in 1952 by K. M. Basker (a.k.a. Bashker), B. N. Rao, V. Girimali and K. R. S. Shastry (a.k.a. Sastry). Joining them in 1956 was Phani Majumdar, and in 1958, Dhiresh Ghosh and Kidar Sharma.

All the Indian directors were initially introduced to the Singapore film industry by the Shaw brothers (except for P. L. Kapur who came in 1959 for only one movie made for Cathay-Keris). A few eventually went to work for Cathay-Keris, including the talented L. Krishnan, who became a

Long House (a.k.a. *Rumah Panjang*) by Phani Majumdar, 1957.

household name there, and B. S. Rajhans, known as the founding father of Singapore cinema, as well as B. N. Rao, who directed the very first pontianak movies.

The contribution of these Indian directors to the history of film in Singapore cannot be overlooked. Even before Cathay-Keris came into existence in 1953, B. S. Rajhans, L. Krishnan and S. Ramanathan had already contributed 36 feature films to Singapore cinema.

Between 1933 and 1964, over a 30-year period which symbolically ended right before Singapore's independence, these 11 Indian filmmakers directed almost 140 Malay movies. L. Krishnan made 30 movies during his Singapore days, B. S. Rajhans 27, B. N. Rao 24, K. M. Basker 18, and S. Ramanathan 17.

They were also very creative, making a number of major breakthroughs. These included the use of colour, the adaptation of local novels and shooting at outdoor locations. They also explored new locations like Sarawak, and made the first monster movies, introducing the "pontianak", a female vampire, and the "orang minyak", or oily man, to the screen. They were responsible for some of the most outstanding box-office hits, including *Pontianak*, *Dendam Pontianak* (lit. Revenge of the Pontianak) and *Mahsuri*.

Whatever the movie genre, Indian film conventions influenced mannerisms and dialogue. Acting was overstylised, songs expressed emotions, dance scenes suddenly broke up the narration. The Indian influence carried over to having initials in names, with Ramlee becoming P. Ramlee, and Roomai Noor transformed into S. Roomai Noor.

Wahid Satay (left) in *Satay* by K.M. Basker, 1958.

Each Indian director had a Malay assistant, who would eventually be credited as assistant director. They helped the directors with their understanding of local culture, and assisted in managing local crews and casts. They learned directly from these directors, and soon started to direct their own movies. When the directors returned to India (except for B. S. Rajhans who died in Singapore, and L. Krishnan who moved to Malaysia), the former assistants turned directors were there to fill the gap.

B. S. RAJHANS LEADS THE WAY
After *Seruan Merdeka* (lit. Call to Freedom), independently produced by Malayan Arts Production in 1946, Balden Singh Rajhans teamed up with the Shaw brothers. He made 20 movies for them between 1947 and 1953. Until 1950, he was the only film director with Shaw, hence the only one working in Singapore. It was in his movies that many of the major Malay actors became stars, such as Kasma Booty, Siput Sarawak, S. Roomai Noor, P. Ramlee and S. Shamsuddin. B. S. Rajhans personified the Singapore film industry and set trends, until he was joined in 1949 by other directors brought from India by Shaw, L. Krishnan and S. Ramanathan.

In the middle of 1953, Rajhans left the Shaw studio for its new competitor, Cathay-Keris. There he made five more movies until his death in 1955 (some accounts say 1957) in Singapore. He holds a very special place in Singapore film history, having made a total of 28 films in Singapore (only the prolific L. Krishnan made more). These include four seminal works: the very first Malay talkie *Leila Majnun* in 1933, the very first post-World War II movie *Seruan Merdeka* in 1946, the very first Singapore studio production for Shaw, *Chinta* (lit. Love) in 1948, and the very first Cathay-Keris movie, *Buloh Perindu* (a.k.a. *Magic Flute*), in 1953. If a founding father

were to be designated, it would certainly be him.

However, with only a handful of India-made features in the 1930s, Rajhans is hardly known in his homeland, and is almost never mentioned in the history of Indian film industry. And even though he paved the way for the Singapore Malay film industry, he is almost totally absent from the annals of the city-state. This may be due to him being from India. Another, perhaps more salient reason, may be that he started very early on, and his career ended not only before Singapore gained its independence in 1965, but before even its autonomy in 1959. Furthermore, the major part of his career (21 out of 28 movies) was achieved before 1953, before the real heyday of Singapore cinema and the golden age of the studios.

L. KRISHNAN, THE MOST PROLIFIC DIRECTOR
Lakshmanan Krishnan was born in Madras, India, in 1922. Arriving one generation after B. S. Rajhans, he travelled first to Penang, and then to Singapore in 1940 where he got his first job at the Cricket Club, and then at the Raffles Hotel. Repatriated to India at the end of World War II, he met Indian film director and producer Shri K. Subrahmanyam, who introduced him to the thriving local film industry. In the late 1940s, L. Krishnan directed his first movie, *Amma*, a Singhalese feature.

The movie was enough of a success, and Krishnan was headhunted by a Shaw talent scout, who was in India to bring back directing talent for their expanding studio in Singapore. Thus, in 1949, L. Krishnan became one of the two new film directors (the other being S. Ramanathan) hired by Shaw. He would stay in the island-city for 10 years before moving to Kuala Lumpur to work for Merdeka Studio.

While in Singapore, Krishnan directed 30 movies, becoming Singapore's most prolific director. He exceeded B. S. Rajhans (28 features) who had started almost 20 years before, and B. N. Rao (24 features) whose career in Singapore continued until the mid-1960s.

In comparison to Malay directors in Singapore, Krishnan's tally was approximately double that of renowned artists like P. Ramlee (16 movies in Singapore), Jamil Sulong (17) and Omar Rojik (15). Only M. Amin, who made 28 features from 1962 to 1972, came close.

This unmatched record was certainly due to the fact that he could churn out a script within a fortnight. In 1958, he and

L. Krishnan.

Sumpah Orang Minyak by P. Ramlee, 1958 (top row) and in-street promotion campaign for the movie (bottom).

P. Ramlee competed to make the first *Orang Minyak* (lit. Oily Man). Krishnan was faster, forcing Ramlee to rename his movie *Sumpah Orang Minyak* (lit. The Curse of the Oily Man). His contribution is also particularly outstanding given the high quality of some of his movies, and for the pioneering role he played in shaping the future of Malay cinema. For one, he was able to talent-spot future stars. He helped many to achieve successful careers in the industry.

Krishnan's directorial debut in Singapore, made under Shaw's Malay Film Productions, was *Bakti* (a.k.a. *Faithfulness*), a mix of numerous Indian stories. It starred established actresses Kasma Booty and Siput Sarawak, both of whom had previously been given lead roles by B. S. Rajhans. The movie also starred the then up-and-coming actor P. Ramlee. It was Ramlee's first lead role, thus marking a major breakthrough in the history of Malay movies.

Many other talents were either introduced to the screen or given career-making roles by Krishnan. The ultimate female icon of Malay filmdom, Maria Menado, was given her first starring role by L. Krishnan, in his third movie of 1950, *Penghidupan* (lit. Life). Rosnani Jamil, whom he first noticed when she was a *joget* dancer, and her husband Jamil Sulong started their careers in his 1952 *Lupa Daratan* (lit. Forgetting the Land). Krishnan also gave many major roles to actors like S. Roomai Noor or M. Amin. These actors also learnt and developed their future directing skills under his expert eye.

In 1952, Krishnan was one of the first to break away from Shaw, whom he had originally signed a three-year contract with. He joined forces with independent producers, directing *Bunga Percintaan* (lit. Love Flower) and *Untuk Sesuap Nasi* (lit. For a Mouthful of Rice). These were the first two feature

Promotional standee for *Orang Minyak* by L. Krishnan, 1958.

Siput Sarawak in *Raden Mas* by L. Krishnan, 1959.

films produced by Ho Ah Loke at his shortlived company, Rimau Film Production, which had been set up with the help of Hardial Singh & Co., which was then distributing Indian movies in Singapore and Malaya.

Krishnan followed Ho when he founded Cathay-Keris together with Loke Wan Tho in 1953. He may not have been responsible for the cult pontianak movies, but Krishnan did bring to the screen one of the strangest creatures of the Malay movie world — the *orang minyak* — with his 1958 *Orang Minyak* (lit. Oily Man) and *Serangan Orang Minyak* (lit. Attack of the Oily Man).

At the beginning of the 1960s, Krishnan moved on again. He teamed up with long-time partner Ho Ah Loke to set up Merdeka Studio, where he directed the first Malaysian feature, *Tun Teja* (a.k.a. *Tun Tijah*) in 1961. Between 1961 and 1962, he filmed *Keris Sempena Riau* (lit. Keris Commemorating Riau), *Selendang Merah* (lit. Red Scarf), *Ratapan Ibu* (lit. Mother's Wails) and *Fajar Menyinsing* (lit. Rising Dawn), thus contributing five movies to the up-and-coming Malaysian cinema scene. Even though Singapore was not independent yet, and was still a part of the Federation of Malaysia (between 1963 and 1965), this late series of movies by Krishnan belongs to Malaysian film history. They symbolically mark a break away from the Singapore-driven Malay film industry.

After having contributed significantly to the expansion of Shaw's Malay Film Productions, to the early days and successes of Cathay-Keris, and finally to the foundation of a Malaysian national cinema with Merdeka Studio's first movie, Krishnan left the cinema industry in 1963. He saw that the future was bright for the advertising and media industry, and launched Gaya Film Berhad in Kuala Lumpur to produce commercials.

B. N. Rao.

B. N. RAO, FATHER OF PONTIANAK

The filmmaker B. N. Rao stands out for four reasons. First, he had a promising career in Tamil filmmaking before coming to Singapore. Second, he contributed some of the most successful movies at the box office in the 1950s and 1960s, including the legendary pontianak series. Third, he was the only Indian director to remain active in Singapore until 1964. And, fourth, together with L. Krishnan, M. Amin and B. S. Rajhans, he was among the most prolific directors in Singapore's film history.

Born in 1908 in Kerala, Bombay-bred Balakrishna Narayana Nair became B. N. Rao when, as a boy seeking admission to school in Bombay, he was mistakenly registered under that name. He kept it when he entered the film industry as an actor and technician in 1926. After working his way into the growing Indian film industry in Tamil, Telugu and Hindi productions, Rao shot his first feature, a Hindi film, *Veer Kumari*, in 1935. He soon directed the maiden production of Tamil's Central Studios in 1937. During this period, the legendary Prabhat Pictures musical production *Sant Tukaram* was making waves all over the country. The movie included 30 songs (another 1930s film, *Sangeetha Lava Kusa*, had 63 songs!), and after its success Rao started making Tamil musicals. His early Indian films included *Rambayin Kaathal*, *Bhooloka Rambha*, *Gumasthavin Penn*, *Madanakamarajan*, *Dasi Aparanji*, *Bhaktha Prahalada*, *Sathi Murali*, and a few others.

When he was hired by the Shaw brothers and came to Singapore, his production suddenly increased. In less than three years, from 1953 to 1956, he directed nine movies for Malay Film Productions, including the renowned *Hujan Panas* (lit. Hot Rain) in 1953, which set high standards for the film industry.

Rao's golden days arrived after he left Malay Film Productions to join Cathay-Keris, for which he directed 14 movies between 1956 and 1964. He created a few box-office hits like *Mahsuri* in 1958, which positioned Cathay-Keris as a serious challenger to Shaw. He also directed *Laila Majnun*, his 1962 remake of Rajhans' seminal film of 30 years before.

Rao left Singapore in 1964, and returned to India, where he resumed his Indian career. He continued shooting movies, including some Telugu movies in the early 1970s, until his death in 1998. But it is as the father of the *pontianak* series that B. N. Rao claims his place in film history, and it is as such that he appears in all the frequently referenced books, articles and websites about horror and vampire movies.

THE PONTIANAK SERIES

B. N. Rao created the series, now a cult classic, in 1957. The first, *Pontianak*, was said to have been produced by Ho Ah Loke in two versions, one Malay, the other Chinese. Unfortunately, the original print is now lost. That same year, he also made *Dendam Pontianak* (lit. The Pontianak's Revenge).

Laila Majnun by B. N. Rao, 1962.

Chinese flyer for *Anak Pontianak* by Ramon Estella, 1958.

Maria Menado as the pontianak in *Dendam Pontianak* by B. N. Rao, 1957 (top); advertisement for the Malaysian release of *Pontianak Gua Musang* by B.N. Rao, 1964 (bottom).

These two films, *Pontianak* and *Dendam Pontianak*, produced by Keris Film and Cathay-Keris, launched the genre. And they made Maria Menado a famous figure in the world of horror and vampire films, Rao having cast her as the pontianak, a female vampire.

The next year, Filipino director Ramon Estella, working for Shaw, would follow with his own *Anak Pontianak* (a.k.a. *Son of Pontianak*). He went on to direct another two more pontianak movies, *Pontianak Kembali* (a.k.a. *The Vampire Returns*) in 1963 and *Pusaka Pontianak* (a.k.a. *The Accursed Heritage*, a.k.a. *The Pontianak Legacy*).

Rao himself also continued the series with *Sumpah Pontianak* (a.k.a. *Curse of the Vampire*) in 1958. And, in 1964, he made *Pontianak Gua Musang* (a.k.a. *The Vampire of the Cave*, a.k.a. *The Vampire of the Civet-Cat Cave*), his last Singapore-made movie.

The pontianak genre he created carried on having a life of its own in Malaysia, with movies like the 1975 *Pontianak* by Roger Sutton (starring Hamid Bond and Jennifer Kaur), or more recently, the 2004 and 2005 *Pontianak Harum Sundal Malam I and II* (lit. Fragrant Tuberose Pontianak) by Shuhaimi Baba, as well as the 2005 *Pontianak Menjerit* (lit. Screaming Pontianak) by Yusof Kelara. In Singapore, a tribute to the female vampire was done by Djinn with his 2001 indie, *Return to Pontianak*, offering a different take on the genre.

Sumpah Pontianak by B. N. Rao, 1958.

THE FILIPINO CONNECTION
Moving away from the overwhelming influence of the Indian film culture inspired by the Indian directors, and in the absence of a sufficient number of local Malay filmmakers, Shaw decided to diversify its talent, importing award-winning Filipinos like Eddy Infante, T. C. Santos, Ramon Estella, Lamberto Avellana and Rolf Bayer (who was apparently also involved in the making of films for Shaw Brothers Hong Kong). They made a total of 16 movies in Singapore, for Singapore.

The Filipinos had a cultural connection with Malay culture, tracing their roots back to the days of the early Malay kingdoms. And, in fact, the Filipinos' Tagalog language and ethnic backgrounds were close enough to Malay culture that they were able to pick up the Malay language easily. As early as 1919, we find the Nepomucemo brothers, the equivalent of the Shaw brothers, starting the first local Filipino company, significantly named Malayan Movies.

These Filipino directors, a whole new group of "foreign talents", worked in Singapore for an entire decade, from 1955 to 1965. They brought in myriad influences, not only from the Philippines, but also from America. Indeed, many of them were very much Hollywood-oriented, and some were even trained by Americans. Their screenplays tended to be remakes of Hollywood films, and their movies were replete with Western themes.

In 1954, Eddy Infante was the first to be brought in by Shaw. His *Gadis Layar* (lit. The Elephant Girl) was screened in 1955. He was followed in 1957 by T. C. Santos, who directed *Taufan* (a.k.a. *Typhoon*), and in 1958, by Rolf Bayer, who directed *Azimat* (lit. Talisman). These men did not make more movies in Singapore. In fact, many of the Filipino directors hired by Shaw did not stay long. Either the studio was not satisfied with their work, or they saw no future in Singapore for their careers, and left of their own accord.

Rolf Bayer's *Azimat* was a very jazzy Hollywoodian film that undeniably moved away from other Singapore Malay movies of the time. The music score, camera angles, lighting, editing, and acting gave it a very particular, and very un-Singaporean, feel. Yet, at the same time, *Azimat* stands out for how it portrayed a very modern way of life in the city, with clubs, bars, smoking, drinking and dining. It also has some interesting location shots along the Singapore River, which today gives it documentary value.

Lamberto Avellana's career began in the Philippines before the war, with his 1939 world-acclaimed *Sakay*. In 1956, he won the Best Director Award at the Asian Film Festival in Hong Kong for *Anak Dalita* (a.k.a. *The Ruins*). In 1957, Lamberto Avellana partnered Cathay-Keris for *Bajau Anak Laut* (lit. *The Badjaos Children of the Sea*), for which he was rewarded with yet another Best Director Award. This movie was, in fact, totally not Singaporean apart from the financial investment by Cathay-Keris who was trying to develop a strategy of international coproductions (this one being done with Dona Narcisa Benvenida de Leon). *Bajau Anak Laut,* beautifully shot in outdoor locations, takes place in Southern Philippines, with a Filipino cast and crew.

Lamberto Avellana was thus a filmmaker already crowned by the industry for his achievements when he was brought to Singapore by the Shaw brothers in 1958. For them, he started directing *Sergeant Hassan* (a.k.a. *Sarjan Hassan*), about World War II, starring P. Ramlee in the lead role. But Lamberto Avellana left midway, leaving P. Ramlee to finish the work. Yet, Lamberto Avellana is usually the only director credited for this movie, as Ramlee had apparently decided to give him full credit. Lamberto Avellana, who was also the first Filipino director selected at the Cannes Film Festival, did not need Singapore to advance his career, which probably explains why he did not pay much attention to the movie.

THE INFLUENTIAL RAMON ESTELLA
Only one Filipino director was as influential as his Indian peers — Ramon Estella. He made a total of 11 movies in Singapore between 1957 and 1965. He started with Shaw's Malay Film Productions in 1957, directing *Kembali Seorang* (lit. A Man is Back). With his ability to tune in to the local culture, and to speedily churn out feature films, Estella was asked to compete with Cathay-Keris' directors such as B. N. Rao in the horror genre, bringing to the screen the pontianak, and other more or less scary monsters.

For Shaw, he directed the famous *Anak Pontianak* (lit. Son of Pontianak) in 1958, and a few more movies, including the very interesting *Mata Hari* (lit. Sun, but a.k.a. *The Rape of Malaya*), which capitalised on the success met by Avellana's *Sergeant Hassan*. *Mata Hari* portrays the life of a *kampong* which is turned into a camp by the Japanese during World War II, with some excellent acting by Maria Menado in the lead role.

In 1963, Estella joined Cathay-Keris for a short period, where he directed *Bunga Tanjung*, *Darahku* (lit. My Blood), and, ironically, one of the pontianak series, *Pontianak Kembali* (a.k.a. *The Vampire Returns*).

He resumed work for Shaw in 1964, and successively shot *Dupa Chendana* (lit. Sandalwood Incense), *Melanchong ke Tokyo* (lit. Going to Tokyo) and his last pontianak movie, the 1965 *Pusaka Pontianak* (a.k.a. *The Accursed Heritage*, a.k.a. *The Pontianak Legacy*), shot the very year of Singapore's independence. It was truly the end of an era. Strangely, the filming of these iconic pontianak movies had always been left to foreigners, whether Indians or Filipinos. It was only in 2001 that a Singaporean, Djinn, would venture into this horror genre with his *Return to Pontianak*.

A *jawi* ad of *Mata Hari* by Ramon Estella, 1958.

As for the Filipino connection, it did not totally disappear, since Filipino John Aristorenas was to direct a feature in Malaysia in 1976, called *Malaysia Five*, shot in Malay. Also, Manila-based producer-cum-director Bobby Suarez would go on to initiate a series of regional coproductions in the late 1970s involving the Philippines, Malaysia and Singapore.

COMING OF AGE OF MALAY DIRECTORS

Due to the success of movies directed by Indian filmmakers, local producers felt the need to slowly introduce Malay directors. Indeed, the 1950s was a nationalistic era for the Malays. Spearheaded by the Singapore Malay Journalist Association, the demand grew for Malay films to be made by Malays. Many recognised the encroachment of foreign Indian culture and denounced the misrepresentation of native Malay culture via adapted films by Indian directors.

The need to have local directors for locally made movies was identified as early as the 1950s by Nusantara Film, an independent production house which, for a while, tried to be the flagship for Malayness in the film industry.

An ad for *Penarek Becha* by P. Ramlee, 1955, mixing Roman and *jawi* scripts.

Nusantara Film placed its productions in the hands of two non-Indian filmmakers, Naz Achnas and A. R. Tompel, both of whom had mixed parentage, but were from within the Malay world. Unfortunately, the first movies made by Nusantara Film, *Pelangi* (lit. Rainbow) and *Sesal Tak Sudah* (lit. Neverending Regret) in 1950, were not successful, partly due to the fact that, unlike Shaw and Cathay, Nusantara did not have its own exhibition circuit.

A new era in Malay film-making began in 1952. Indeed, not only did Nusantara Film persist in its efforts to introduce more Malayness, producing two more movies directed by Tompel, *Norma*, and *Seniyati* (lit. Film Star), and one by Naz Achnas, *Dian* (lit. Candle), but its example was followed by another independent producer, Ho Ah Loke.

Under his newly created company, Keris Film Productions, he churned out in one year three movies made by first-time director Jaafar Wiryo, an ex-Shaw artist. The movies were *Ramli Ramlah*, *Setia* (lit. Faithful) and *Perwira Lautan Teduh* (lit. Warrior of the Calm Seas), sometimes said to be Singapore's first colour movie.

That very same year, the Shaw themselves, observing what their competitors were doing, and taking into account that true representation of local culture would bring more satisfaction to local audiences, appointed one of their former actors-cum-assistant directors, Haji Mahadi, whose real name was Mahadi Mohamed Said, as director. He was responsible for Malay Film Productions' first Malay-directed movie, *Permata di Perlimbahan* (lit. The Jewel in the Valley) in 1952. Unfortunately, according to some accounts, it was unsuccessful and business takings were poor.

Jaafar Wiryo would subsequently, in 1953, make two more movies, one for Keris Film Productions, *Berbahagia di Singapura* (lit. Happy in Singapore), and another, *Nelayan* (lit. Fisherman), for the newly set-up studio, Cathay-Keris.

The first Malay directors lacked experience, and the studios felt that they needed to learn their craft from the more renowned Indian filmmakers in Singapore. But neither Haji Mahadi nor Jaafar Wiryo were given a chance to direct again. The studios preferred to look for new talent. In the meantime, Shaw and Cathay turned to their in-house Indian directors, who were once again the only ones to direct in 1954. They dominated the industry for a few more years, until 1959, when there were finally as many Malay-directed movies as Indian-directed movies, i.e., six movies each.

Aziz Jaafar and Rahmah Rahmat in *Batu Belah Batu Bertangkup* by Jamil Sulong, 1959.

Between 1955 and 1959, Indian directors still reigned supreme, and only three new Malay directors emerged. The first was P. Ramlee in 1955 with his *Penarek Becha* (a.k.a. *Trishaw Puller*) which would become a historical success; then S. Roomai Noor with *Adam* in 1956; and finally, Jamil Sulong with *Batu Belah Batu Bertangkup* (lit. Stone Splits Stone Closes) in 1959. Of the three, Ramlee would be the most outstanding.

THE VERSATILE P. RAMLEE

The Indian connection may have exerted a huge influence, but if one person embodied perfection during the golden age of the Malay studios, it was a Malay — P. Ramlee. Singer, musician and composer turned actor and director, he was the most versatile talent of the era. This multifaceted artist sung almost 360 songs, acted in 63 movies (40 in Singapore, 23 in Malaysia), and directed 34 features (out of which 16 were shot in his Singapore days between 1955 and 1964, and 18 during his Kuala Lumpur period from 1964 to 1973). Ramlee truly made history, and if one name stands out, it is his.

P. Ramlee.

Ramlee bin Puteh was born Teuku Zakaria bin Teuku Nyak Puteh, in Penang, northern Malaya, in 1929. He is said to have naturally taken to singing and playing music during his childhood. His steady, resonant voice impressed relatives and neighbours and he was often asked to take the muezzin's role in making the call to prayers from the Kampung Jawa Baru mosque.

Ramlee was under the tutelage of the brass band head at the Penang Free School when the Japanese invaded Malaya. He was compelled to stop school, and he attended the Japanese navy school, the Kaigun, where he learned Japanese songs, as well as the violin, piano and ukulele. After the war, he picked up the guitar and started to play in a local band named Teruna Sekampung. Just as he was turning twenty, he wrote the song *Azizah* which brought him some measure of local fame.

Ramlee was spotted by B. S. Rajhans, who was scouting for talent throughout Malaya on behalf of Shaw, at an agricultural show where he was performing with his band. Taken by his voice, Rajhans asked him to audition for Shaw's Malay Film Productions. And that was how Ramlee bin Puteh made it to the Singapore stage.

Rajhans, then the only active filmmaker in the island-city, gave Ramlee his first role in *Chinta* (lit. Love). He was a supporting actor playing a villain constantly threatening the virtue of the heroine Siput Sarawak, and also a background singer. Ramlee was not known at first for his good looks, since he had a rather pockmarked face as L. Krishnan himself facetiously recalls. He could have been typecast as the ubiquitous villain, or remained a background singer for other stars.

However, even though he did not get the lead role in movies, his talent in composing and performing music, as well as singing, soon gave him

P. Ramlee as an apprentice actor in his *Seniman Bujang Lapok,* 1961 (top); release of *Anak-ku Sazali* by Phani Majumdar at Shaw's Empire Theatre in 1956 (bottom).

an edge over many of his contemporaries. Indeed, Indian directors like B. S. Rajhans and L. Krishnan were always on the look out for "voices" as much as "faces", and sometimes would even hire actors based on voice rather than looks. Ramlee also proved to be a versatile actor, equally adept at drama and comedy.

P. Ramlee became more famous when Krishnan gave him the lead role in the first movie he made in Singapore. In the 1950 *Bakti* (a.k.a. *Faithfulness*), he co-starred with popular favourites Kasma Booty, Siput Sarawak and S. Roomai Noor. Two more lead roles in L. Krishnan's *Penghidupan* (lit. Life) and *Takdir Ilahi* (lit. Divine Decree) followed. Ramlee's career immediately

Musang Berjanggut by P. Ramlee, 1959.

skyrocketed. He acted in more and more movies by B. S. Rajhans, L. Krishnan and S. Ramanathan.

His fame as a multitalented artist grew to such an extent, that as early as the 1951 *Juwita*, he acted as himself (something he would very often do throughout the rest of his career), the script of the movie being closely inspired by his own life. The audience started relating to him in a very different way, because he was both a face and a voice, one of the first Malay stars who did not need a background singer. He also went on to learn more about the craft behind the movies, taking on art direction for S. Ramanathan's *Juwita* in 1951. He later started composing more and more hit songs and

music for movies, as he did for Krishnan's *Rayuan Sukma* (lit. Longing of the Soul) that same year.

Finally ready to become a filmmaker, Ramlee made his directorial debut in 1955 with *Penarek Becha* (a.k.a. *Trishaw Puller*), which tells the story, in an almost neorealist way, of a poor trishaw puller who falls in love with a rich girl. This movie revisited the *majnun* lover genre inherited from B. S. Rajhans' inaugural *Leila Majnun* of 1933. However, the movie was not directly inspired by Indian cinema, but rather by a Japanese movie called *Jin Rickshaw* which had already been adapted in Hong Kong. *Penarek Becha* was a success, and convinced Shaw's Malay Film Productions to give Ramlee and

Pendekar Bujang Lapok by P. Ramlee, 1959.

other Malay artists more opportunities to direct. Ramlee was the only Malay who shot a film in 1955. His career subsequently took an upward swing.

The year after, he directed his second feature, *Semerah Padi*, which showed signs of various influences, from the Italian neorealism of Giuseppe De Santis' 1948 *Riso Amaro*, to Japanese postwar movies like Akira Kurosawa's 1954 *Seven Samurai*. Lavish tracking shots, baroque angles and fast-tempo editing appeared to be Ramlee's signature, in the manner of Kurosawa himself. Even though *Semerah Padi* did not make world film history like De Santis' or Kurosawa's films have done, Ramlee showed great artistic ambition and integrity. He set new and higher standards for the up-and-coming Malay cinema. Unfortunately, these standards were rarely followed, particularly in Shaw movies, where efficiency and profitability ruled over artistic attempt, unless the studio decided otherwise.

With both *Penarek Becha* and *Semerah Padi*, Ramlee broke away from the overwhelming Indian influence, even though he was and would remain greatly indebted to directors like B. S. Rajhans, L. Krishnan and S. Ramanathan, whom he had learnt the basics of filmmaking from. If there was any Indian influence in his first movies, it might have come just as much from directors like Satyajit Ray or Guru Dutt, who were politically aware, and committed to social realism (although such lofty influences have not been proven).

Although a few of his peers like S. Roomai Noor joined Cathay-Keris, Ramlee always remained true to Shaw until he left Singapore for Kuala Lumpur. With many talents leaving Shaw for Cathay, Ramlee enjoyed much freedom and support from the Shaws themselves, who saw in him their most faithful and successful household artist. The late 1950s and early 1960s were his heyday. Every movie he filmed or acted in seemed to fit him to perfection, and most became perennial classics.

As an actor, his crowning glory came when he won the Best Actor Award at the 1957 Asian Film Festival held in Tokyo for his double roles

P. Ramlee bringing back a Golden Harvest Award from the 10th Asian Film Festival, 1963.

in *Anak-ku Sazali* (lit. My Son Sazali), a powerful drama directed by Phani Majumdar. That same year, during which he was once again the only Malay to direct, Ramlee filmed *Pancha Delima* (a.k.a. *Five Rubies*), a period drama, as well as his first comedy, *Bujang Lapok* (a.k.a. *Confirmed Bachelor*), which was filled with innuendoes and themes focusing on Malay society's shortcomings and failings.

The comedy was such a success that it became the first of a whole series of *bujang lapok* movies that would become Ramlee's trademark: *Pendekar Bujang Lapok* (lit. The Bachelor Warrior) in 1959, for which he won the Best Comedy Award at the 1959 Asian Film Festival held in Kuala Lumpur; *Ali Baba Bujang Lapok* (lit. Ali Baba, the Confirmed Bachelor) and *Seniman Bujang Lapok* (a.k.a. *The Nit-Wit Movie Stars*), both in 1961.

Finally, in 1963, he received an extraordinary award as Asia's Most Versatile Talent for his performance in *Ibu Mertuaku* (a.k.a. *My Mother-in-Law*), the story of a successful and adored musician, which was one more take on his own life.

A year later, Ramlee left Singapore for Kuala Lumpur, where he joined Merdeka Film Productions which was just about to be taken over by the Shaw brothers themselves. In the second decade of his directing career, Ramlee managed to make 18 movies. None, however, was as successful as those from his Singapore days. Things were more difficult, and the Merdeka Studio offered fewer possibilities compared to Shaw's Jalan Ampas studio back in Singapore. Ultimately, his career withered away, and P. Ramlee died in 1973. He was only 44.

Hussain Haniff.

HUSSAIN HANIFF
Hussain Haniff (his first name sometimes being spelt Hussein) wanted to be an actor, but started as a film editor for Cathay-Keris in the late 1950s. He worked on some of the studio's major movies, such as L. Krishnan's *Chinta Gadis Rimba* (a.k.a. *The Virgin of Borneo*, lit. Love of the Jungle Girl), and B. N. Rao's *Sumpah Pontianak* (a.k.a. *Curse of the Vampire*), both in 1958, on L. Krishnan's *Rasa Sayang - Eh* (lit. The Feeling of Love) in 1959, and on K. M. Basker's *Noor Islam* (lit. The Light of Islam) in 1960, which indeed stand out for the quality of their editing.

At the age of 27, in 1961, he made his directorial debut with *Hang Jebat*, a very ambitious period drama renowned for its cinematic qualities and for the way it revisited Malay classical history. It immediately positioned him as a first-rate filmmaker. While P. Ramlee remained with Shaw's Malay Film Productions, Hussain Haniff stayed on with Cathay-Keris, where he became

Dang Anom by Hussain Haniff, 1962.

a household name for a few years. Sadly, his career was shortlived as he died in 1966 at the age of 32. However, in five years, he had managed to direct no less than 13 movies.

Hang Jebat and *Dang Anom*, his first two films, were instant box-office hits. *Dua Pendekar* (lit. Two Warriors), in 1964, earned him great respect, due to its high contrast photography, its audacious angles, and its pace. The movie certainly remains one the best made in Singapore during that era. He also directed *Istana Berdarah* (lit. The Bloody Palace) that same year, a film which was loosely adapted from Shakespeare's *Macbeth*. He generally demanded a lot from the studio for his movies, some of which were costly to produce.

Period dramas seem to have been his forte in his early years as a director, whereas his movies set in contemporary Singapore did not do so well at first, and are not generally regarded as historically significant. In that sense, Hussain Haniff was quite the opposite of P. Ramlee, whose screenplays — at least, the most successful ones — were usually of a more personal nature, and staged contemporary life as it was. Hussain Haniff, on the other hand, managed to address modern issues even in his period dramas, and often took a progressive stand, questioning what remained of feudalism in Malay society.

It was only towards the end of his career, and after P. Ramlee had left Singapore, that he fully mastered the art of contemporary social drama and successively shot two excellent movies in 1965, a year of great change for Singapore as it gained independence.

Chinta Kaseh Sayang (lit. My Darling Love) is the story of a young woman, Normah, who is married to a painter more focused on his art than on her. When he leaves for a trip abroad, she does not reject the attentions of Jamal,

A classical silhouette shot in *Dang Anom*, 1962 (left) and *Hang Jebat*, 1961 (right), both by Hussain Haniff.

a car dealer who starts courting her. Jamal is himself married with two children, but does not tell her. The movie is an acute social study of Singapore at the time of its independence. It deals with the attempts to come to terms with modernisation — phones, Fiat cars, escalators and sewing machines. It also very subtly addresses the clash of cultures and the different habits and customs affected by Westernisation.

As for *Jiran Sekampong* (lit. Village Neighbours), it intertwines stories of different low and middle-class *kampong* families in the Singapore of 1965, in a very pre-Eric Khoo way. Rohani's mother, although sick, must go back to work in the bourgeois family where she serves as a maid. Saloma invites some friends home for a dance session one afternoon, while her parents are out. Hassan's parents do not want him to marry Suryani, because they find her too *"seksi"*. Here again, the movie captures with great sensitivity the changing times of the mid-1960s, and the clash between tradition and modernity, the growing gap between generations.

Hussain Haniff's movies undeniably showed good or even sometimes outstanding artistic qualities. Even in a minor comedy like *Gila Talak* (lit. Crazy) shot in 1963, he maintained high standards, with an excellent mastery of photography and editing. His untimely death and shortlived career contributed to his legendary status. It also affected Cathay-Keris, which was unable to find a suitable replacement.

No Malay filmmaker was going to be his match in the few years that remained ahead of them, before studio closed its doors in 1972. It is said that had he not died, Singaporean cinema, or to be more accurate, Singapore Malay cinema might have taken a different turn, and known a different fate. Yet, had he lived, Hussain Haniff might also have done what most of his peers like P. Ramlee did — leave Singapore for Kuala Lumpur, pursuing his career there, and contributing to the development of Malaysian cinema.

MARIA MENADO, THE FIRST PONTIANAK
Along with a few seminal and influential directors, Maria Menado came to embody perfection during the golden age of Singapore Malay cinema, because she was more than just a beautiful actress.

S. Roomai Noor and Maria Menado in *Selamat Hari Raya* by L. Krishnan, 1955 (top); Maria Menado in *Sumpah Pontianak* by B. N. Rao, 1958 (bottom).

Born in Menado (now also known as Manado), North Sulawesi, Indonesia, in 1932, her real name was Libeth Dotulong. She changed it early on, when she moved from Menado to Jakarta, and then from Jakarta to Singapore in 1949 where she became a model and a *kebaya* queen.

Her acting career began in 1950 with *Penghidupan* (lit. Life), a movie by L. Krishnan. She would go on to work with him on many films, including *Tas Tangan Wanita* (lit. A Woman's Handbag), *Nafsu* (lit. Desire), *Pertaruhan* (lit. The Gamble), *Selamat Hari Raya* (lit. Festive Day Greeting), *Orang Lichin* (lit. Slippery Man), etc. She also acted in S. Ramanathan's 1951 *Pulau Mutiara* (lit. Pearl Island) and B. S. Rajhans' 1952 *Gadis Peladang* (lit. The Farm Girl). Her first roles owed much to these three Indian directors.

She shot to international fame when B. N. Rao cast her as the pontianak, a local female vampire, in the two 1957 horror movies that launched the new pontianak genre: *Pontianak* and *Dendam Pontianak* (lit. The Pontianak's Revenge). Maria Menado took on the role again the next year in *Sumpah Pontianak* (a.k.a. *Curse of the Vampire*), also directed by Rao.

Seemingly unmatched by any other actress in those days, Maria Menado decided to gain a bit of artistic freedom within the studio system that had made her. In 1959, she became her own producer, founding Maria Menado Productions. Her first film as such, made in association with Cathay-Keris, was *Korban Fitnah* (lit. Victim of Slander), an excellent social drama set in contemporary Singapore. Renowned Indian filmmaker P. L. Kapur was specially hired to direct it, while Maria Menado herself acted in it, along with

The opening cycling and singing scene in *Korban Fitnah* by P. L. Kapur, 1959.

a very cosmopolitan cast made up of actors coming from all over the region, such as A. N. Alcaff or Sukarno M. Noor.

Menado followed up on her Indian connections, which she developed while acting for L. Krishnan, and while producing *Korban Fitnah* directed by P. L. Kapur. She teamed up with the Indian film industry on a 1960 movie called *Singapore*. This fully Indian production made by F. C. Mehra and Eagle Films was directed by Shakti Samanta. It starred major Bollywood artists like Shammi Kapoor, Shashikala and Rajen Kapoor, along with Maria Menado herself as the local Singaporean beauty (whom the lead male actor meets on the plane bringing him to Singapore). Just as it had been in the late 1920s and early 1930s, Singapore was an attractive film location in the 1960s, not only for the Indian film industry, but also for projects from Hong Kong, Great Britain, France and Italy.

While pursuing her career as an actress, Maria Menado coproduced with Cathay-Keris a 1961 B. N. Rao movie, *Siti Zubaidah*; and in 1963, both K. M. Basker's *Raja Bersiong* (a.k.a. *The King With The Fangs*), and Ramon Estella's *Darahku* (lit. My Blood). With Estella, she also ventured into a belated sequel to the pontianak series, with the 1963 *Pontianak Kembali* (a.k.a. *The Vampire Returns*), in which she played the role once more, for the last time.

The pontianak series remains her major legacy. If anything at all is sometimes known on the international scene about Singapore-made cinema at the turn of the 1950s through to the 1960s, it is very often Maria Menado as the pontianak.

A.N. Alcaff, Maria Menado and Sukarno M. Noor, all of Indonesian origin, in *Korban Fitnah* by P.L. Kapur, 1959.

CHINESE MOVIES IN SINGAPORE

The demand for Chinese movies in Singapore was nothing new to players like Shaw or Cathay, and even more for Kong Ngee and Eng Wah (both of which had started by distributing and exhibiting only Chinese films). They usually struck deals with producers from mainland China (mostly from Shanghai and Hong Kong) to secure a steady flow of products for the large population of overseas Chinese in Southeast Asia. Singapore itself was already predominantly Chinese, with the Chinese making up more than 70% of the population.

The Shaw brothers also supplied themselves with their own Chinese films, produced by their Hong Kong sister companies such as the Unique Film Company in the 1920s and 1930s, the Nanyang Film Company in the late 1930s to the early 1950s, the Shaw and Sons Company in the 1950s.

Their competitors would adopt the same strategy in the 1950s, with Cathay, Kong Ngee and Eng Wah soon venturing into production, at a time when mainland China had already been taken over by the Communists. This shows that, if Chinese movies flooded Southeast Asia, it was not merely because of the need to find new markets. It was more because the local demand for Chinese films (be it in Mandarin, Cantonese or, although more rarely, Hokkien) was rapidly growing with the simultaneous growth of the overseas Chinese population and its increasing spending power.

CATHAY'S MP&GI IN HONG KONG

Cathay was going to be one of the first to really make its move into massive production of Chinese movies. Loke Wan Tho, who had settled in Singapore to control his growing Southeast Asian empire, had also developed close ties with the Chinese film industry in the mid-1940s. In 1949, many Shanghai filmmakers and producers were moving to Hong Kong to escape the Communist takeover, and Loke went into partnership with one of them, Lee Tsu Yung.

Cathay's MP&GI logo.

At first, Cathay only distributed films like the 1954 *Mei Gui Mei Gui Wo Ai Ni* (a.k.a. *Rose, Rose, I Love You*) made by Yung Hwa Motion Pictures in Hong Kong. It was Cathay's very own supplier of Chinese movies, allowing it to cater to the growing Chinese population in Southeast Asia, as well as competing directly with Shaw in that market.

Yung Hwa proved to be a good, innovative partner. It produced movies like *Singing under the Moon* in 1953 (which introduced a new actress, Lin Dai), *Wife and Husband* the same year (introducing Liu Enjia, a.k.a. Lau Yan Kap) and *Golden Phoenix* (in which King Hu debuted as an actor, before becoming a renowned director for Shaw Brothers in the mid-1960s).

Grace Chang and Peter Chen in *Mambo Girl* by Yi Wen, 1957.

However, Yung Hwa Motion Pictures slowly developed insurmountable financial trouble, and in 1955, Loke Wan Tho had to progressively take over the business to recover his investment and preserve his supply of Chinese movies. Yung Hwa ceased operations to make way for a new company named Motion Picture & General Investment Co. Ltd (MP&GI), with which Cathay opened its very own Hong Kong studio.

In Hong Kong, Loke relied on the help of Albert Odell, a Eurasian born in the territory who was fluent in both Cantonese and Mandarin. A former manager of Frieder Films, Odell joined Cathay in Singapore in 1951 as a distribution manager. When Yung Hwa started facing difficulties, he was appointed joint receiver and manager there. He took full charge of Cathay's operations in Hong Kong after 1955, coordinating the construction MP&GI's studio.

Over a 15-year period, from 1956 to 1970, Cathay's MP&GI (also known as "Dianmao", a shortened version of Dianying Maoye, Chinese for "motion picture and general investment") would produce around 250 titles and thus greatly contribute to the foundations of the postwar Hong Kong industry. MP&GI films were widely distributed in Hong Kong, Taiwan and Southeast Asia.

Some of the first films made by Cathay's branch in Hong Kong were *The Magic Monk and His Double*, *Gloomy Sunday*, *Girl in Disguise* or *Miss Kikuko* (starring Lin Dai) in 1956. Then *Mambo Nu Lan* (a.k.a. *Mambo Girl*), directed by the talented Yi Wen (a.k.a. Evan Yang), became Cathay's first hit in cinemas in the region, propelling its lead actress, Ge Lan (a.k.a. Grace Chang), to superstardom in 1957.

Loke Wan Tho was not just interested in making money. What he was looking for was regional and even international artistic recognition (although

The two sides of the Cathay "family", Loke Wan Tho and Ho Ah Loke (back row, 7th and 8th respectively from left, both wearing glasses) with MP&GI and Cathay-Keris stars at the Sixth Asian Film Festival held in Kuala Lumpur in 1959.

he produced flicks like *Booze, Boobs and Bucks*, a.k.a. *Wine, Women and Money*, directed by Ma Tsui Wai Bang in 1957, starring none other than Grace Chang). Critical acclaim and festival success came as early as 1957, when Lin Dai won the Best Actress Award for her part in *Golden Lotus* at the fourth Asian Film Festival held in Tokyo.

The next year, in Manila, *Si Qian Jin* (a.k.a. *Our Sister Hedy*), directed by Tao Qin and starring Julie Yeh Feng and Jeannette Lin Tsui, was named Best Picture. Cathay's Chinese movies, made in Hong Kong by MP&GI, made history, and became milestones in world film heritage.

Mambo Girl, in particular, has remained highly influential, continuing to inspire moviemakers. A few of them paid tribute to the movie, such as Malaysia-born and Taiwan-based Tsai Ming-liang, in his 1997 feature, *The Hole*. In Singapore, Royston Tan himself re-enacted *Mambo Girl's* famous

"I love cha cha cha" song, initially performed by Grace Chang, in his 2001 short movie, *Hock Hiap Leong*.

Within three years, that is, 1953 to 1956, Loke Wan Tho had established two new studios: one in Singapore, Cathay-Keris, and the other in Hong Kong, MP&GI. In doing so, he secured a steady flow of movies produced in-house for his fast-expanding exhibition circuit. He also took Cathay Organisation, which was initially just a film distributor and exhibitor, to a new level, by getting involved in film production, both in the Malay and the Chinese worlds.

Until the early 1960s, MP&GI had hardly any competition in the Hong Kong production business, since the Shaw brothers themselves had momentarily gone out of business, and took time to come up with a totally refurbished studio and new strategy. It was only in 1964, when the new Shaw

Choo Kok Leong receiving Lee Kuan Yew, then Prime Minister of Singapore, at a charity premiere at the Odeon in 1964.

Air Hostess, one of MP&GI's productions filmed both in Hong Kong and Singapore, 1958.

Brothers movies proved to be highly profitable, and earned artistic recognition by winning awards at the 11th Asian Film Festival held in Taipei, that MP&GI suffered from fierce competition and started losing its market share. It was also during the same Taipei film festival that Loke Wan Tho, together with some of his staff, unfortunately died in a plane crash.

In 1965, MP&GI was renamed Cathay Organisation HK, and went on to make a few more movies (which did not meet the same success). In 1970, Choo Kok Leong, Loke's brother-in-law who had succeeded him at Cathay, closed the Hong Kong studio — at a time when Hong Kong cinema was growing rapidly.

Even though they are the product of a Singapore-driven company, the MP&GI films, generally shot in Hong Kong in Mandarin or Cantonese with

Hong Kong actors, pertain more to Hong Kong film history than to Singapore's. They are usually seen as such.

At the same time, one cannot overlook the fact that the movies' MP&GI logo bore the very identifiable silhouette of Singapore's Cathay Building, or that some of them were partly shot in Singapore. One such is the glamorous 1958 *Air Hostess,* in which director Yi Wen conscientiously included aerial shots of Singapore... and the Cathay Building. Thus, Singapore film history certainly does not come across as clear-cut. Rather, its elements and events are blurry, organic, complex and merge into one another.

CATHAY-KERIS' *LION CITY*

Another strategy momentarily adopted by Loke Wan Tho was to produce a fully Singapore-made Chinese movie. Cathay-Keris did this in 1960, with its first Mandarin film, *Shi Zi Cheng* (a.k.a. *Lion City*), shot by Yi Sui (also known under his real name Tang Pak Chee). Since it was obviously targeting the local audience, its language was a local variant of Mandarin, sometimes known as Malayan Mandarin. Its cast was entirely Chinese, largely from an acting school Tang Pak Chee had set up a few years before (where

Yi Sui.

renowned Singapore dramatist Kuo Pao Kun was also trained). The film showed a totally different picture of Singapore — whereas Singapore Malay movies had hardly any Chinese actors, except for those playing stereotypical roles, this Singapore Chinese movie had hardly any Malays.

The movie looked at Singapore with a new eye, and certainly did not resist the temptation of numerous location shots. It featured long panoramas of the city's modern landscape, as seen either from the top of the first high-rise buildings or from atop Mount Faber. It also included its fair share of references to the political and social changes taking place then. Hence, *Shi Zi Cheng,* with its slightly neorealist touch, remains a highly valuable record of Singapore in 1960. In

Promo picture of *Shi Zi Cheng* (a.k.a. *Lion City*) by Yi Sui, 1960.

Chinese advertisement for *Shi Zi Cheng* (a.k.a. *Lion City*) by Yi Sui, 1960 which also carries its Malay title, *Bandar Raya Singapura*.

order to reach a wider audience, including the Malays, it was also released under the title *Bandar Raya Singapura* (lit. Singapore City), and advertised as such in Malay magazines. *Shi Zi Cheng* was followed by another film by Yi Sui in 1962, titled *Black Gold*, shot partly in the mines in Malaysia.

Such attempts at making local Chinese movies were thus very few. Even though the movie industry had long been in the hands of Chinese business entities who ran the studios and production houses (Shaw Run Run, Loke Wan Tho, Ho Ah Loke, etc), there was a dearth of local Chinese creative talents. This was simply due to the fact that hardly any Singapore-made Chinese movie had been attempted in the past, and thus no local Chinese had had the opportunity to learn and garner artistic experience in the making of films. It seemed somehow easier to set up a sister company in Hong Kong and take advantage of the large pool of talents available there.

KONG NGEE'S NANYANG TRILOGY
Somehow forgotten by history, there was a third studio, along with Shaw and Cathay. The Ho (also called He) family's Kong Ngee Company indeed constituted one of the three big cinema chains in Singapore and Malaya. Like the other two, its business soon straddled Singapore and Hong Kong.

In Singapore, where it had initially started in the late 1930s to early 1940s as an exhibitor and distributor, the company was running cinemas such as the Majestic (before it was taken over by Cathay), and the Metropole, in the heart of Chinatown. These were strategically located to give the best possible exposure to the company's newly made movies, since Kong Ngee saw a niche market in Chinese viewers who only or mostly spoke a dialect such as Teochew, Hokkien or Cantonese.

Kong Ngee's logo.

Therefore, it distributed in Singapore movies made in Hong Kong by production houses such as the Huaye Company, the Minsheng Company, the Yinhai Company or the Bihu Company, for films in the Amoy dialect; the Longhua Company for films in Chaozu dialect; and the Yingpeng Company for features in Mandarin or Cantonese.

Kong Ngee was not the only one to cater to this market in Singapore. Xinhua or Eng Wah did the same, importing many Chinese movies, mostly in Cantonese or Hokkien. Yet, none went as far as Kong Ngee who, just like the other two main cinema groups, Shaw and Cathay, soon ventured into production.

Looking for some specific products, Kong Ngee started commissioning works directly from Hong Kong producers. Such was the case with the Cantonese film *Du Juan Hun* (a.k.a. *The Cuckoo*) directed in 1954 by Chun Kim, which was commissioned from Artland Films.

Soon after, in 1955, Kong Ngee decided to move to in-house production. Following the example of Loke Wan Tho in exploring the production of Chinese language movies, one of the He brothers, He Qirong (better known under his Cantonese name Ho Kai Wing), who apparently had lived both in Singapore and Malaya, teamed up with famous director Chun Kim (a.k.a. Jian Qin) from Hong Kong to establish there the Kong Ngee Film Production Company, more commonly known under the shortened name Kong Ngee Company. Just like Cathay did with MP&GI, Kong Ngee opened a production arm in the Territory, while fully retaining its head office in Singapore.

Its early movies, in Cantonese, like its inaugural *Yan Zhi Hu* (a.k.a. *The Pretty Tigress* or *The Rouge Tigress*), a melodrama shot in 1955, starred up-and-coming Cantonese actors like Patsy Kar Ling (a.k.a. Jia Ling), Wu Fung (a.k.a. Hu Feng), Nam Hung (a.k.a. Nan Hong), Patrick Tse Yin (a.k.a. Xie Xian or Tse Yin) and Kong Suet (a.k.a. Jiang Xue).

Kong Ngee also cultivated new writing and directorial talent, with Chor Yuen (a.k.a. Chu Yuan) who made his true directorial debut with *Hu Pan Cao* (a.k.a. *The Natural Son*, a.k.a. *Grass by the Lake*) in 1959. Very much involved in the process, Ho Kai Wing is generally credited as executive producer on those movies.

As a matter of fact, the Singapore and Hong Kong-driven Kong Ngee, together with the Union, Overseas Chinese Films and Sun Luen, soon became one of the Big Four of Cantonese cinema. Kong Ngee's biggest draw was their staple of matinee idols such as Patrick Tse Yin, Patsy Kar Ling, Nam Hung and Kong Suet.

Its Hong Kong studio served the distribution networks in Southeast Asia (especially targeting the growing Chinese population there), a strategy also adopted by Shaw with its Shaw Brothers studio and Cathay with its MP&GI studio. The in-house productions being in Cantonese, Kong Ngee still retained the habit of commissioning movies in other Chinese dialects, such as *Peach Blossom Weeps Wood* (a.k.a. *Tao Hua Qi Xue Ji*) in 1957, in the Amoy dialect, directed by Chen Huanwen (a.k.a. Chan Wun-man). *Peach*

Xue Ran Xiang Si Gu (released in Singapore as *Blood Valley*)
by Chun Kim and Chor Yuen, 1957.

Blossom Weeps Wood was adapted from a stage play by Singapore's Yingian Fujian Opera Troupe, and its troupe of players went to Hong Kong for filming.

All in all, from the mid-1950s to the mid-1970s, Kong Ngee is said to have produced about 80 Cantonese movies. Among them were *Qiu Feng Can Ye* (a.k.a. *Autumn Leaf*) by Chor Yuen in 1960, *The Adventures of Genius Boy* in 1961, and *Hua Hua Gong Zi* (a.k.a. *The Beau*) by Chun Kim in 1964.

Kong Ngee's productions remained closely linked to Singapore, as the company's general manager, Ho Kian Ngiap, born in 1933, lived in the island-city part of the time. Even though most of Kong Ngee's movies were Cantonese, and deeply rooted in Cantonese culture, a number of them were either totally or partly shot in Singapore, particularly for some exterior scenes. This is worth noting, as the Cantonese film industry was not particularly used to filming outside of China during the 1950s.

Three movies, in particular, known as the "Nanyang San Bo" (or the "Nanyang Trilogy") were produced back-to-back in 1957. Indoor scenes were most likely shot in some Hong Kong studio. Outdoor scenes were all shot on location in Singapore. The quality of these exotic outdoor scenes strongly established the reputation of the Kong Ngee studio.

The three movies were *Ye Lin Ye* (a.k.a. *Ye Lum Yu*, lit. Coconut Grove at Night, a.k.a. under its English title *The Whispering Palms*), *Xue Ran Xiang Si Gu* (a.k.a. *Blood Stains in the Valley of Love* or *Bloodshed in the Valley of Love*, released in Singapore as *Blood Valley*) and *Tang San A Shao* (a.k.a. *She Married an Overseas Chinese*, released in Singapore as *China Wife*). The cast comprised major Hong Kong stars like the then up-and-coming Patrick Tse Yin. Chun Kim codirected these features with the soon to be famous Chor Yuen who, at the time, was still a scriptwriter and an assistant director. These three Singapore-made movies did well at the box office. They also familiarised the mainland Cantonese audience with the island-city.

In 1969, Kong Ngee was involved in the coproduction of two other Hong Kong films shot back-to-back in Singapore. *Niang Re Zhi Lian* (a.k.a. *Love with a Malaysian Girl*, a.k.a. *Romance of a Nyonya*) and *My Love is Like a Spring Breeze* were both directed by Lui Kei (a.k.a. Lui Kay) from Hong Kong. Both movies starred the same cast made up of Connie Chun Bo Chu (a.k.a. Chan Poh Chu), Lui Kei (a.k.a. Loy Kay) himself, Chan Leung Chung, Leung Bo Chu and Chan Bo Yee.

In *Romance of a Nyonya*, Ting-han, a dashing writer from Hong Kong, is invited by a friend of his to visit Singapore. He goes there in search of inspiration. In Singapore, he meets a local Chinese woman, Siu-wan. Singapore was obviously still an exotic tropical setting not only for Westerners, but also for mainland Chinese in search of sun, heat and orchids. *Romance of a Nyonya* portrayed Singapore in a more touristy

Tang San A Shao (released in Singapore as *China Wife*) by Chun Kim and Chor Yuen, 1957.

Romance of a Nyonya, 1968: Hong Kong stars Chun Bo Chu and Lui Kei filming at MacRitchie Reservoir (top) and the Kong Ngee magazine cover for the movie (bottom).

manner than the Italian or French movies of around the same time, which gave it extra documentary value. It also shows that the exotic perception of Singapore was not the same in the East as in the West.

Yet, after almost 15 years of success, Kong Ngee suffered from fierce competition both in its exhibition business in Singapore, with Shaw and Cathay focusing on that aspect of the film industry, and in its production business in Hong Kong, from the new Hong Kong cinema initiated by Golden Harvest. Production activities of its Hong Kong studio slowly came to a halt in the early 1970s, although it continued with its distribution and exhibition business in Singapore until the 1980s.

ENG WAH Eng Wah started as a distributor and exhibitor in 1945, under the direction of its founder, Goh Eng Wah. It specialised in Chinese movies, mostly in Hokkien and in Cantonese (and consistently did so until 1988, when it also started showing English movies). Following the examples of Cathay and Kong Ngee, though on a smaller scale, it moved to production by establishing the Eng Wah Film Production Company in Hong Kong.

Speaking volumes about the Southeast Asian origin of the company, among its first Hokkien (Amoy dialect) films were significant titles like *Peranakan Nonya* in 1958, as well as *Ma Lai Ya Zhi Lian* (a.k.a. *Love of Malaya*) and *Xin Jia Po Xiao Jie* (a.k.a. *Miss Singapore*), both shot in 1959.

Love of Malaya was directed by Chen Yiqing (a.k.a. Chan Yik-ching) and starred Ding Lan, Chen Lie and Shangguan Luyun. It contained six song numbers. As for *Miss Singapore*, it was directed by Yan Qiufeng (a.k.a. Yuen Cho-fung), with Xiao Juan (a.k.a. Ivy Ling Bo) and Huang Ying (a.k.a. Wong Ying) as leads.

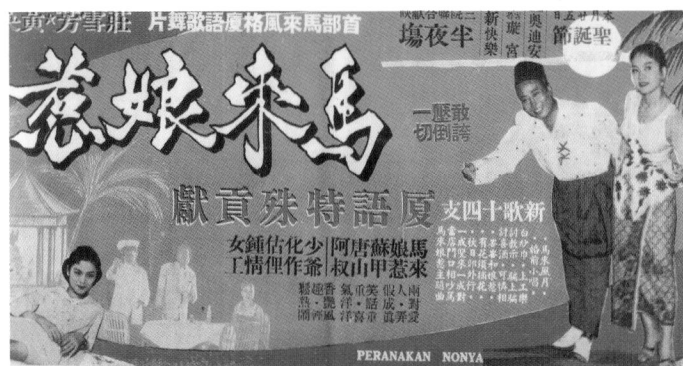

Peranakan Nonya in 1958, advertised as "specifically presented in Hokkien".

The same year, a productive one indeed for the new company, it made other Hokkien movies in Hong Kong, such as *Ye Chi Cha Mou Gang Nan Zi* (a.k.a. *The Shrew and the Blockhead*), *Dai Jia Gu Ku Du Hao Xi Fu* (a.k.a. *The Malicious Mother-in-Law Poisons the Dutiful Daughter-in-Law*), *A Xiu Mai Yan Zhi* (a.k.a. *Axiu Peddles Rouge*).

In the 1960s, Eng Wah would also start producing Cantonese movies in Hong Kong, including *Autumn Melancholy* in 1962 by Ng Wui, and *The Magic Whip* in 1968, directed by Wong Fung.

SHAW RUN RUN GOES TO HONG KONG

The Shaw empire had always kept a foot in China (originally Shanghai, and later on, Hong Kong), and another in Singapore. While Shaw Runme and Shaw Run Run continued to run the Singapore branch of the family, Shaw Runde, who had remained in China, moved to Hong Kong in the mid-1930s, so as to escape the unrest and troubles created by Japan's expansionist policy.

In 1937, during the Japanese invasion, the original Shaw production house in Shanghai had to close, leaving the Shaws with their smaller studio in Hong Kong, the Nan Hua Film Company. There, Shaw Runde resettled the family and resumed production, with the help of his Singapore-based brothers.

They soon started another studio, headed by Runde, and named the Nanyang Film Company. Nanyang meaning "South Seas", it was a highly symbolic name, because Southeast Asia was becoming more important to Shaw as a market for their productions, while the China market was shrinking.

Du Li Qiao Zhi Lian by Chow Sze Luk, 1958.

In 1950, the studio, still headed by Shaw Runde, changed its name once again and became Shaw Father and Sons Film Company (Shaw Runde had 10 sons), which continued producing films in Cantonese, as well as in Mandarin, mainly for the overseas Chinese in Southeast Asia. This was because Shaw had to supply its large number of highly profitable theatres in Southeast Asia, which was where the real financial strength of the family lay ever since mainland China was taken over by the Communists in the late 1940s.

Yet, Shaw Runde never had as much success as a producer as his Singapore-based brothers. Also, in the mid-1950s, when competition grew in Hong Kong, especially after both Cathay (with MP&GI) and Kong Ngee moved in and started their own production lines, Shaw Runde seemed unable to adapt to the fast pace of the film industry.

As the city rapidly modernised, the film industry boomed, partly due to the fact that, unlike in Taiwan, Singapore and South Korea at that time, Hong Kong operated largely free from government interference. It was also an aggressively capitalistic environment. Shaw Father and Sons soon lost out to the competition, and finally left the movie production business in 1957, only retaining activities in local distribution and the exhibition of foreign language films.

This was when Shaw Run Run, who had been in Singapore for 30 years, decided to fully return to Hong Kong. In 1958, he took over the reins and started Shaw Brothers, as it is known till today. Shaw Run Run was an entirely different kind of businessman from Runde. A film buff who worked in his youth as a cameraman at Unique Film Productions, he also possessed a lot of business savvy, which can be seen in the way he built Shaw's empire in Southeast Asia.

Soon after its inception, the newly established Shaw Brothers studio produced a series of Cantonese movies partly shot in Singapore and Malaysia, thus entering into direct competition with Cathay's MP&GI as well as with Kong Ngee Film Production Company.

Du Li Qiao Zhi Lian (a.k.a. *The Merdeka Bridge*, a.k.a. *Chinta di Jambatan Merdeka*) tells the story of two lovers who meet on the Merdeka Bridge, to conduct their sweetheart talks. *Guo Bu Xin Niang* (a.k.a. *Bride from Another Town*) is another melodrama where a bride-to-be Chun arrives in Singapore only to discover that her fiancee has died in a car accident, and consoles herself with a caring cyclo-driver. Finally, *Liu Lian Piao Xiang* (a.k.a. *When Durians Bloom*, a.k.a. *The Fragrance of the Durians*) recounts the hardship of a young man taking over the rubber plant business from his uncle in Singapore.

All three movies were directed by Chow Sze Luk (a.k.a. Chow See Luk) and had the same cast comprising of Patricia Lam Fung, Cheung Ying Choy, Lung Kong, Lee Pang Fei. In the manner of what Kong Ngee had done two years before with its "Nanyang Trilogy", they had been shot back-to-back.

Shaw Run Run had also made the audacious decision to leave behind the thriving studio in Singapore simply because he felt the conditions were ripe for the film industry in Hong Kong. He was right. He invested a lot of capital to build the infrastructure, recruit up-and-coming artists and cultivate new talent in all aspects of filmmaking.

Shaw Run Run (centre) at a festival.

Hong Kong, flooding all of Asia with its productions, and winning most of the film festival awards (which up to then had been swept by Cathay).

Shaw Brothers also revolutionised film history by making martial arts a highly successful and popular genre. Chang Cheh's *Du Bi Dou* (a.k.a. *One-armed Swordsman*), starring Jimmy Wang Yu, was the first film to gross more than HK$1 million and to score big in Taiwan, Singapore and Malaysia.

It is also worth noting that Shaw Brothers in Hong Kong found inspiration as well in their old Malay catalogue when ideas were badly needed. For instance, the figure of the *orang minyak* or oily man, which had been a successful monster in three 1958 Malay movies (two by L. Krishnan for Cathay-Keris, and one by P. Ramlee for Shaw's Malay Film Productions), was the reference for their 1976 Hong Kong feature directed by Hoh Mung-wa (a.k.a. Ho Meng Hua), *You Gui Zi* (a.k.a. *Oily Maniac*), starring Danny Lee and Lily Li.

Most of these movies were brought into Singapore by the Shaw theatres, thus giving its exhibition circuit a huge advantage over other local competitors such as Cathay, Kong Ngee or Eng Wah. The Shaws had a major influence on the local audience and contributed greatly to local film culture.

The success of their newly revamped and relaunched Hong Kong studio also meant that the Shaw would focus less on their Singapore productions, which were far less profitable and in a much smaller market.

While major changes were taking place in post-1965 Singapore, Shaw Brothers in Hong Kong was about to meet huge success with a movie that would make history and carve itself a permanent place in the annals of film, the world-famous and now cult *Come Drink With Me* by King Hu, released throughout Asia in 1966.

By the end of 1961, Shaw's brand new, gigantic studios opened in Hong Kong and started production. In a few years, Shaw Run Run had revolutionised the way the family did business. In another few years, he would revolutionise Hong Kong cinema. He started competing against long-time rival Loke Wan Tho, whose MP&GI had been thriving in Hong Kong for five years.

As early as 1964, a year also saddened by Loke Wan Tho's accidental death in a plane crash, Shaw Brothers was able to dominate the market in

The Shaws' pragmatism and shrewd business sense led them to make drastic choices, such as the abrupt closure of their Singapore studio at Jalan Ampas in 1967, five years ahead of the closure of the Cathay-Keris studio. On the other hand, the Shaws' stay in Hong Kong was to last far longer than Cathay's. Indeed, Cathay Organisation (ex-MP&GI) closed down its Hong Kong studio as early as 1970. Shaw Brothers continued producing movies there until 1985, the year it restructured its activities in Hong Kong.

APOGEE OF MALAY DIRECTORS
It was around the period 1959 to 1963 that both Indian and Filipino directors slowly started leaving the scene. In 1964, B.N. Rao shot his last movie in Singapore, *Pontianak Gua Musang* (a.k.a. *The Vampire of the Cave*, a.k.a. *The Vampire of the Civet-Cat Cave*). In 1965, Ramon Estella also ended his Singapore film career with *Pusaka Pontianak* (a.k.a. *The Accursed Heritage*, a.k.a. *The Pontianak Legacy*). With their departure, the presence of Indian and Filipino directors in the Singaporean film industry came to an end. In doing so, they were giving way to the Malay filmmakers who had once started as their assistant directors. Only then did the number of Malay filmmakers in activity seriously expand.

S. Kadarisman in *Tiga Abdul* by P. Ramlee, 1964.

From 1950 to 1954, Naz Achnas, A. R. Tompel, Jaafar Wiryo and Haji Mahadi were the only active Malay directors, responsible for just a handful of titles. They were followed, between 1955 and 1959, first by P. Ramlee, then by S. Roomai Noor and later on by Jamil Sulong. From 1960 to 1964, they were joined first by Salleh Ghani, Omar Rojik, Hussain Haniff, and S. Kadarisman, then by M. Amin, and at a later stage by Mat Sentol and Noordin Ahmad. Most of them, apart from Hussain Haniff, were former actors.

The years 1961 to 1966 were the most prolific and successful for the entire group of Malay directors. They had a regular annual output of roughly 17 to 19 movies over 1961 to 1964, including major titles such as: *Ali Baba Bujang Lapok* (lit. Ali Baba, Confirmed Bachelor), *Labu dan Labi* (lit. Labu and Labi) or *Ibu Mertuaku* (a.k.a. *My Mother-in-Law*), by P. Ramlee; *Hang Jebat*, *Dang Anom* and *Dua Pendekar* (lit. Two Warriors) by Hussain Haniff; *Puteri Gunung Ledang* (lit. The Princess of Mount Ledang) by S. Roomai Noor; *Sri Mersing* and *Tun Fatimah* by Salleh Ghani; *Darah Muda* (a.k.a. *Young in Heart*) and *Mambang Moden* (lit. Modern Partner) by Jamil Sulong.

It was the heyday for Malay stars, not only for the abovementioned actors-cum-directors, but also for a whole range of actors and actresses like Wahid Satay, Maria Menado, Jins Shamsudin, Zaiton, Rose Yatimah, Saloma, Rosnani, Sarimah, etc., all taking part in the triumph of this increasingly homegrown pop culture phenomenon.

Symbolically enough, 1965 was to be not only the year of Singapore's independence, but also the year when Malay filmmaking was fully handed over to Malay directors (bearing in mind that the financial dimension remained in the control of Chinese producers-cum-exhibitors). It was exactly around the time of independence, in the few months that preceded it, and that followed it, that made-in-Singapore Malay cinema delivered a few gems which managed to capture the numerous changes experienced by the island-city-state.

In 1965, Hussain Haniff made two noteworthy social dramas, *Chinta Kaseh Sayang* (lit. My Darling Love) and *Jiran Sekampong* (lit. Village Neighbours), both subtly encapsulating the ambiguities of modernisation.

In the same genre, Jamil Sulong also came up in early 1966 with a fine feature, *Kacha Permata* (lit. Glass and Gems), showing how an outwardly progressive society can retain strong conservative elements. Around the same time, Jamil Sulong gave Singapore its own version of James Bond, with the character of Jefri Zain played by the dashing Jins Shamsuddin. With the new hero's first adventure on screen, *Gerak Kilat* (lit. Moves in a Flash), Jamil Sulong made local film a little bit trendier and funkier, keeping it in tune with the latest evolutions of world cinema.

Yet, 1965 and 1966 were also the years that overall production started its decline, falling to 14 and then 11 feature films, never to return to the grandeur of the pre-independence years. Paradoxically, the decline in production of Malay films in Singapore came almost at the same time as it reached its full maturity. If some Malay filmmakers were to have long-lasting careers, it would not be in Singapore anymore, but in neighbouring Malaysia, except for a handful of them like M. Amin, who remained in Singapore until 1972.

THE BEGINNING OF THE END
Although Singapore had, for many years, made the choice to be part of a larger Malay entity, major changes were on the way. Key figures in the movie industry, like Ho Ah Loke and L. Krishnan, foresaw the way the industry was going, and even anticipated it. And by anticipating it so much, they made it happen.

In 1960, H. M. Shah bought over a piece of prime land on the fringe of Kuala Lumpur and, with the help of Ho, who had broken away from Cathay-Keris, set up Merdeka Studio, also known as Merdeka Film Productions Ltd.

L. Krishnan followed and shot the new studio's first feature, and officially the first Malaysian feature made in the newly independent Malaysia, *Tun Teja* (a.k.a. *Tun Tijah*). He went on to make, between 1961 and 1962, *Keris Sempena Riau* (lit. Keris Commemorating Riau), *Selendang Merah* (lit. Red

Lethal *keris* in *Hang Jebat* by Hussain Haniff, 1961 (top); Maria Menado (right) in *Tun Fatimah* by Salleh Ghani, 1962 (bottom).

over Merdeka Film Productions in 1966. They carried on with producing Malay movies at Merdeka until the late 1970s. Merdeka would be taken over in 1985 by the newly created National Film Development Corporation of Malaysia (a.k.a. FINAS). That would mark the end of the Studio Era of Malay cinema in the region, which had coincided with its golden age. It had lasted almost 40 years, and Singapore had played a most instrumental role in it.

FOREIGN-PRODUCED MOVIES IN THE 1960s The 1960s saw a surge of interest for Singapore as a shooting location for international projects (just as it had very briefly been in the 1930s). It was exotic enough to attract the attention of producers and directors from India, France, Italy or the USA, who were in search of inspiration for escapist adventures and romances.

Not only was the island-city used as a convenient hub, and the backdrop for Italian B-movies recounting the adventures of fierce Malay pirates, as in Umberto Lenzi's 1964 *I Pirati della Malesia* (a.k.a. *The Pirates of Malaysia*), it was also valued for its own mystique, the mere name of Singapore speaking volumes about Southeast Asia to foreign audiences.

The first international project came from India, in 1960. Simply titled *Singapore*, this production very clearly focused on the island-city itself. Directed by Shakti Samanta, it starred a string of Indian actors like Shammi Kapoor, Rajen Kapoor or Padmini, as well as Maria Menado herself. But most significant of all, it was filmed almost entirely on location in Singapore.

In the mid-1960s, two European features were shot, almost at the same time. They were B-movies in the spy genre then much in vogue, ripping off James Bond. The 1966 *Goldsnake Anonima Killers* (a.k.a. *Suicide Mission to Singapore*, a.k.a. *Singapur, hora cero*, a.k.a. *Mission suicide à Singapour*) directed by Ferdinando Baldi, a prolific Italian filmmaker, tells the story of American secret agent Kurt Jackson who is sent to Singapore to rescue Professor Wang Li and his son, who have escaped from China. Prof. Wang Li has discovered a way to produce a small atomic bomb, and he is being threatened by Chang Tu, a villain trying to get the secret. Those were the days of the Cold War. This coproduction involving Italy, France and Spain is of great interest because it was largely shot on location in Singapore, with a cast that included local actors, such as Salleh Melan.

A year later, in 1967, a French production, directed by Bernard Toublanc-Michel, *Cinq gars pour Singapour* (a.k.a. *Five Ashore in Singapore*, a.k.a. *Singapore, Singapore*), was shot entirely on location in Singapore. It was adapted from an eponymous original story by Jean Bruce, with a music score by famous French New Wave composer Antoine Duhamel.

Here again, many local actors and extras were used, such as Lim Hong Chin, Abdullah Ramand, Ismail Boss and See Foon. The leads were Western though, starring Sean Flynn (the son of Errol Flynn, who had a shortlived movie career from the mid-1950s to the mid-1960s, before disappearing

Scarf), *Ratapan Ibu* (lit. Mother's Wails) and *Fajar Menyinsing* (lit. Dawn Breaks). Merdeka Studio had a meagre beginning, but once the top stars began their exodus from the two Singapore studios, its growth surged dramatically.

Of the two Singapore studios, the Shaw brothers, anticipating the changes ahead and certainly planning to move their production of Malay movies to Kuala Lumpur, were the first to let go some of their major artists, including, as early as in 1964, the prominent Salleh Ghani and P. Ramlee.

Jamil Sulong, Omar Rojik, S. Kadarisman and Jins Shamsudin followed, around 1967 to 1968, when Shaw closed their Singapore studio. Others like M. Amin or Mat Sentol kept on working for Cathay-Keris as long as they could, but finally also had to make the move to Kuala Lumpur in the early 1970s.

The Shaws, to facilitate their swift move to Kuala Lumpur, simply bought without a trace in Cambodia in 1970), Marika Green (who had started in 1959 in Robert Bresson's *Pickpocket*, and who would later play in the 1974 French erotica *Emmanuelle in Bangkok*), Marc Michel (who had played in some of the most famous French movies of the early 1960s, including some by Jacques Demy), Denis Berry (the son of film director John Berry).

Just like with the Italian *Goldsnake Anonima Killers*, the plot was simple, Cold War-oriented, and packed with action. Captain Art Smith, from the CIA, is sent to Singapore to investigate the disappearance of some Marines. He meets four Marines who are willing to assist him in his task so as to avenge their missing friends. But Art Smith also crosses the path of the mysterious Monica.

This movie shows a lot of Singapore in the mid-1960s, with 50% shot directly in the streets and in 52 different settings (black-and-white villas, nightclubs, villages, etc.). And it does so in full colour, a rather rare thing in Singapore in those days. Interestingly enough, it seems to have been shot around National Day, since most buildings in the streets carry the flag, and some even have banners with the words "Majulah Singapura" (lit. Onward Singapore) which is the island-state's national anthem.

END OF THE STUDIO ERA
The early to mid-1960s saw major upheavals for Singapore. Becoming autonomous in the late 1950s, the island-city turned city-state momentarily joined the Federation of Malaysia between 1963 and 1965. Along the way, it encountered racial and social unrest. This included agitation by the left-wing unions under SATU (Singapore Amalgamated Trade Unions) which controlled the workforce of both studios (the tone had been set as early as 1957 with a huge strike at Shaw's Malay Film Productions).

This was also a time of modernisation, marked by the advent of television in 1963. Its popularity after 1965 made it a major competitor to the movie industry. But television was not the only change. The cinema audience was no longer flocking to local Malay films, but to Malay-dubbed or Malay-subtitled Filipino and Indian movies.

As a matter of fact, both the Filipino and the Indian industries managed to reach very high standards of production, combining popular scripts with great artistic quality. Technically speaking, with their ability to produce more and more colour movies, they were also far ahead of the Singapore film industry, which was unable to catch up and still mostly shooting in black-and-white.

Only one Singapore-made colour feature was produced in the whole of the 1960s, at a time when the use of colour in movies was becoming the norm all over the world. Indeed, the introduction of colour in films was a strategic move made by studios everywhere else but Singapore, so as to remain one step ahead of television and maintain a competitive advantage. This was something Singapore studios did not do, thus reducing the capacity of local movies to compete with television, or with other film industries which had been swifter at switching to colour production.

SHAW CLOSES ITS SINGAPORE STUDIO
Seen strictly from an exhibitor's point of view, the movie business was doing quite well in Singapore, with attendance of 28.2 million in 1968. However, this growth was benefiting mostly Western and Hong Kong films, whereas the box-office revenue for Singapore Malay movies had been declining since the mid-1960s. This downward trend forced the Shaw brothers to take action rather swiftly. From 1963 onwards, they started cutting down their production in Singapore and eventually decided to close their Singapore studio at Jalan Ampas in 1967.

One of the last movies made was the outstanding *Raja Bersiong* (a.k.a. *King with The Fangs*), shot by Jamil Sulong in Singapore and Kedah. A lavish production, it was filmed in colour and cinemascope, with the help of a Japanese assistant director and a number of Japanese technicians. No colour movie had been produced in Singapore since the late 1950s, and the know-how had been lost. It was as if Shaw had tried to leave one last testimony of its lost Singaporean grandeur. As Jamil Sulong himself puts it in his memoirs, it was to be the "swan song" for Malay Film Productions. However, it was a major box-office failure which never recouped its cost.

Shaw's decision to stop production in Singapore had been carefully planned. With Shaw Run Run's move to Hong Kong in 1958, and his founding of the new Shaw Brothers there, the Shaws' focus in terms of movie production switched from Malay movies made in Southeast Asia to Chinese movies made in Hong Kong

Yet, Shaw did not totally give up on Malay moviemaking. However, instead of staying in Singapore, they moved to Kuala Lumpur where, in 1966, they took over Merdeka Studio. This was not much of a surprise since they had partly orchestrated the migration of their most famous household names there.

Shaw was the distributor for the first Merdeka Studio productions ("A Shaw Organisation release" generally being seen in the opening credits). And the newly created studio, Merdeka Film Productions, even had the advantage of having the exact same initials as the soon-to-be-closed Malay Film Productions.

Shaw would thus head Malaysia's main studio for quite a few years. However, Merdeka's production dwindled drastically in the late 1970s. So, in effect, Shaw's only real production activity was in Hong Kong making Chinese movies. In Malaysia, Shaw eventually sold everything to FINAS (Malaysia's national film development board) in 1985. That same year, they also put a halt to their Chinese movie production in Hong Kong.

Shaw remains a legend in the industry. From 1924 onwards, over a period of more than 60 years, the Shaws, under the different companies they had set up and owned, had actively produced hundreds of movies, leaving behind them an unmatched record and an amazing legacy.

SHAWS MALAY FILM PRODUCTIONS LTD., presents
TUNKU ABDUL RAHMAN'S

Raja Bersiong

(KING WITH THE FANGS)

in
SHAWSCOPE
and
EASTMANCOLOR
DIRECTED BY JAMIL SULONG

MILLION-DOLLAR PRODUCTION!
TWO YEARS IN THE MAKING!

35 CENTS

Flyer for *Raja Bersiong* by Jamil Sulong, 1967

CATHAY-KERIS STOPS PRODUCTION

Cathay took longer to face reality, but when a decision had to be made, all links with production were severed. They, unlike Shaw, did this without any back-up plans. The sudden accidental death of Loke Wan Tho in 1964 had come at a time when Cathay faced new challenges both in Hong Kong and in Singapore. In 1970, Choo Kok Leong, Loke's brother-in-law who had been put in charge of Cathay after the 1964 incident, decided to first close down its Hong Kong studio.

Cathay's former facilities were not destroyed, but leased to someone else, who happened to be Raymond Chow, who had just left Shaw Brothers and started his own company, Golden Harvest. The first movies he produced in the ex-Cathay studio were no less than *Big Boss* (a.k.a. *Jing Wu Men*) in 1971, *Fist of Fury* (a.k.a. *Meng Long Guo Jiang*) in 1972, and *Enter the Dragon* (a.k.a. *Long Zheng Hu Dou*) in 1973, which shot to stardom a newcomer named... Bruce Lee. Significantly, *Big Boss* and *Fist of Fury* were both directed by Lo Wei (a.k.a. Law Wai or William Lowe), a Chinese director from Jingsu who had worked with the Shaw Brothers in Hong Kong since 1965, and directed numerous James Bond rip-offs for them, including some sequels to the adventures of Jefri Zain, the Malay James Bond first created by Jamil Sulong in 1966. Strangely enough, these partly Malay movies are almost never listed in Lo Wei's biography. A new era was emerging for Hong Kong cinema, of which Singapore (except for the Shaw connection) was going to be left out after having paved the way for it in more than one way.

Between 1968 and 1972, Cathay-Keris thus remained the only supplier of Singapore-made Malay movies, churning out a total of 22 features, with only three directors still under contract with the studio — Noordin Ahmad, Mat Sentol and M. Amin.

Bruce Lee's *Big Boss* being shown at Cathay's Majestic in the early 1970s.

Noordin Ahmad made five movies in 1968, 1969 and 1970. His 1968 social drama *Kekaseh* (lit. Lover) stands out for addressing women's issues in a modernising society, at a time of change, when Singapore was in the process of nation-building.

Mat Sentol directed five movies as well, including the slapstick Mat series, with *Mat Lanun* (lit. Mat the Pirate), *Mat Toyol* (lit. Mat the Mischievous Demon), *Mat Karong Guni* (lit. Mat the Gunny-Sack Man) and *Mat Magic*, all rather silly, and badly — or hastily — put together. His last Singaporean feature, in 1972, was not a Mat movie, but a very unexpected postpontianak genre movie, the title of which, *Dara-Kula* (after the names of the two female leads, one called Dara, the other Kula... yes!) also made explicit reference to the then internationally popular Dracula movies. It is definitely a B-movie (or even Z). Mat Sentol would later go on to a not-so-successful career in Malaysia, appearing on television and occasionally directing and

M. Amin.

acting on the big screen, like in his 1979 *Mat Tenggek* (lit. Someone too lazy to do his own work), a last take on the Mat genre, done for Maju Film.

As for M. Amin, an ex-actor turned director (like P. Ramlee, Noordin Ahmad, Mat Sentol and most of the Malay filmmakers of that era), he became highly prolific in the mid-1960s, and remained so until the end of Cathay-Keris, directing a total of 28 movies between 1960 and 1972.

In his last years in Singapore, between 1968 and 1972, M. Amin

Mat Magic by Mat Sentol, 1971.

directed no less than 12 features, including valuable dramas like *Satu Titik di Garisan* (lit. A Drop at the Line) and most significant of all *Hati Batu* (lit. A Heart of Stone), a movie capturing Singapore in the early 1970s like almost no other. But having been produced at a time of decline, they immediately fell into oblivion, together with their director. As a matter of fact, M. Amin, quite unjustly, remains one of the most underrated filmmakers in Singapore cinema history.

M. Amin carried on with his career in Malaysia throughout the remainder of the 1970s, making no less than nine feature films there between 1973 and 1979. Some were for Merdeka Film Productions: *Harimau Jadian* (lit. Tiger Man), *Satu Penentuan* (lit. A Determination), *Satria* (lit. Warrior) and *Penyamun Si Bongkok* (lit. Si Bongkok, the Thief) in 1973, *Pertiwi* in 1974. He also made some for a new company called Sabah Film Production — *Hapuslah Air Matamu* (lit. Wipe Away Your Tears) in 1976, *Pendekar* (lit. Warrior) in 1977, *Sumpah Semerah Padi* (lit. Curse of Semerah Padi) in 1978, *Kisah Seorang Biduan* (lit. A Male Singer's Tale) in 1979. With a total of 37 movies directed by him in Singapore and Malaysia, plus all the ones he acted in, M. Amin has left one of the most prolific legacy in the history of classic Malay cinema.

In 1972, Cathay finally ended its Malay film studio operations. Competition was coming not so much from Kuala Lumpur where Merdeka Film Productions was not doing so well either, but rather from Indonesia, where Malay moviemaking had entered a new era and was fast expanding.

Cathay restructured its core activities to focus on the exhibition and distribution businesses, which were thriving. Ironically enough, the very same year, 1972, that the closure of the last homegrown studio marked the end of Malay filmmaking in Singapore, the local box office boomed to 36.7 million patrons. The growth particularly benefited the Hong Kong film industry which, in the early 1970s, became the biggest supplier to the Singapore market, with imported Chinese movies from Hong Kong even outnumbering films coming from the USA.

All in all, the golden age of the Studio Era in Singapore had lasted 25 years, from 1947 to 1972. Both leading studios had had a 20-year period of activity. And each had been on its own, without any other competitor, for a period of three to six years; in the case of Shaw, when Malay Film Productions first opened, and for Cathay-Keris, at the very end. Within those 25 years, around 300 movies were made, out of which roughly 280 were produced by the two major studios, and the rest by a few smaller companies.

It had, at one point, been one of the major regional film industries in Asia. Yet, having attained regional status, it had hardly ever gone beyond this, and never made an impact on the international scene. Apart from P. Ramlee, and occasionally Maria Menado, almost no Malay actor was known outside Southeast Asia. Even when it came to P. Ramlee, there was very little mention of him and his works in the international film reviews or magazines of the 1950s to 1970s, and there is very little about him in more recent books about world film history.

Hati Batu by M. Amin, 1972.

Malay movies seemed to have had no market beyond the Malay market (Malaysia, Singapore, Indonesia), and it is also worth noting that hardly any Malay actors had a chance to act outside of the local industry, apart from Maria Menado who acted in the Bollywoodian production aptly titled *Singapore* in 1960. But it was Bollywood, not Hollywood... Two years later, in 1962, Ibrahim Pendek would be the first to act in an American film, *The Spiral Road*, directed by Robert Mulligan, starring alongside Rock Hudson and Gena Rowlands. Strangely enough, Ibrahim Pendek was credited in this movie as Ibrahim bin Hassan, his real name — as if Malay cinema, even at its height, was just too distinct, and too far apart, from international cinema to meet it in any way.

They Call Her... Cleopatra Wong by George Richardson, 1978

DECAY AND OBLIVION
1973-1986

THE END OF THE STUDIO ERA did not mean the end of Singapore cinema. In the aftermath of the highly symbolic closure of the Cathay-Keris studio, a number of independent producers felt it could be time to move away from Malay-based cinema.

CHANGE AND DECLINE By the mid-1970s, Singapore had changed quite significantly. Ten years of full independence had greatly reshaped Singaporean society. The *kampong* or village was slowly becoming a thing of the past. Malayness was not the only cultural reference, since Singapore was out of the Federation of Malaysia. Singapore society and the political party in power were placing greater emphasis on the Chinese sector of the population. And rapid modernisation had brought many changes in terms of lifestyle and taste. The few movies that would be made between 1973 and 1978 were in Chinese or English, and not in Malay anymore, hence reflecting different aspects of the changes that were taking place.

Instead of pursuing the pontianak genre or the *kampong* drama, Singapore producers and filmmakers copied American or Hong Kong ideas. The fact that they were largely unsuccessful at doing this, and could not beat the other film industries at their own game, further contributed to the decline of film production in Singapore.

Moreover, the government did not come to the aid of the once vibrant but now decaying film industry. Its policies for the newly independent country

Ring of Fury by Tony Yeow and James Sebastian, 1973, features fight scenes by karate master Peter Chong (seen here being kicked over the bike).

Actor Peter Chong and director Tony Yeow in 1973.

were generally based on developmental economics. As industrialisation and modernisation were of vital importance, culture and entertainment became an afterthought. The government's new social engineering policies also led to increasingly strict media censorship, which would adversely affect movies like the 1973 *Ring of Fury*. Due to all these factors, Singapore film production would, by the late 1970s, come to a halt.

RING OF FURY

Two Singaporeans unknown to the world of filmmaking produced and directed their own martial arts movie in 1973. Tony Yeow, who had been involved in TV production since the mid-1960s, teamed up with James Sebastian to make *Ring of Fury*, which was inspired by, and paid tribute to, the then recently deceased Bruce Lee. It was a quick endeavour aimed at capitalising on the success of the kung fu genre. Trying to break away from what was done in the last years of the Studio Era (i.e. low-budget, black-and-white movies which sometimes looked like they had been shot in the 1930s), *Ring of Fury* was produced in colour and in widescreen.

Ring of Fury was not only the first 1970s indie movie, but it also stood out because of its narrative. It tells the story of a hawker who, because he refuses to pay for 'protection', is threatened by gangsters who accidentally kill his mother. He is also beaten up, but manages to escape. He goes on to learn martial arts, and later returns to exact revenge. The plot certainly sounds like a Bruce Lee or a Charles Bronson movie.

The lead role of *Ring of Fury* was not performed by a professional actor but by an actual karate master, Peter Chong, who, coincidentally, looks like a mix of Bruce Lee and Charles Bronson. Chong played opposite a cast of real martial arts practitioners — experts in karate, shaolin, tai chi, etc.

The fight scenes were, for the most part, not prechoreographed or simulated. The codirectors let the artists fight any way they liked, for as long as they could. This resulted in very realistic shots, where one can feel that there are no tricks but only real kicks, albeit with an unavoidable touch of amateurism in the cinematography.

This B-grade film had all the makings of a cult movie. As such, it could have become a landmark in Singapore film history, signalling the shift to a new era. However, local censorship standards were not as relaxed as in Europe, the USA or Hong Kong, and censors cracked down on films that had themes centred on sex and violence. *Ring of Fury* had both, a bit of sex (with a rape scene in the forest, which was immediately cut and forever lost) and a lot of violence. After much talk and a few cuts, it was banned.

One of the main reasons for banning the movie was not only because it featured gangsterism, but also because it seemed to advocate self-defence. Local authorities perceived it as condoning vigilantism, taking the law into

Peter Chong faces a bad guy in *Ring of Fury* by Tony Yeow and James Sebastian, 1973.

one's own hands, very much in the manner of Bruce Lee and even more of Charles Bronson. As this appeared to be the main point of contention, an extra scene was shot showing a policeman warning the hero not to act on his own. This inserted scene, however, was not sufficient to stop the ban.

As early as the mid-1970s, *Ring of Fury* had already been shown theatrically elsewhere, in Malaysia, Hong Kong and other countries in the Asia-Pacific region. However, Singaporeans had to wait another 25 years to see the movie. It was shown once on television in the late 1990s, but with hardly any promotional advertising. And, to date, it has never been commercially released in a Singapore theatre.

Ring of Fury had its first festival screening in 2005, at the first "Screen Singapore" festival, which was held in conjunction with Singapore's 40th anniversary of independence. The festival had unearthed the film, and duly included it in a comprehensive retrospective of local cinema.

Ring of Fury's main codirector, Tony Yeow, was to have an on-and-off career in the film industry much later on. He was involved as a unit manager in the shooting of Peter Bogdanovich's infamous *Saint Jack* in 1978, then in the preparation of *Medium Rare* in 1991 and, finally, in the production of *Tiger's Whip* in 1998, not to mention numerous uncompleted projects.

As for Peter Chong, who acted rather well for a first-timer, he unfortunately had no chance of becoming a Singaporean "Bruce-Bronson". Instead, he carried on with his martial arts practice, and went on to become one of a very few eight-dan karate masters in the world.

THE TWO SIDES OF THE BRIDGE

Chongay Organisation, founded by Koh Tian Kit, specialised in the distribution and exhibition of movie imports from Taiwan, Hong Kong and China. It catered to the local Singapore Chinese market, capitalising on the slow demise of industry players like Kong Ngee.

Following the collapse of studio film production, its then director, Lim Jit Sun (a.k.a. Lim Zhi Xiun) decided to venture into production. Unlike *Ring of Fury*, this was not supposed to be a shoestring affair with a limited crew. Since talent was now lacking in Singapore (most of the Malay film artists and crew had left for Malaysia or opted to forget about their movie careers), and Chongay was more Chinese-oriented, some technicians were brought in from Hong Kong.

Chongay's film production unit thus started off with Hong Kong experts, who soon trained a team of local technicians. It also employed about 10 fulltime actors with stage (not film) experience. The initial plan was to churn out three Mandarin movies a year. Yet, in the end, it did not make more than three movies in total. The first two seemed to have been *Yi Jia Zhi Zhu* (a.k.a. *Crime Does Not Pay*) and *Huang Tang Shi Jia* (a.k.a. *Hypocrite*, a.k.a. *Family Degeneration*) in 1974, both directed by Hong Kong filmmakers. However, very little information is available about those two titles.

After learning from the Hong Kong experts, locals were given the opportunity to make a third movie, *Qiao De Liang An* (a.k.a. *The Two Sides of the Bridge*) in 1976. It was directed by Lim Ann (a.k.a. Lim Meng Chew, originally from Malaysia), and used local actors and crew, except for a few foreign lighting and camera technicians. This movie tells the story of a young man, Yu Fei, from Kelantan in Malaysia, who wants to marry a Singaporean girl and work in the city-state. But once in Singapore, he has difficulty coping with the modern world and ends up getting dragged into all sorts of mishaps.

Since *Ring of Fury* did not make it to Singapore screens, *The Two Sides of the Bridge* became the first truly Singaporean production (after the closure of Cathay-Keris) to do so. Interestingly enough, it moved away from what had been the norm in the film industry.

Shot entirely in Mandarin, mostly by, with and for Chinese locals, it portrays a very "un-Malay" Singapore. Malay characters appear only in scenes taking place in Malaysia. And in the case of Fatimah, Yu Fei's childhood friend,

The Two Sides of the Bridge by Lim Ann, 1976.

Bionic Boy by Leody M. Diaz, 1977.

she does not even speak in Malay but in Mandarin (with a very cute Malay accent). This truly reinforced the fact that the Malay days of the movie industry were over, and Singapore cinema was now exploring new avenues in step with a changing society and a new target audience.

The Two Sides of the Bridge also shows interesting aspects of Singapore's fast-paced modernisation: Shenton Way, the financial district, under construction; Boat Quay still bustling with bumboats (before the Singapore River was entirely cleaned up); and new residential areas for the growing middle-class population sprouting up. The movie also captures what still remained then of the old days in the rural areas.

Chongay ceased production operations after three films because of increasing costs. What could have become the new small film studio of the 1970s was shelved and forgotten. However, Lim Jit Sun, who left Chongay to create his own company, Overseas Movie Pte Ltd, did not totally give up on film projects and started talking to a Shanghai film studio about the possibility of coproducing Mandarin films. Unfortunately, he passed away before anything materialised. After his death, his son Lim Fang Hua took over and carried on with Overseas Movie's main distribution and exhibition business, showing Chinese language movies, as well as Korean, Japanese and European films in Singapore. Following in his father's footsteps, he would later

venture into production, as with *Bailiu Libai* (a.k.a. *Lucky Number*) in 1999.

BIONIC BOY AND *CLEOPATRA WONG*

In 1977, Filipino producer Bobby A. Suarez, then chairing R. J. R Film Exchange and Bobby A. Suarez Film Production Inc. in Manila, sought new opportunities. He decided to partner with Malaysian Mohamed Ashraf, director of Zahraine Films, and Singaporean Sunny Lim Peng Hock who was from Intercontinental Distributors.

The three men incorporated a new company, B. A. S Films International, with the goal of reviving filmmaking both in Singapore and in Malaysia, and to do so on a regional level (like in the old studio days), with strongholds in Singapore, Kuala Lumpur and Manila. They even had dreams of grooming new talent with an international profile, and of entering both the Hong Kong and U.S. markets. Once again, Singapore was in a regional venture that would bring in a mix of talent from all over. It seemed like the old Filipino connection of the 1950s and the 1960s had been reactivated, in a most unexpected manner.

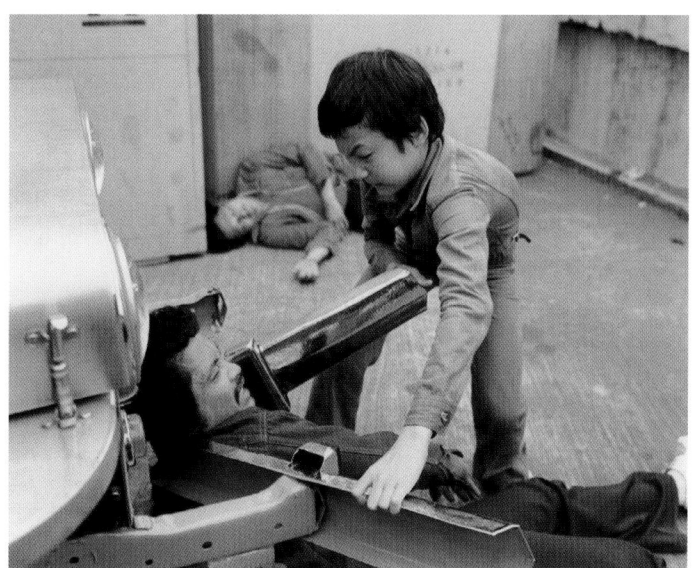

Dynamite Johnson by Bobby A. Suarez, 1978.

B. A. S Films International had no intention of producing either Chinese or Malay language movies. It planned to produce English films, so as to immediately reach out to a larger market. It wanted to capitalise on the success of spy and action movies popular in many places, particularly in Hollywood and in Hong Kong.

Feature films made by B. A. S were a mishmash of influences ranging from the James Bond and the OSS series, and all the B-grade spy movies that followed, to the kung fu wave that came after Bruce Lee. They also drew from the blaxploitation genre (black-oriented films emphasising sexuality

Devil's Angels by Bobby A. Suarez, 1979.

Marrie Lee, during her Cleopatra Wong days in the late 1970s.

and violence) that had taken the US by storm in the early to mid-1970s, as well as nunsploitation movies, a genre which featured nuns, and was characterised by its mix of action and soft porn, another craze in the 1970s (particularly in Japan and Italy). In fact, their famous "Cleopatra" Wong and "Dynamite" Johnson characters may have been named after the two seminal blaxploitation features, the 1973 *Cleopatra Jones* by Jack Starrett and the 1974 *Willie Dynamite* by J. J. Johnson.

They may also have been inspired by Shaw Brothers' infamous *Nu Sha Shou* (a.k.a. *The Lady Professional*) in which Lily Ho is perfectly cast as a gun-for-hire. Shaw had also produced in 1975 *Cleopatra Jones and the Casino of Gold*, which was also known under the French title, *Dynamite Jones et le Casino d'Or*. Shaw had thus already put together both the "Cleopatra" and "Dynamite" components which B. A. S would later make famous; Bobby A.

They Call Her... Cleopatra Wong by George Richardson, 1978.

Suarez and his colleagues had not been the first in Asia to capitalise on the action flick craze.

B. A. S inaugurated its trilogy of absolutely cult B-grade if not Z-grade movies in 1977 with *Bionic Boy*, starring young taekwondo black belt Johnson Yap from Singapore. *Bionic Boy* was loosely based on the TV action series, *Six Million Dollar Man*, with Bruce Lee and Chuck Norris thrown into the mix. In 1978, two more films were produced, *They Call Her... Cleopatra Wong* directed by George Richardson, and *Dynamite Johnson* (a.k.a. *Bionic Boy II*)

directed by Bobby A. Suarez himself (who had in fact more or less been behind the camera for the previous movies as well).

Cleopatra Wong, in particular, exploded across movie screens in Singapore and the Philippines. It became quite a phenomenon across Asia, and quickly reached cult status among film buffs all over the world. The film starred Singaporean booted-queen Marrie Lee, who was presented as a sort of Asian sister to Tamara Dobson (the original 1973 *Cleopatra Jones*), whose brother would have been Bruce Lee. This was actually how Bobby A. Suarez and

Sunny Lim came up with her screen name — they were looking for Bruce Lee's sister. Nineteen-year-old Doris Young (her real name) from Singapore's East Coast suddenly became the internationally known Marrie Lee who "purrs like a kitten... makes love like a siren... fights like a panther" (according to a poster advertising the film). *Cleopatra Wong*'s main asset was definitely Cleopatra Wong herself, who could surely wear a skirt much better than Bruce Lee or Peter Chong.

The plot was simple. Cleopatra Wong, a woman fighter who always gets her man in more ways than one, is asked to squash a counterfeiting ring in Singapore, Hong Kong and Manila. It starts out in Singapore (with excellent location shots) and moves to Hong Kong, then Manila, and back to Singapore for the climax, in a combination of action and seduction scenes. One of the best parts is when the villains are dressed up as gun-toting nuns, and Cleopatra Wong fiercely massacres them. She also has to dress up as a nun, once again a direct reference to Shaw Brothers' *The Lady Professional* in which Lily Ho also masqueraded in such a costume.

Soon after, both Cleopatra Wong and Bionic Boy (the former being characterised as the latter's "auntie") were brought together in *Dynamite Johnson*, where they teamed up against another group of villains. More kicks, more explosions... *Dynamite Johnson* took the entire series one step further by featuring two action-flick heroes; and it remains the only Singapore-made movie to do so. This movie, together with *They Call Her... Cleopatra Wong*, left a lasting impression and inspired many. An Australian rock band from the early 1990s even named itself "Cleopatra Wong", and Quentin Tarantino cites the movie as a reference for his own *Kill Bill*.

The first three movies being successful, a fourth one was initiated soon after *Dynamite Johnson*. Shot in Malaysia, its title was *Code Name: The Destroyers*, featuring Marrie Lee alongside Sarimah Ahmad, a famous Malaysian actress and businesswoman who had started her movie career 15 years earlier, in P. Ramlee's *Ali Baba Bujang Lapok* (lit. Ali Baba Confirmed Bachelor). However, due to production difficulties, it was never completed.

Marrie Lee, for the last time, reprised her role as Cleopatra Wong in another little-known but nonetheless enjoyable Bobby A. Suarez movie, *Devil's Angels* (a.k.a. *Devil's Three* or *Pay or Die*) in 1979, in which she is sent on a mission that takes her to Manila, where she finds the support of some of her old partners, a flamboyant gay martial arts master (who seems to be more into disco than anything else, though), and an enormous female buddy who kicks butts like no one else when she is not busy eating. The movie is packed with over-the-top action, gadgets and jokes.

Yet, Marrie Lee ended her career when she was only about twenty, before she ever fully realised that she had become a star. She had been Singapore's first and only action lady. And, for quite a few years, she remained one of the only, if not the only, Asian action lady to earn international recognition, way before actresses like Michelle Yeoh came on the scene.

Sunny Lim, unable to carry on with such projects in Singapore, moved to Kuala Lumpur (like many Malay artists had done 10 to 15 years before him). There, he went on to produce around 15 features, most belonging to the same Z-grade genre.

Bobby A. Suarez, who had been the main driving force, went back to Manila, where he has remained, occasionally directing and producing feature films, such as *One-Armed Executioner* in 1983 or *Manila Tattoo* in 1988.

The *Cleopatra Wong* and *Dynamite Johnson* films were definitely not first-rate productions. Shot on a shoestring budget, these films were not meant to be taken seriously. Nonetheless, they were memorably loaded with energy, campiness and quirkiness. And, in particular, *They Call Her... Cleopatra Wong*, the only one shot in Singapore, is a rare testament to a very scantily documented era for Singapore. The on-location scenes, the fashion styles, the music and the ambience all give this movie undeniable documentary value.

These Bobby A. Suarez films were also among the last to be produced, either wholly or partly, in Singapore, with Singapore artists in lead roles. This was at the very end of the 1970s when local cinema production was to disappear from Singapore for almost fifteen years.

THE POLITICALLY INCORRECT *SAINT JACK* *Saint Jack* was adapted by renowned American arthouse director Peter Bogdanovich from Paul Theroux's eponymous novel (written while he was in Singapore teaching at a university in the late 1960s and early 1970s, and first published in 1973). The movie serves as a very interesting and symbolic closure to the golden age of the Studio Era and the few years of decline that followed.

A low-budget feature produced by Roger Corman, the king of American B-grades, it draws a very unexpected and unofficial picture of Singapore. It is definitely not a Singapore-made movie, although shot entirely in the island-state. The story is about an easygoing expatriate, Jack Flowers. He makes a living in early-1970s Singapore, both legally and illegally, by looking after the needs of American and British businessmen visiting the city-state. Quickly expanding his business, Jack opens a successful brothel in an old colonial house, but physical threats from local gangsters soon drive him out of business. Not giving up, he starts working for GIs on breaks from Vietnam, at a time when Singapore was being used as a base and recreation camp by the US Army, which was then involved in the Vietnam War.

Saint Jack gives an unusually gritty portrayal of the city, showing what some would call its dark side. Because of this, and also because Peter Bogdanovich had tricked the censorship bureau by submitting a different script called *Jack of Hearts,* thus not revealing his intentions, the movie was immediately banned in Singapore and remained so for 20 years. *Saint Jack* was finally screened at the Singapore International Film Festival in the late 1990s. Abroad, even though not a box-office hit, *Saint Jack* met with something of a *succès d'estime* and even won the Italian Journalist Award for Best Film at the 1979 Venice Film Festival. It also gained cult status for the way it was produced, the way it portrayed Singapore, and the way it was banned.

Even though hardly seen by Singaporeans, *Saint Jack* seems to have been a rather seminal movie in the history of cinema in Singapore. Clearly an auteur's work created in a very independent and carefree way, it explores the at first unseen aspects of Singapore's multilayered and multifaceted society, and exposes its dark and gloomy — if not sleazy — sides. It also focuses on a character who is not much of a winner, but who comes across as a sort of anti-hero.

Saint Jack was very much in the tradition of 1970s American independent filmmaking, and definitely not what Singapore was used to. Yet, it is a style that would resurface 10 to 15 years later in the works of young local filmmakers like Djinn, who were attracted by

Ben Gazzara (centre) as Jack Flowers in *Saint Jack* by Peter Bogdanovich, 1979.

the fringes and underbelly of Singapore society. It would be an approach to filmmaking that would mark the revival of Singapore cinema after a period of collapse.

UNTIMELY COLLAPSE
Raising private money was difficult, public funding was nonexistent and censorship was becoming heavier. The 1970s was definitely not a conducive era for filmmaking in Singapore. The fact that both the very first local indie movie shot in 1973 (*Ring of Fury*) and the very last foreign indie movie shot in 1979 (*Saint Jack*) ended up being banned is extremely revealing and emblematic.

While Singapore's film production was collapsing, the situation was improving in Malaysia, and the film industries in Hong Kong and Indonesia were growing rapidly. In neighbouring Malaysia, things changed in 1975 when Deddy M. Borhan produced for Sabah Films the colour movie, *Keluarga Comat* (lit. The Comat Family), which was a hit at the box office. Its success led to the mushrooming or reactivation of many other companies such as Perfina, Syed Kechik Productions, Indra Films and Jins Shamsudin Production.

More and more Malay films followed in the late 1970s, an era which would later be labelled the revival of Malaysian cinema. The 1980s solidified that trend when a vital step forward was made with the creation of the National Film Development Corporation of Malaysia (known as FINAS) as early as 1981. FINAS regulated and stimulated the growth of local film production by setting up funding and advisory services.

As for Hong Kong, things could not be better. The kung fu craze reached another level with the rise of a new superstar — Jackie Chan. His 1978 *Snake in the Eagle's Shadow* and *Drunken Master* met with huge international success. Also, the first signs of what was going to be the Hong Kong New Wave were heralded by two very influential movies: *The Secret* by Ann Hui and *Cops and Robbers* by Alex Cheung.

However, in Singapore, things could not be worse, rather inexplicable given that the film distribution and exhibition sectors in Singapore were thriving as never before. More than 46 million tickets were sold in 1979, the very same year that film production ceased. After that, the film production industry would remain inactive for 12 to 15 years, resuming only in the first half of the 1990s. A rather long period of silence.

International film critics were swift, as always, at declaring the death of Singapore cinema. Renowned film critic Roy Armes wrote in his 1987 book, *Third World Film Making and the West*, that "Singapore is thus the only country in East or Southeast Asia without a local film industry". He was certainly right. Singapore had once been first in terms of Southeast Asian film production, now it was not even in the running.

Mee Pok Man by Eric Khoo, 1995

FROM SURVIVAL TO REVIVAL
1987–2005

IN 1987, THE VERY SAME YEAR that film critic Roy Armes declared Singapore filmmaking's premature death, signs began to emerge that cinema in Singapore may have survived a long coma, and would soon slowly revive.

SINGAPORE INTERNATIONAL FILM FESTIVAL In the absence of filmmakers, a group of film buffs slowly paved the way for better times to come. Among them was Geoffrey Malone, an Australian who settled down in Singapore in 1981 after taking part in the 1970s Australian New Wave. He saw the need to promote film culture in the city-state and stimulate the environment for future film directors.

He decided to set up the Singapore International Film Festival (SIFF) with the help of two Singaporeans, Philip Cheah, who handled programming, and Teo Swee Leng, who took charge of administration.

The Festival was first held in 1987, and swiftly positioned itself as a platform for Asian movies, strongly exposing, promoting and supporting new talent such as those from the Chinese Fifth Generation (Zhang Zemin, Zhang Junzhao, etc.) and the Taiwanese New Wave (Hou Hsiao-hsien, Tsai Ming-liang, etc.). Being ahead of its time in doing so, it quickly established an international reputation. The Festival also saw itself as a bridge between generations. It paid homage to the long-gone filmmakers of the distant golden age, in order to educate new talent, and give Singapore a sense of heritage, legacy and identity. In 1989, the biennial Festival, held only for the second time, presented a small

Geoffrey Malone, Philip Cheah and Teo Swee Leng (standing, respectively first, third and fifth from left) together with guests from Japan at the Singapore International Film Festival in 1995.

providing cash and support to the burgeoning industry. Many benefited, forging ahead with their careers in filmmaking.

MEDIUM RARE Produced by Singaporean Errol Pang, *Medium Rare* was initially supposed to be directed by a Singaporean, Tony Yeow (who had survived *Ring of Fury's* cataclysm), then by an American, Stan Barret, and finally by Arthur Smith, who was British, and by that very fact, roused postcolonial sentiments in Singapore.

Medium Rare, made in 1991, was thus the first local, or at least partially local, film made in Singapore since *They Call Her... Cleopatra Wong* and *Dynamite Johnson* in 1978. Initially, when the movie project was made public, it was seen as a revival. Alas, once completed, the disillusionment and disappointment were great. Singapore itself partly rejected it, seeing it as a rather un-Singaporean film.

Medium Rare was adapted from the true story of Singaporean Adrian Lim, who supposedly had spiritual powers which he used to abuse men and women, financially and sexually. He murdered two children and was sentenced to death in 1988. The lead role was, however, given to an American actor, Dore Kraus, who did not look or sound like the typical Singaporean that Adrian Lim was. Kraus tried hard but was miscast. Apart from a few other Caucasian roles (including the lead actress), the rest of the cast and the majority of the crew were Singaporeans.

However, considering that its director was British, its lead roles were played by Americans, and its understanding of local culture and society questioned by Singaporeans themselves, *Medium Rare* did not have the qualities to kick off the revival of local cinema.

Medium Rare was not to be the seminal movie that some expected, out of which the future revival of the local film industry would emerge. On the contrary, it caused everything to come to a standstill — not only because of its poor artistic value (revealing a lack of local filmmaking talent and professional expertise), but also because it was a box-office failure. This probably discouraged local producers from venturing into such a risky business — they are likely to not only lose money, but may also receive harsh criticism and lose face.

Despite this, *Medium Rare* remains interesting for its documentary value, with its shots of the Singapore of the early 1990s, when the city was undergoing a surge of change once again. Was it because it was the first movie shot after so many years of inactivity, or was it because the director was a foreigner, that *Medium Rare* is loaded with sights of the city-state, including many outdoor shots?

There are glimpses of the Giok Hong Tian temple on Havelock Road, a number of beautiful colonial and Peranakan houses near Tong Watt Road, the East Coast Park, and the Pan Pacific Hotel during its heyday. These local scenes so flooded the movie that it was almost like a tourism board video,

Opening ceremony of the 1997 Singapore International Film Festival held at the old Capitol Theatre.

retrospective of P. Ramlee's works through titles such as *Semerah Padi*, *Seniman Bujang Lapok* (a.k.a. *The Nit-Wit Movie Stars*) and *Labu dan Labi* (lit. Labu and Labi)

In 1997, its 10th anniversary, the Festival recollected once more Singapore's past, with a special programme called "Singapore Rediscovered". Films screened were *Hang Jebat* and *Dang Anom* by Singaporean Hussain Haniff, *Orang Minyak* (lit. Oily Man) by India-born and now Malaysian citizen L. Krishnan, *Sumpah Pontianak* (a.k.a. *Curse of the Vampire*) by Indian B. N. Rao, together with *They Call Her... Cleopatra Wong* and *Dynamite Johnson* by Filipino Bobby A. Suarez.

New avenues for future generations of filmmakers were opened by the Festival's endeavours, giving them the exposure, encouragement and support they needed for their work. A major step was made in 1990, after Philip Cheah discovered the first few homemade video or super-8 short movies by young local filmmakers. He decided to open a section dedicated to Asian short films, which gave him the opportunity to include those early films in the Festival programme.

Another important step was taken the following year (the Festival had by then become an annual event). In 1991, the Festival introduced the Silver Screen Awards. For the first time, local and regional moviemakers had the opportunity to showcase their productions and compete in two categories, Asian Feature Film, and Singapore Short Film.

The Singapore International Film Festival would remain the only one with a purely Asian competition until 1996, when the Pusan Film Festival in South Korea did the same. Furthermore, for a few years, until the Singapore Film Commission was established in 1998, the Festival was the only organisation and lowered the already poor standards of production. Lip service is paid even to the Merlion, in a scene by the Singapore River.

In trying too hard to make a marketable product that will appeal to an international audience looking for cheap, exotic escapism, and, at the same time, please the local authorities and business partners, the producer simply ended up with a failure, definitely not making film history. And it certainly did not help Singapore much in its endeavour to, on the one hand, lure foreign filmmakers and producers and, on the other, open up avenues for any up-and-coming local talents.

THE HONG KONG CONNECTION I
Having left the scene and seen its place taken by Hong Kong through the 1960s and into the 1970s, Singapore in the mid-1980s grew envious of Hong Kong's success story, and eventually saw it as a model and an inspiration.

The city-state tried to reactivate its connections in the movie business with the then British Crown colony, so as to benefit from the overspill of Hong Kong's booming film industry in the mid-1980s. At the back of the mind, there was the idea that Singapore should be prepared for the delocalisation of the movie industry that was expected to follow Hong Kong's handover to China by the British in 1997. The handover happened, but the delocalisation to Singapore never really did.

Recognising the need to reactivate things, the Singapore government did its best to attract Hong Kong investments and projects as early as the mid-1980s. In 1987, a special committee for the promotion of the movie industry was set up, and facilitated the building of infrastructure that would draw in foreign productions.

In 1989, Hong Kong businessman and former president of Asia Television, Deacon Chiu, ventured into the construction of a new studio in the western part of Singapore. The Tang Dynasty Village studio was fashioned after the Sung Dynasty Village in Hong Kong, but on a bigger scale. The Tang Dynasty Village, soon renamed the Tang Dynasty City, was a huge 12-hectare theme park replicating the city of Xi'an (a.k.a. Chang An) in China, the ancient capital of the Tang dynasty (AD 618 to 907).

The park had three gigantic indoor studios, and was a manifestation of Deacon Chiu's dream to make at least three movies a year (which rings a bell as Chongay had similar dreams in the 1970s).

This venture coincided with the first full Hong Kong production shot in Singapore, in 1991, thus apparently opening the way for further partnership. The movie was *Jing Tian Shi Er Xia Shi* (a.k.a. *The Last Blood* or also *12 Hours of Fear*), directed by Jing Wong and starring Eric Tsang Chi Wai, Andy Lau Tak Wah and Alan Tam Wing Lun. It was a full-fledged Hong Kong team, cast and crew. With its many outdoor location shots, this movie, like *Medium Rare*, captured Singapore's everchanging landscape. There was the cable car at Sentosa, the airport, the hospital, and so forth.

Since its opening in 1992, Tang Dynasty City has, unfortunately, not seen that many productions making use of its facilities. The only noteworthy one was the Hong Kong comedy *All's Well Ends Well Too*, directed by Clifton Ko Chi Sum and Raymond Wong Pak Ming, with Leslie Cheung, Sandra Ng and Stephen Chow. The official launch of the studio, however, did attract some measure of attention for Singapore as a place to shoot movies.

Sadly, the closer the handover drew, the less the Hong Kong producers seemed willing to invest in Singapore. What had once happened in the 1950s to 1960s, with a flow of Singaporean investment (Cathay, Shaw, Kong Ngee, etc.) going to Hong Kong, alas did not happen the other way around in the early 1990s. As a matter of fact, if there were to be collaborations with Hong Kong, it was going to be left to Singaporean producers to pump in the money that would attract renowned Hong Kong filmmakers to Singapore, a situation rather the reverse of what might have been initially hoped for.

THE AUTEURESQUE ERIC KHOO
Born in 1965, Eric Khoo is the same age as independent Singapore. His mother brought him to his first movies when he was only two years old. Around the age of eight, he chanced upon his mother's super-8 camera, and started making short animated films. This was in 1973, when the Studio Era had just come to an end.

His interest in filmmaking took him to the City Art Institute in Sydney, Australia, where he studied cinematography. Back in Singapore, he resumed making homemade videos, before venturing into award-winning short films, and then feature films. He was Singapore's first true auteur. Khoo usually admits to being influenced by movies like *Taxi Driver*, *Midnight Cowboy*, and the films of Aki Kaurismaki.

As early as 1990, Khoo's animated short film, *Barbie Digs Joe*, garnered no less than five prizes at the Singapore Video Competition. It went on to be the first Singapore short film officially presented at international festivals throughout the world. In 1991, his next short film, *August*, the story of an adulterous relationship seen through the eyes of a dog, won Best Singapore Short Film at the Singapore International Film Festival.

Khoo pursued his career by successively directing three more short films, *Carcass* in 1992 (a 50-minute video drawing parallels between the life of a businessman and the life of a butcher which was the first local film to be given an R(A) rating), *Symphony 92.4* in 1993 (about solitude and loneliness, and having nothing to do but live in the past), and *Pain* in 1994.

Pain by Eric Khoo, 1994.

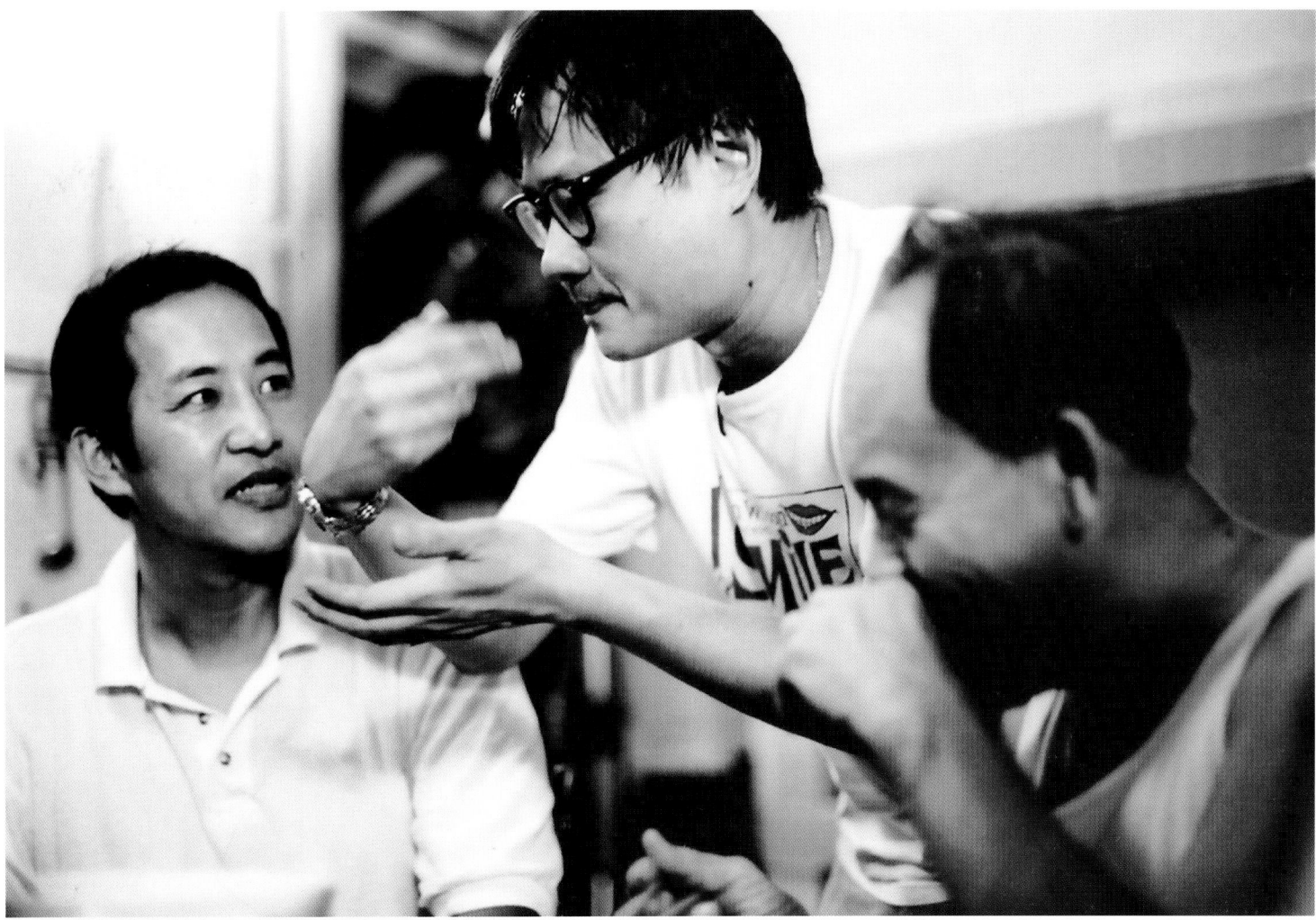

Eric Khoo (centre) directing *Be With Me*, 2005.

Pain was the movie that brought him trouble and notoriety, notoriety generally coming after trouble. This highly graphic portrait of a sado-masochistic young man who is obsessed with pain attracted attention because of its dark and gritty melancholic mood, and its artistic treatment. It was on the verge of being an experimental film. It also had all the elements of what would be Khoo's style and signature, with its portrayal of a misfit unable to find his place in society. *Pain* won Khoo the Best Director and Special Achievement Awards at the 1994 Singapore International Film Festival. It was, however, banned from public viewing in Singapore for its graphic portrayal of a person who commits a hideous crime involving brutality and torture. Twenty years after *Ring of Fury*, censorship was still very active. That did not discourage Eric Khoo. The ban was finally lifted and *Pain* was screened in Singapore in 1998. It was shown at the 11th Singapore International Film Festival (The Festival is known for its persistent efforts to give local filmmakers a chance to have their works shown).

MEE POK MAN In 1995, the 30-year-old Khoo went one step further in his career and in his exploration of Singapore's dark urban landscape and lifestyle. Using the prize he won when he received the Special Achievement Award for *Pain*, he directed his first feature film, *Mee Pok Man*. It was the mid-1990s, the turning point for Singapore cinema. It was also exactly 30 years after Singapore's independence. If a time and a movie were to mark the onset of the new Singapore cinema, it would be the 1995 *Mee Pok Man*.

Shot in Cantonese and Hokkien, and directed by a Chinese Singaporean without any experience of Singapore before its independence, *Mee Pok Man* kicked off a new era. This new period for Singapore cinema has little in common with the past golden age of the studios. Malay, which had been the dominant language in films, gave way to Chinese (Mandarin, Cantonese or Hokkien). And the Chinese, who were once mainly the producers (Shaw Run Run and Runme, Ho Ah Loke, Loke Wan Tho, Lim Jit Sun) controlling the business side of the industry, would now be in charge of the whole process, including directing and acting.

Indeed, after Eric Khoo's trailblazing efforts, many of the film directors in the decade between 1995 and 2005 were Singaporean Chinese. It also gave the new Singapore cinema an auteurist twist which remains highly influential. In positioning himself as an auteur making personal, intimate and non-mainstream movies, mindless of the market, he was able to enter the international arena, and contribute to placing Singapore back on the map of world cinema. *Mee Pok Man* was invited to over thirty film festivals including Berlin and Venice.

Michelle Goh *in Mee Pok Man* by Eric Khoo, 1995.

his home. However, the *mee pok* man is unable to let go of her and begins a relationship with her corpse. It is revealed later in the film that he had known her virtually all his life as they were classmates.

It was the first Singaporean movie to be entered for the Singapore International Film Festivals' Silver Screen Awards. Eric Khoo had set the tone with this sombre, modern-city tale, and inspired a trend that other filmmakers would follow.

12 STOREYS Two years later, in 1997, he directed *12 Storeys* (a.k.a. *Shi Er Lou*), a social drama in the vein of *Mee Pok Man*. It was almost a sequel, as reference is made to incidents from the previous film. Bunny's pimp, Mike Kor (played by Lim Kay Tong in *Mee Pok Man*) makes an appearance at the neighbourhood coffeeshop. He has a brief conversation with a few customers, and makes it clear that he has knowledge of Bunny's death. He blames the *mee pok* man for it. In a very interesting manner, the two films find an interface.

However, *12 Storeys* revolves around a whole new set of characters, and its structure is far more intricate than *Mee Pok Man*. It unveils the lives of four different families living in the same 12-storey block (hence the title), in public housing built by Singapore's Housing Development Board or HDB. Their lives intertwine to make up one single portrayal of Singapore society in the mid-1990s. Ah Gu is a chubby, middle-aged man who has lured a woman from mainland China through his lies, and married her. However, he is taken aback when she turns out to be a gold-digger with zero commitment to marriage. San-San is a single woman who is plagued by her late mother's contemptuous voice ringing in her ears. It becomes so unbearable that she contemplates suicide. Trixie and her younger brother rebel against their elder brother Meng, who talks like he is making a public service

Joe Ng in *Mee Pok Man* by Eric Khoo, 1995.

Mee Pok Man is a bleak, melancholic psychological drama about a noodle (known in Chinese as *mee pok*, hence the title) seller who had inherited an all-night noodle stall in a seedy district of clean and green Singapore. He is ridiculed by some of his regular customers for being mildly mentally disabled, and unable to understand what goes on around him. He is a lonely figure, living in public housing, in a small, one-room flat. However, this rather innocent man, bullied and taken advantage of by many, is not devoid of feelings. He is secretly in love with Bunny, a prostitute who often drops by at night to have a drink and a bite before going back to work. Bunny is also one of the few people to treat him in a friendly manner. One night, there is a hit-and-run accident outside his stall, and he finds Bunny injured and lying unconscious on the ground. He then decides to bring her home to nurture her back to health. However, fate deals a cruel blow and she dies at

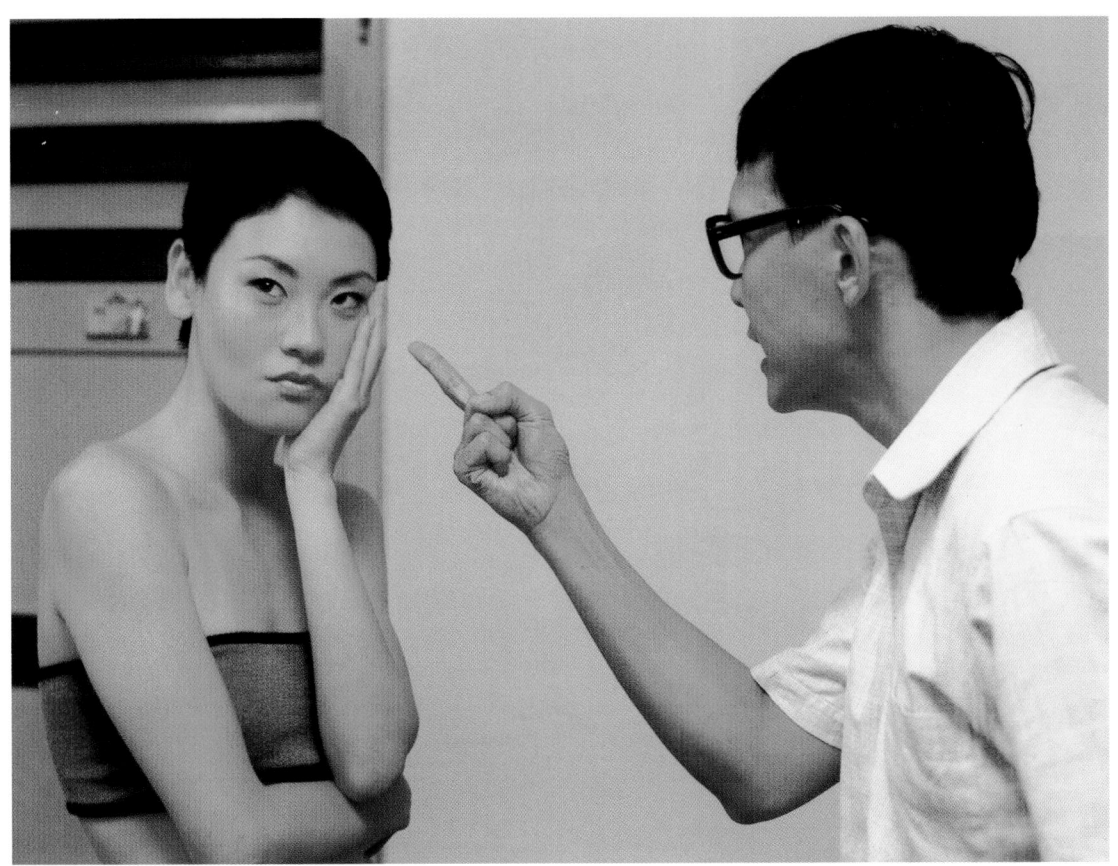

Lum May Yee and Koh Boon Pin in *12 Storeys* by Eric Khoo, 1997.

announcement and has a real problem with his authoritarian impulses and his sexual desires. The movie cleverly cross-cuts between these stories, building a picture of the destructive and dark side of Singapore society. The whole narrative is confined to a 24-hour period, a Sunday, and to one anonymous apartment block (though it was in fact shot at three different locations, for production reasons).

This multilayered script style would become Eric Khoo's signature, although he would not be the only filmmaker to use it. In *12 Storeys*, it enabled him to unravel a panorama of unspoken problems and anguish faced by a large number of Singaporeans (80 per cent of whom live in government-built housing blocks, generally designed with a degree of sameness). He would use it again in 2005 for *Be With Me*.

12 Storeys arrived at the right time, when Singapore, like the rest of Asia, was hit by the 1997 financial crisis, and all the social fears hidden under the official economic success story surged. Life did not seem as rosy as before. Without economic stability and comfort, what would Singaporeans be left with, knowing that they have lost many traditional values and reference points along the way? What would be left of the Singaporean dream? The movie

addresses these questions in a timely and honest way, thus giving a sincere and accurate portrayal of the island-city-state.

Along with its merciless portrayal of Singapore society, *12 Storeys* stood out for its artistic qualities, without which it would have never made it to the international scene and festival circuit. It is a finely photographed and edited movie, which sometimes relies less on its storytelling than on its cinematic savoir-faire to unveil emotions. *12 Storeys* also revealed a masterful direction of actors, managing to get out of first-timers some excellent delivery of speech and body language.

Always on the lookout for new talent, Eric Khoo offered Jack Neo his real debut on the big screen. Neo had already spent many years working in television, and was known mainly for his comedic skills. However, in this movie, he revealed the ability to underplay and be at ease in social drama. His portrayal of Ah Gu remains his best performance on screen, exceptionally contained and intimate.

With *12 Storeys*, not only did Eric Khoo refine his trademark dark humour, he also established in no uncertain terms the leading role played by auteur cinema in modern Singapore. It was the second Singapore-made movie to be entered the Singapore International Film Festival's Silver Screen Awards. It was also the first Singapore film to be screened at the Cannes Film Festival, having been selected for the *Un certain regard* programme. *12 Storeys* also won the Federation of International Film Critics (FIPRESCI) award. It was commercially distributed to the international market, including France. All this strengthened Khoo's international stature, positioning him among the ranks of top up-and-coming Asian directors, along with the likes of Edward Yang, Tsai Ming-liang, Fruit Chan and a few others.

Less than two years later, *Asiaweek* magazine named him to its list of 25 influential and exceptional Asians in the fields of cinema and television (Khoo had also directed and produced numerous music videos, television productions and television commercials). Khoo had given Singapore a face

Mark Lee (above) and Sharon Au (below) in *One Leg Kicking* by KhooKoh, 2001.

comprising three different episodes which displayed very uneven qualities. Not finding an audience, it played for one month and did not recoup its production cost.

Under the combined name "KhooKoh" (as stated in the film poster and title credits), Khoo also collaborated with first-timer Wei Koh on *One Leg Kicking* in 2001. Once again coproduced with Raintree Pictures, the movie tried to capitalise on the growing trend of soccer-related movies (*Shaolin Soccer* by Stephen Chow in 2000, *Bend it Like Beckham* by Gurinder Chadha in 2002). *One Leg Kicking* revolves around recently widowed Tai Po who is left on his own to take care of his children. He hopes to win an amateur football game to make some money to take his family for a holiday. His team, called the Durians, includes Handsome the goalkeeper and Kim the tomboy. The team they play against is mean and fierce. The cast featured popular television actors (Gurmit Singh as Tai Po, Sharon Au as Kim, Mark Lee as Handsome, Fiona Xie as Gwen) in a bid to attract the audience.

After having more of less successfully ventured into commercial films, Khoo returned to projects more in tune with his personality and image. As a producer, he was responsible for Royston Tan's first feature *15* (a.k.a. *Shi Wu*) in 2003, and Toh Hai Leong's unidentifiable filmic object, *Zombie Dogs* (a.k.a. *Eat Shit, Fuck and Die*) in 2004. Both delved deeper and deeper into the unseen and unspoken fringes of Singapore society, following up nicely on Khoo's own movies of the 1990s.

BE WITH ME   In 2005, and in time for the 40th anniversary of the independence of Singapore, Eric Khoo delivered a new opus, *Be with Me*, which would once again win him international recognition. *Be with Me* has won numerous international awards and has been sold to Europe, the United States and Asia for general distribution.

The movie was immediately selected for the Cannes Film Festival, where it was not only given a coveted spot in the Directors' Fortnight, but was chosen to open the programme. Ten years after his first feature, *Mee Pok Man*, Eric Khoo had pushed his cinematic ambition one step further, and set the bar very high for the local film industry. He had also brought to a close the first decade of the new Singapore cinema, which he himself had started with his first feature in 1995.

Be with Me is another tale of loneliness (or one should almost say "lonelinesses"), a genre which Eric Khoo excels in. It intertwines the lives of average Singaporeans from different generations, different backgrounds, and different personal histories. They all have their own issues to deal with, and most of them are alone. One old man cannot get over the death of his wife, particularly the fact that she had asked him to help her terminate it (it is left to the audience to decide whether he did indeed hasten her death). A solitary young man, who earns a meagre living as a security guard, is obsessed with his inability to find love. Two confused teenage girls

in the prestigious arena of world-renowned cinema. Khoo had also proven that he was able to make more than one feature, and a critically acclaimed one at that. Many of the filmmakers who would come after him would rarely make it past one movie.

It did, however, take Eric Khoo a long time to direct a third movie of his own. Keeping himself busy with a number of television series and commercials, he took on the role of producer. He teamed up with the newly created Raintree Pictures, and coproduced, under his company Zhao Wei Films, a very commercial comedy, *Liang Po Po — The Movie*.

He also produced the first fully digital film from production to projection. The film, *Stories about Love*, introduced a few budding filmmakers, Cheek, James Toh and Abdul Nizam, to the big screen. It ended as an omnibus film,

Be with Me by Eric Khoo, 2005: Ezann Lee and Samantha Tan (top); Seet Keng Yew eating alone (middle); Chiew Sung Chin in his shop (bottom).

search for their sexual identity by exploring lesbianism. The whole movie is infused with despair, with hope being seen only in the story of an ageing blind and deaf woman, Theresa Chan, who overcomes her handicap to become a teacher. Theresa Chan happens to be a real blind and deaf woman. The story told is her true story. With it, documentary suddenly overwhelms fiction, and life walks in.

Highly subtle and sensitive, *Be with Me* portrays a caring Singapore, and its everyday people who make it what it is. It is far less voyeuristic than Eric Khoo's first two features, both of which had a colder feel about them. Maturity has come, and, with it, the understanding that life does not hold much unless shared with others.

KHOO'S TALENT SCOUTING
As a film director-cum-independent producer, Eric Khoo has been able to retain artistic freedom through the years, and he holds a very influential position in the revived Singapore movie industry. Not only did he pave the way for auteur cinema in Singapore, but he was also a major talent scout, like L. Krishnan 40 years before.

Many film technicians began their careers with Khoo, before going on to work on other people's movies. A variety of actors were spotted by him and given their first roles on screen. A number came from television (Jack Neo, Gurmit Singh and Sharon Au, etc.), others from the music industry (for example, Joe Ng, formerly from the early 1990s' local rock band, The Padres), and yet others from nowhere, or the street. For some of them, shooting with Eric Khoo allowed them to become something else, even if only for that moment.

Transforming Jack Neo from a humorous television host to a movie drama actor in *12 Storeys* was a brilliant move, giving Neo his best role on screen. It also enabled Neo to move on to an impressive career in film. Similarly, Sharon Au's role as a tomboy in *One Leg Kicking* elevated her from bubbly TV host to actress. She later starred in some of Jack Neo's movies such as *Homerun* in 2003, and *I Do I Do* in 2005, quite an achievement in Singapore where very few actresses make more than two films.

Michelle Goh, who played Bunny, the lead role in *Mee Pok Man*, became a fulltime actress in the US; mostly in television scifi series like *Seven Days* and *Dark Angel*. She also took on the Asian babe role in the Z-grade Steven Seagal action movie, the 2003 *Out for a Kill*. Lum May Yee, who was Trixie in *12 Storeys*, went on to play — three years later, while pursuing her modelling career — Audrey Chan, the female lead role in Cheek's (a.k.a. Cheah Chee Kong) *Chicken Rice War*. *Be with Me* gave TV actress Ezann Lee the opportunity to debut on the big screen.

Some of the talent scouted by Eric Khoo, however, did not go on to pursue acting careers. Joe Ng never acted again after *Mee Pok Man*, even though he had given one of the best underplayed performances of Singapore cinema. He remains a quietly seminal figure in local film history.

THE VERSATILE JACK NEO   Jack Neo could be said to be the new P. Ramlee, a Chinese version. Like P. Ramlee, Neo started off as a multitalented entertainer, then went on to acting in film, before becoming a prolific director still playing in his own movies. Also like P. Ramlee, he is highly versatile, acting in both drama and comedy, as well as being involved in scriptwriting, directing and singing (although not as melodiously...)

Jack Neo was initially an entertainer who became a household name in the early 1980s on the Chinese channel of the then Television Corporation of Singapore (TCS). He hosted one of its most successful shows, *Comedy Night* (a.k.a. *Gao Xiao Xin Dong*) from 1995 to 2002. He hosted another popular Chinese TV variety show, *Top Fun* (a.k.a. *Huan Xiao Dian Feng*) from 2002 onwards.

Jack Neo in *I Not Stupid,* 2002.

Even though he turned to a career in movies, as an actor, then a director, Neo remained active in television. By doing so, he was able to retain popular support, which in turn benefited his ventures into films, at least commercially, if not always artistically. Indeed, after making his acting debut in 1997, he would become the most profitable artist in the whole of the Singapore movie industry of the late 1990s and early 2000s.

He may have started on the big screen in a typically auteuresque film, but after that Neo immediately embarked on another kind of project, more in tune with what he was usually doing on television. He went on to do popular comedies, some of them turning out to be national blockbusters.

His first venture into this new genre was the 1998 *Money No Enough* (a.k.a. *Qian Bu Gou Yong*). It was a huge success, becoming the top-grossing movie ever in the country. It shot Jack Neo to cinema stardom and gave the Singapore film industry a gigantic boost, reaffirming that the long-awaited

renaissance was in effect. Produced by J. P. Tan from JSP Entertainment, and directed by ex-TV producer Tay Teck Lock, *Money No Enough* was also Jack Neo's very own success. He not only played one of the lead roles, but also wrote the story.

Money No Enough revolves around the life of three characters. Chew (Jack Neo), a middle-class Chinese Singaporean is Chinese-educated (as opposed to the English-educated populace), does not speak fluent English, and does not have high educational qualifications or "diplomas". As a result, he faces professional hardship. Ong, well-played by Mark Lee, is a contractor in debt to loan sharks who keep threatening him. Hui, played by the hilarious Henry Thia, is a waiter in a coffeeshop with only one obsession — impressing girls. In the manner of other local directors' multilayered style, Jack Neo intertwines different personal stories of men caught in everyday troubles.

Neo put together a "band of brothers" made up of three silly buddies (Mark Lee, Henry Thia and himself). It was a recipe he would subsequently use in *Liang Po Po — The Movie* and *That One No Enough*. These were similar to P. Ramlee, S. Shamsuddin and Aziz Sattar's four *Bujang Lapok* (lit. Confirmed Bachelor) movies in which they formed a comic trio; and to the team of P. Ramlee, Haji Mahadi and S. Kadarisman in *Tiga Abdul* (lit. The Three Abduls), one of the last P. Ramlee movies made in Singapore in 1964.

The comic trio became one of Jack Neo's trademarks, a formula he used even when not starring in a particular movie. *I Not Stupid*, which he shot in 2002, revolves around three 12-year-old classmates, Koh Pin, Boon Hock and Terry. *The Best Bet*, which he directed in 2004, takes on the same structure inherited from *Money No Enough* and *That One No Enough* — three men, Mark Lee (Huang), Richard Low (Richard) and Christopher Lee (Shun) face more and more hardship. But, unlike other local movies, people are not solitary souls. They bind together and help each other, forming a group, a band of brothers. And Jack Neo's endings, like in *Money No Enough*, are generally happy and cheerful.

LIANG PO PO — THE MOVIE   After his excellently underplayed character of the bucktoothed Ah Gu in *12 Storeys* and his successfully overplayed middle-class man in *Money No Enough*, Jack Neo worked with Eric Khoo again. He was actor, scriptwriter and coproducer for the 1999 *Liang Po Po — The Movie*, made in association with the then newly formed Raintree Pictures. It was Raintree's first production.

The film was directly adapted from the Liang Po Po character, an 85-year-old granny played by Neo himself in his television show *Comedy Night*. Just like *Money No Enough*, it was directed by an ex-TV producer, Teng Bee Lian. This movie did not reach high artistic standards. It was, nevertheless, very carefully produced and technically adept. It successfully made use again of the comic trio, played by Jack Neo, Mark Lee and Henry

Liang Po Po — The Movie by Teng Bee Lian, 1999: Mark Lee, Jack Neo and Henry Thia (picture on the left) and Patricia Mok (picture on the right).

Thia, albeit in the unexpected context of a gangster movie. It resembled a number of the action comedies that Hong Kong efficiently churned out for a few decades. *Liang Po Po* also allowed Patricia Mok to make her convincing debut on the big screen. She played a very aggressive Ah Lian, a local version of a female gangster.

Liang Po Po poked fun at Singaporean particularities, and insisted on bad English (with switching to Hokkien or Cantonese) at a time when the government was pushing forward its "Speak Good English" campaign. The movie benefited from a massive advertising and promotion campaign. Jack Neo disguised as Liang Po Po could be seen everywhere in Singapore. The film was another box-office hit, even though it did not break *Money No Enough*'s record.

Lucky Number by Gao Lin Pao, 1999.

After trying out a nine-minute short movie called *Replacement Killers* (about a man who hires a contract killer to murder his boss) which won him the Best Director Award at the Singapore International Film Festival, Neo's next step was directing a full-length feature. Playing it safe, he tried to capitalise on the previous success and style of *Money No Enough*. The title of this first Jack Neo-made movie, *That One No Enough* (a.k.a. *Na Ge Bu Gou*), said it all.

As a matter of fact, *Money No Enough* had already set a trend that others would follow. Within a few months, it had been copied by *Lucky Number* (a.k.a. *Bailiu Libai*), and *Where Got Problem*. Both had themes of financial troubles faced by middle and upper-class Singaporeans, very much in the manner of *Money No Enough*. Ironically, they were major failures at the box office. They were released at a time when competition, coming from Jack Neo himself, was fierce. Not only was he everywhere with *Liang Po Po*, but he was also putting together *That One No Enough*.

The cast of *That One No Enough* comprised the usual heroic trio (Neo, Lee and Thia), plus Patricia Mok, and a few television actors and actresses such as Tan Kheng Hua or Hong Huifang. This time, the movie was not only about money, it was also about women. The three good friends have problems of their own. Guo Rong's wife becomes fat after giving birth, and so he cheats on her constantly and spends all his money on karaoke bars. Hao Ren is married to a beautiful, successful wife but she is too busy with her career to think about sex and children, despite his family's demands for grandchildren. He begins to have an affair with his wife's secretary from mainland China. Ah Kua is a 30-something virgin who falls for his boss's daughter.

Although released in theatres, where it did rather well, recouping its costs and more, the movie was more a telemovie than anything else. Jack

Neo would later try to move away from this type of formula with *Homerun*, to finally come back to it, at least occasionally, with *I Do I Do* and *The Best Bet*.

I NOT STUPID Right after *That One No Enough*, Jack Neo decided he had had enough of the "no enough" money-comedies, and came up with a new genre in Singapore — the children movie. Not just a movie for children, but a movie about children.

Hossan Leong (left) and Jack Neo (right) in *I Not Stupid* by Jack Neo, 2002.

I Not Stupid (a.k.a. *Xiaohai Bu Ben*) is a simple story with universal appeal. Three 12-year-old classmates, Koh Pin, Boon Hock and Terry, are not academically successful and are placed in the EM3 stream (for slower learners). Koh Pin is a gifted artist, but his parents want him to focus on mathematics. Boon Hock comes from a poor family and has a hard time balancing school and work at his parents' restaurant. Terry is a spoilt, rich kid who has never been left on his own. Their parents also have problems of their own. Neo, once again, intertwines families and their destinies, portraying Singapore society with all its idiosyncrasies.

I Not Stupid, successfully released for Chinese New Year in early 2002, was produced by Raintree Pictures. It was another major blockbuster which garnered a series of regional releases in Malaysia, Taiwan and Hong Kong. It was only missing festival and international recognition. Some said that such recognition eluded it because it was too locally rooted to be understood and accepted by foreign audiences, even festival audiences generally eager to discover movies from faraway countries. Yet, other movies were just as locally rooted, but made it to the international scene. The truth is that *I Not Stupid*, however well-crafted, still lacked a few cinematic qualities.

HOMERUN Realising this, both director, Jack Neo, and producer, Daniel Yun, agreed to make their next movie artistically more ambitious. They did so in 2003 with *Homerun*, a remake of Iranian Majid Majidi's 1997 *Children of Heaven*, a famous arthouse movie which had garnered much international recognition.

For Singapore's revival cinema, *Homerun* explored new territory by being the first period movie. It went back to the very symbolic year of 1965, when Singapore became an independent nation-state. At that point, the 1960s had been revisited only by Hong Kong's Yon Fan, with his 1995 *Bugis Street*. Glen Goei's *Forever Fever*, shot in 1998, referred to the late 1970s.

Yet, instead of staging the major political and social events that took place in 1965, *Homerun* uses them as the background (on the radio) and focuses instead on the intimate story of a brother and sister from a poor family. The plot is roughly the same as in Majidi's movie: a young boy (Ah Kun) accidentally loses his sister's school shoes. To avoid trouble at school and with their parents, they decide to secretly share his shoes. Seow Fang, the little sister, wears them to school in the morning, then runs back home to pass them to Ah Kun for his afternoon classes, and so on. One day, at a school running competition, Ah Kun wins a brand new pair of shoes.

Patricia Mok in *Homerun* by Jack Neo, 2003.

Homerun has an old-world, rustic charm, with its scenes of *kampongs* (villages), fields and muddy tracks, long vanished from the Singapore landscape. The movie had to be shot in neighbouring Malaysia, where these remnant features from the past could still be found. Locations were carefully selected, giving the whole movie a sense of authenticity worth noting. The atmosphere is suffused with nostalgia. In a sense, it could be seen as a historical and social commentary on how fast the modernisation process has

Megan Zheng in *Homerun* by Jack Neo, 2003.

proceeded since the days of independence, and how much has been left behind. Old memories are something Singaporeans are very sensitive to, especially when they see how the lifestyle and the landscape have dramatically changed.

With *Homerun*, Neo and Yun delivered a very well-crafted movie. It may have lacked some of the sensitivity and subtlety of Majid Majidi's original feature, but it was still far more refined than Jack Neo's previous attempts (except for *I Not Stupid*, which already had good standards in terms of content) and, alas, most of his next movies.

The cast proved themselves with excellent acting, particularly from Shawn Lee (Ah Kun) and Megan Zheng (Seow Fang). Zheng won the Best

New Performer Award at the 40th Golden Horse Film Festival (the Chinese equivalent of the Oscars). It happened to be the first ever Golden Horse Award garnered by Singapore, bringing great attention to both her and Jack Neo. *Homerun* was also nominated for Best Music. It went on to win the Best Director prize at the International Children Film Festival in Iran. Such international festival recognition came as a consecration for Singapore's reborn cinema industry.

The only part where director and producer ventured into unsteady ground and aimed a little too high was in inundating *Homerun* with heavy symbolism. It had unsubtle jokes about Singapore's current affairs and relationship with Malaysia. That made the film lose a bit of focus (no pun

Christopher Lee, Richard Low and Mark Lee in *The Best Bet* by Jack Neo, 2004.

intended), sacrificing the original freshness and innocence of Majidi's opus. The above-average child performances, not only by Shawn Lee and Megan Zheng, but by all the children in the movie, were *Homerun's* saving graces. This artistically ambitious Raintree production was another box-office hit, even though its local takings were inferior to *Money No Enough*, *I Not Stupid* and *Liang Po Po*. But it certainly did better than *That One No Enough* and the movies that were to follow. It also managed to be sold internationally.

With that movie, both director and producer moved away from their trademark satirical comedies, and set higher standards. Yet, instead of capitalising on *Homerun's* commercial and international success, Jack Neo and Raintree Pictures went back to low-value productions that they would churn out (in roughly three months) for a Chinese New Year release (just like in the old days when popular Malay movies were released for Hari Raya).

JACK NEO BACK TO SQUARE ONE In 2004, *The Best Bet* (a.k.a. *Tu Ran Fa Cai*) saw the return of the typical Jack Neo social comedy, focusing on middle-class issues, and particularly money. It also featured once again a comic trio. This time neither Jack Neo nor Henry Thia played in it, only the ever-so-popular Mark Lee. Richard (played by Richard Low), a white-collar executive, aims to be a good father and a good husband. However, indecisive and wimpy, he is easily influenced by the people around him. Shun (played by Christopher Lee) works with Richard in the same company. Unlike Richard, Shun is ambitious, outspoken and full of ideas. However, down on his luck, Shun seldom succeeds at what he does. Huang owns a *bak kut teh* (pork bones soup) stall. An avid gambler, Huang (played by Mark Lee, as good as ever, even though typecast) not only places heavy bets on 4D (the local lottery), he also is a part-time debt collector for the "4D King". It is his sister, Hui Min (nicely acted by Joanne Peh), who sees to the

running of the *bak kut teh* business. Their friendship is put to the test when one of them strikes 4D and decides to keep the winnings to himself.

The Best Bet added nothing to what had been better said and filmed in *Money No Enough* and *That One No Enough*. Even the local audience — perhaps because it had grown tired of this formula and could see the lack of innovation — was less responsive. In the end, *The Best Bet* did not really meet the expected success.

In early 2005, Raintree Pictures released a new Jack Neo movie. Learning a lesson from *The Best Bet*, Daniel Yun (of Raintree) and Neo made it a popular romantic comedy. The timing of *I Do I Do*'s release fell nicely within both the Chinese New Year and Valentine's Day period.

Peng (convincingly played by Adrian Pang), a truck driver, falls deeply in love with Hui (Sharon Au), a senior executive at a food company. Hui is a career-minded woman who is of marrying age but feels there is no suitable man meeting her requirements. Peng confesses his love for Hui but is rejected. Meanwhile, Hui suddenly falls for her colleague, Feng.

Although highly enjoyable as a witty take on the way love is perceived in modern Singapore, this good-hearted film did not even do better than local telemovies. With no visible production value and clearly no cinematic ambition, *I Do I Do* once more lowered the standards of local filmmaking and incidentally met with very moderate success.

In early 2006, once again in time for Chinese New Year, Yun and Neo released *I Not Stupid Too*, which tackled almost exactly the same issues as its 2002 predecessor, spicing it up with elements directly borrowed from local indie movies. It met with popular success, putting Neo back on track. Jack Neo's career seemed to be following an unexpected cycle, bringing him back to where he had started — giving the audience a bit of tears and a lot of laughs.

HISTORICAL STUDIOS ON THE SIDELINES The historical studios, Shaw and Cathay, took very little part in the revival of local film production. Shaw remained an exhibitor. As for Cathay, the temptation was always there to play a role. But it did not venture again into filmmaking, apart from two projects, *Army Daze* in 1996, and *That One No Enough* in 1999.

The signs of a revival in local filmmaking prompted Cathay to consider a comeback into production. In 1996, Choo Meileen, daughter of Choo Kok Leong and niece of Loke Wan Tho, the then head of Cathay Organisation, decided, under the name Cathay Asia Films, to go for *Army Daze*, Ong Keng Sen's very first — and so far, last— feature.

Army Daze was adapted from the eponymous play, which had been successfully staged the year before by the same director. Cathay tried to capitalise on an existing success, giving a new filmmaker his first chance. Produced as early as 1995, it was only the second truly Singaporean movie of the revival era. And it anticipated the comedy craze that would follow once Jack Neo entered the film industry

The story, about a group of young Singaporean men from different backgrounds and origins having to do their National Service, was simple and accessible to all. The movie was overacted and lacked cinematic qualities, thus proving that Ong Keng Sen was more a theatre director than a film director.

Army Daze was, nevertheless, the first local box-office hit of the 1990s. Its theme appealed to the local male audience, and it featured the unashamed use of Singlish, the local slang, at a time when this was officially discouraged by the government.

Cathay Asia Films' next venture was with Jack Neo himself, for his directorial debut in 1999. *That One No Enough* revealed more production value than *Army Daze*, and a more refined direction of actors. Even its sense of humour was subtler. It did just as well as *Army Daze* at the box office, but far less than was expected of Jack Neo. After all, he was supposed to be the most bankable talent of the time after the huge takings of *Money No Enough* and *Liang Po Po*.

Sheikh Haikel with Choo Meileen at the time of *Army Daze* in 1996.

Cathay has not ventured into any other local production since. Like Shaw, it has been focusing on its far more profitable exhibition business. However, it does still keep an eye on regional opportunities for coproduction in hopes of reaching out to a larger market.

RAINTREE, THE MINI STUDIO
While Shaw hardly played any role in the renaissance of local film production, and Cathay cautiously ventured into only two projects, a new player came into the picture. The Television Corporation of Singapore, known as TCS, renamed Media Corporation of Singapore (MediaCorp) decided to take part in the resurgence of the cinema business in order to leverage on its pool of local TV talent.

In 1998, the production branch of MediaCorp was set up, aiming first to make mainstream commercial movies. Headed by Daniel Yun, MediaCorp Raintree Pictures (a.k.a. Raintree Pictures, commonly referred to as Raintree) explored many different avenues, trying out new strategies to position itself in both the local and regional markets. However, unlike the major studios of the past, Raintree Pictures was not backed by its own theatre chain (usually the source of a studio's strength). It thus resembled more what is sometimes called a mini studio.

Daniel Yun's first approach was to make locally rooted commercial films, with the aim of turning them into high-earners in the local market. Raintree Pictures teamed up with existing talents in the burgeoning film industry. It coproduced, in its first year of business, *Liang Po Po*. Jack Neo wrote the script and took on the lead role. Raintree produced one more comedy in 2001, *One Leg Kicking*. Jack Neo was not involved in the project, and this was perhaps the reason it did not meet with the same success as *Liang Po Po*. Having learnt its lesson from *One Leg*

Daniel Yun of MediaCorp Raintree Pictures.

Kicking, when it came to putting together a mainstream local comedy in the following years, Raintree Pictures would always team up with Jack Neo.

With Neo as director and actor, there emerged the successive — but not always successful — movies: *I Not Stupid* in 2002, *Homerun* in 2003, *The Best Bet* in 2004, *I Do I Do* in 2005 and *I Not Stupid Too* in 2006. One Jack Neo movie a year became Raintree Pictures' core strategy. It aimed to secure at least one commercial success a year in the local market (mainly targeting the Chinese audience, the largest segment of Singapore's population).

The second approach by Raintree Pictures was to produce local movies with a slight arthouse feel, while retaining a few mainstream elements (such as the cast). Its first experiment was a coproduction with an independent company called Oak3, which had already made one film on its own in 1997 called *The Road Less Travelled* (a.k.a. *Gui Dao*).

Together, they produced in 2000 *Chicken Rice War* (a.k.a. *Jiyuan Qiaohe*), directed by Cheek (a.k.a. Cheah Chee Kong). Born in 1966, Cheek had started with two short films, *Married* in 1994, and *Beansprouts and Salted Fish* in 1996. Both won him a number of awards at the Singapore International Film Festival.

Shot in English and Cantonese, *Chicken Rice War* loosely adapts the story of Romeo and Juliet to modern-day Singapore, and thus very indirectly the *majnun* lover genre of the 1930s to the 1960s.

In *Chicken Rice War*, two young lovers are entangled in an interfamily feud which had been sparked off by chicken rice. Both families, the Wongs and the Changs, have been in the chicken rice business for the last two decades, which is how far the rivalry spans. In the midst of the bitter feud, close friends and chicken rice, love begins to blossom.

Lum May Yee and Pierre Png in *Chicken Rice War* by Cheek, 2000.

Rather well-acted by Pierre Png and Lum May Yee, *Chicken Rice War* also displayed interesting cinematic qualities. Cheek resorted to a wide range of filming and editing techniques, with multiple shots, slow motion, and so on; so varied that they sometimes gave the movie a clipped feel. This was perhaps due to the fact that Cheek was also working for MTV Asia. Unfortunately, the movie, which overstretched both local references and high-class literary inspirations, looked a bit forced and artificial. It was neither a commercial nor a critical success. Cheek did not direct another feature but went back to doing another short movie, titled *576*, a few years later, which was hardly noticed.

In 2001, Raintree Pictures produced, with the support of MediaCorp's Chinese Drama Division, a totally in-house movie, *The Tree* (a.k.a. *Haizi Shu*). It was directed by Daisy Chan, and cast Hong Kong talent Francis Ng together with MediaCorp actresses, Zoe Tay and Phyllis Quek.

The psychological drama revolves around a young boy whose mother is arrested for the murder of his father (her husband). The pathologist, played by Francis Ng, befriends the young boy, who is the sole witness in the murder case. *The Tree* was Daisy Chan's only attempt at directing a real movie, but unfortunately, it did not draw the crowds. They preferred to watch the same sort of telemovie on local television. It did not recoup its costs, and proved that local TV stars, however popular, like Zoe Tay, could not be turned into movie stars overnight. It also proved that bringing in a talented actor from Hong Kong was not enough to help the project.

In 2005, Raintree Pictures teamed up with local independent company, Boku Films, to produce a Singapore horror movie called *The Maid*. It was filmed by Kelvin Tong, who had previously codirected *Eating Air* in 1999. *The Maid* was inspired by the Japanese and Korean horror films which had met with great success in the late 1990s and early 2000s. It was only Singapore's second serious attempt at exploring the horror genre, after Djinn's *Return to Pontianak* in 2001. It gave Singapore cinema a new style and flavour, as well as developed a new type of regional product, involving — through its cast and crew — Hong Kong, the Philippines and Singapore (a combination reminiscent of the good old days of *Cleopatra Wong*…).

RAINTREE'S REGIONAL STRATEGY Raintree Pictures' third approach was to venture into regional artistic coproductions with strategic and high value-added partners, mostly from Hong Kong. The first such venture was the 1999 *The Truth about Jane and Sam* (a.k.a. *Zhen Xin Hua*, a.k.a. *Zun Sum Wah*) with Hong Kong company Film Unlimited. It was directed by Derek Yee, and starred Singapore actress Fann Wong along with Hong Kong's Peter Ho. This arthouse movie tried too hard to beat Wong Kar-wai at his own game, something not easily achieved, and was a failure. It prompted Raintree Pictures to look for less ambitious projects to coproduce. Its next artistic coproduction, less arty, but more action-based, was *2000 AD* (a.k.a. Gongyuan 2000 Nian), directed by Gordon Chan from Hong Kong.

Both *2000 AD* and *The Truth about Jane and Sam* tried to have a Singaporean component in the cast as well as in the locations. It was an ambitious way of approaching coproduction, providing not just financing, but also getting involved in the artistic dimension. Unfortunately, it was also a very difficult approach, with many experiencing failure, Raintree Pictures included. Insisting on having part of *2000 AD* shot in Singapore was well-intentioned, but ended up making the movie appear forced. Both movies were not particularly successful.

Learning from its mistakes, Raintree Pictures ventured into a fourth approach, focusing on financial coproductions, and not forcing any Singaporean element into it. Such an approach enabled Raintree Pictures to tap into the greater Asian film market, thus earning a name for itself in the vast Asian filmmaking network. It was also a way to get the business going without waiting for good projects to come out of Singapore.

Daniel Yun, for Raintree Pictures, invested in *The Eye I* (which starred MediaCorp actors Pierre Png and Edmund Chen) and *The Eye II* by the Pang brothers in 2002, *Turn Left Turn Right* by Johnny To and *Infernal Affairs II* in 2003, among others. The choices were excellent and the strategy proved to be commercially more viable. Raintree Pictures was able to recoup its investment in those high-profile movies. None of these movies, however, contributed to having a Singapore identity on screen.

While Raintree Pictures continued to capitalise on the successful Jack Neo trademark formula to gross money, it moved on to a fifth strategy. In 2005, it brought in Western directors to shoot in Singapore. *One Last Dance*, shot mostly in Cantonese, was directed by Brazil-born filmmaker Max Makowski, who had previously made *The Pigeon Egg Strategy* in 1998 (in

Hong Kong), and *Taboo* in 2002 (in the US). Both were loaded with sex and violence, and garnered mixed reviews.

One Last Dance was Max Makowski's third feature, a film noir very much in the manner of Johnny To, but more mannerist and postmodern, like how Quentin Tarantino revisits Jean-Pierre Melville's *Samurai*. It starred Francis Ng (for the third time in a Raintree Pictures production) along with Taiwanese actress Vivian Hsu, and Harvey Keitel himself in a cameo role. As for local Singapore talent, it gave the excellent Sunny Pang another chance to act after his very good performance in Djinn's *Perth* shot in 2003.

INDEPENDENT DIRECTORS OF THE LATE 1990s

The late 1990s saw the burgeoning of new local talent, particularly self-produced independent filmmakers. The film industry in Singapore was taking a very different turn from what it was in the golden age of the studios. Many of these young directors remained one-timers, unable to make a second feature, at least for the longest time. Four of these movies, of varying standards, were made successively in 1997, 1998 and 1999, contributing to the slow maturing of the newly revived local film industry.

The first of these filmmakers was Lim Suat Yen who came as early as 1996, when she started her own production house, Oak3, with fellow partners Jason Lai and Zaihirat Banu. After her short movie, *Sense of Home* (1996), won her the Best Short Film award at the Singapore International Film Festival, Lim went on to produce and direct her first full-length film, *The Road Less Travelled* (a.k.a. *Gui Dao*), in 1997. Lim, born in 1976, was then in her early twenties, and leading the way for a whole generation of eager young filmmakers.

Shot entirely in Mandarin, it confirmed Singapore's trend of having a partly Chinese-oriented film industry. *The Road Less Travelled* starred a bunch of talented, young actors like Robin Goh, Lilian Chua and Jackie Lui.

The story is about a group of four friends struggling to realise their aspirations in the music scene. In its own way, it paved the way for the teenage-cum-young-adult films that were to follow from 1998 onwards in Singapore. Although it was not commercially successful, *The Road Less Travelled* is a sincere first movie, totally dedicated to Singapore, strongly believing in local talent, and in the city itself as a location worth shooting. It also remains Lim Suat Yen's only feature film so far.

The true story of Adrian Lim, the so-called medium who was hanged in 1988 for the ritual murders of two children, made a deep impression on people's minds. It had already been adapted in 1991, rather unsuccessfully, and was again made into a movie in 1997. This time, the director was not British, but a Singaporean who had achieved some measure of success in Hong Kong.

The Eye II by the Pang brothers, 2002.

The Teenage Textbook Movie by Phillip Lim, 1998.

Hugo Ng (a.k.a. Ng Doi Yung) had made his debut as an actor for the Singapore Broadcasting Corporation, before moving to Hong Kong where he became a director and successfully made *Fatal Encounter* and *Island of No Return* in 1994, as well as *Husband and Wife* in 1996.

In 1997, he returned home to direct his first Singapore feature, *God or Dog* (a.k.a. *Dabayao Shatongan*). Shot in a mixture of Mandarin, Cantonese, Hokkien, English and Singlish, it gave a fair representation of the city-state's linguistic reality. It also explored the life of the average man living in public housing, portraying a somewhat bleak picture. Ng cast himself in the — some say cursed — lead role of Adrian Lim, after other actors turned it down. He gave a far more convincing performance than Dore Kraus did in the 1991 *Medium Rare*. Tammy Chan, an 18-year-old student playing one of the criminal's mistresses, successfully brought out the psychological fragility of her character. A rather costly production, *God or Dog* was a commercial failure and largely ignored by film critics. However, it deserves to be reassessed. As for Hugo Ng, it was his only attempt at making a film in Singapore.

The following year, 1998, another independent movie was completed by stage actor-turned-director Glen Goei. *Forever Fever* was produced by his own company, Tiger Tiger Productions, together with Jeffrey Chiang's Chinarunn Pictures. Having made a large part of his stage career in Great Britain, Goei returned to Singapore in 1994. He was inspired by John Badham's *Saturday Night Fever*, which was shot 21 years before, in 1977, and released in Singapore one year later, in 1978. *Forever Fever* is precisely set then. It tells the story of an idle young man, who dreams of buying a nice motorcycle. He is suddenly hit by the disco craze, and takes part in a dance competition.

Forever Fever is both a remake and a parody of *Saturday Night Fever*, Singapore style. It starred Adrian Pang, who proved to be excellent, along with Annabelle Francis and Pierre Png. It was far from breaking even in the local market, but fortunately it was bought by Miramax, who also signed Glen Goei to a three-picture deal. However, the US release of *Forever Fever* went sour and the production deal void. Glen Goei did not get a chance to direct after that, for a long time. Together with *Bugis Street*, released a few years before, and *Homerun*, a few years later, *Forever Fever* was one of the rare features of the revival era to revisit the past, returning to where the first age of local cinema had ended — the late 1970s.

That same year, in 1998, a teenage film was produced, riding on a current trend in Singapore. It was adapted from the locally famous *Teenage*

Adrian Pang in the lead role in *Forever Fever* by Glen Goei, 1998.

Alvina Toh in *Eating Air* by Kelvin Tong and Jasmine Ng, 1999.

Textbook, and its sequel, *The Teenage Workbook*, both written in the late 1980s by Adrian Tan. The books had captured the attention of thousands of adolescents, and the film was named *The Teenage Textbook Movie*, to capitalise on that success.

This all-local production was directed by first-time filmmaker Phillip Lim, a former MTV Asia producer. It starred a number of up-and-coming actors like Caleb Goh, who did rather well, and who

also acted in *Forever Fever* that same year. Melody Chen delivered an interestingly emotional performance, but had a shortlived career in film, acting only in *Street Angels* the following year. She went on to focus on telemovies and shows. Lim's background in MTV made the movie too much like a hip and glib video, and did not set the standards high enough to make it either a commercial or a critical success. It remained Lim's only and rather forgettable contribution to Singapore film history.

Eating Air by Kelvin Tong and Jasmine Ng, 1999.

EATING AIR The fourth independent movie was the arthouse *Eating Air* (a.k.a. *Chi Feng*) codirected by Kelvin Tong Wen Kia and Jasmine Ng Kin Kia. They first joined forces in 1996, working on a short movie titled *Moveable Feast* with Sandi Tan. *Eating Air* was produced by Multi-Story Complex, a company set up for that purpose.

Once again, the movie partly belonged to the growing teenage movie genre. It had a mixture of motorcycles racing in fluorescent tunnels, gaming culture, kung fu nostalgia, urban decay and postmodern melancholy. But positioning itself as a trendy, arty movie moved it away from *The Road Less Travelled*, *The Teenage Textbook Movie* and *Street Angels* which were shot around the same time.

The movie's impressive cinematic qualities, with excellent photography and editing, made *Eating Air* even more noteworthy. It had a cast of unfamiliar, largely amateur actors, whose natural, spontaneous delivery gave the movie a refreshing and authentic feel. The few professional actors included in the cast seemed almost totally out of place. Mark Lee's caricature of an old gangster was very much overplayed. The successful non-professional cast inspired many young filmmakers making their first short movies in the next few years. Kelvin Tong and Jasmine Ng deftly revealed one aspect of many of Singapore's contemporary melancholia, so deeply felt by their generation.

Eating Air was, sadly, not a commercial success, even though it received rather good international reviews. This was not enough to help the codirectors carry on with their careers, though they both remained involved in the movie industry. Jasmine Ng never directed again, but edited other people's works. Kelvin Tong took six to seven years to direct a film again, a rather long lapse during which he wrote cinema reviews, and ventured into television.

In 2001, he was invited by Singapore television station SPH MediaWorks to direct two 48-minute telemovies. *Aspiration* and *Fantasy* were shot in 1:85 letterbox format — a first for Singapore television. But Tong was seeking a comeback to cinema. His 2005 horror feature, *The Maid*, moved away from independent filmmaking. His own company, Boku Films, went into coproduction with Raintree Pictures — leaving *Eating Air*'s experience a distant memory.

OFFICIAL RECOGNITION FOR FILM For a very long time, film in Singapore did not receive any support from the local authorities. The only action taken by the government and its agencies was to regulate the industry, through laws and censorship. The halt of film production in the late 1970s did not prompt the government to revive the dying industry. When the question was raised in the early 1980s, no action was taken. In neighbouring Malaysia, however, a local film commission, known as FINAS, was established in 1981 to aid the revival of its film industry.

With only 15 to 20 years of independence, Singapore's government felt the country still had more urgent challenges to face, including fierce competition with other Asian economic dragons. If any national identity and pride were to be forged, it was through economic success rather than artistic expression.

It also seemed pointless to revive the old Malay movie industry after breaking away from the neighbouring Malay world. As for Chinese filmmaking, Singapore was not ready to start almost from scratch and compete with the then booming Hong Kong industry. Film production was reduced to a non-profitable niche market, not worth exploring or taking a risk in. Pragmatically, the government decided to leave cinema aside and focus its efforts on

Harvey Keitel (centre) in a cameo role in *One Last Dance* by Max Makowski, 2005.

television. Introduced in 1963, television had become widespread in the 1970s, with homes switching to colour between 1974 and 1976.

The early 1980s to the mid-1990s saw high growth in the audiovisual industry. However, for cinema, independent producers and filmmakers were turned off by the strict censorship which made it difficult to make movies with creative flair.

Tony Yeow did not recover from the misfortune of his banned *Ring of Fury* in 1973. Sunny Lim, who was involved in the production and creative process of B-grade films like *Bionic Boy* and *They Call Her... Cleopatra Wong*, found it easier in Malaysia, where he faced less obstacles. *Saint Jack*, completed in 1979, remained an example of the difficulty faced by local and international producers and directors when making a movie in Singapore.

The 1980s was less conducive in Singapore history for filmmaking. Although a number of local video clubs and government-authorised associations managed to make a few amateur short movies, this was a lost decade. The filmmaking industry was dead. And everybody contributed to its demise — the studios who gave up on it, with no intention of resuming, and the government, who was not ready to take the lead.

Interest from the local authorities grew in the late 1980s and early 1990s, but only from a strictly industrial and economic point of view. The leading agency was the Economic Development Board, which set up a committee in 1987 to promote the movie industry. Its main goal was to attract foreign investment. The creation of a special fund for film was announced in 1990, but was never really implemented. The focus was also on turning Singapore into a regional and international platform for filmmaking, with state-of-the-art world-class infrastructure.

The Tang Dynasty Village was built by Hong Kong businessman Deacon Chiu. Fully completed in 1992, it was hardly ever used. Another grandiose project was initiated by Italian businessman Vittorio Cecchi Gori, who had successfully produced Bernardo Bertolucci's *The Last Emperor* in 1987, and Gabriele Salvatores' *Mediterraneo* in 1991. His plan was to invest heavily in a gigantic production complex which could churn out 10 feature films a year. It never happened.

While the authorities were obsessed with luring unrealistic projects doomed to fail, the renaissance of local cinema was budding without the support of any public money. This was because film was not included in the newly created National Arts Council, and a film commission not established yet.

The only support came from the Singapore International Film Festival. It started filling the gap by setting up, in 1991, its Silver Screen Awards for Short Films, which would help many filmmakers like Cheek and Lim Suat Yen, among others. For six years, the Awards were the only form of support given to local directors, along with the training organised by the Substation, a local arts centre.

Official recognition of cinema, and its support by the government, came in 1997 when the National Arts Council opened its cultural grants to film. This was 50 years after the opening of Shaw's Malay Film Productions, 30 years after the closure of Shaw's studio in Singapore, 25 years after the exit of the Cathay-Keris studio, and 10 years after the launch of the Singapore International Film Festival. The National Arts Council, however, was not fully dedicated to film alone, and may therefore not have been the most appropriate agency to take care of it.

SINGAPORE FILM COMMISSION

In 1998, a major step forward was made with the setting up of the Singapore Film Commission, initially under the umbrella of the National Arts Council. In 2003, the Film Commission merged with the Singapore Broadcasting Authority and the Films and Publications Department to form the Media Development Authority. Its focus was on establishing Singapore as a media hub, internationalising its media companies, developing digital media, and, most importantly, producing and exporting Singapore content. With this boost, the Singapore Film Commission managed, over just a few years, to put together a very consistent and coherent system of support for the film industry. It introduced a wide range of activities deemed necessary for the growth of the local movie industry.

The Film Commission's main focus was on funding short and feature film projects through various schemes. In order to nurture up-and-coming talent, attention was placed on short film. Without an active studio system grooming its own artists, this appeared to be the natural path for young filmmakers. In its first year of activity, the Film Commission supported 11 short film projects through its Short Film Grant. This increased steadily to 23 in 1999, 34 in 2000, and then around 40 short films a year, making a total of more than 200 short films supported between 1998 and 2005 — a rather substantial amount.

The Singapore Film Commission also had a Feature Film Investment Programme (FFIP) in order to raise the professional standards of the local film industry. This was in the form of substantial investment in production, to be repaid with revenue from the movie after its commercial release. Films like *Chicken Rice War*, *One Leg Kicking*, *City Sharks*, *15* and *Perth* benefited from it.

To help Singapore producers venture into coproduction with Asia and the rest of the world, the Singapore Film Commission announced in 2002 the launch of its Coproduction Investment Programme (CPIP). The programme provided funding in the form of investment that would match local funds raised for a coproduction feature film. The core objective was to increase the exportability of Singapore film through collaborations with foreign producers and investors. The idea was to reach out to markets beyond Singapore, thus gaining international exposure and expertise.

Through both its Feature Film Investment as well as its Coproduction Investment Programmes, the Film Commission, in the mid 2000s, supported an average of three to four feature films a year. It also developed long-term partnerships with core local production companies. MediaCorp Raintree Pictures signed a five-year and ten-movie memorandum of understanding with the Media Development Authority in 2003 to jointly invest in movies such as *One Last Dance* and *The Maid*.

The Singapore Film Commission introduced, in December 2003, two more schemes. The aim of the Film Incubator Programme was to help aspiring directors make their first film, by providing guidance and funding from preproduction, through to production and postproduction. Benefiting from this were three digital feature films: *Unarmed Combat*, *The High Cost of Living* and *S11*. The Script Development Grant, launched simultaneously, provided filmmakers and scriptwriters with financial support for developing a good story. In less than two years, almost a hundred applications were received by the Film Commission for its new Script Development Grant, out of which 25 projects were selected. The Singapore Film Commission had, in less than five to six years of existence, covered almost all areas of filmmaking.

In July 2005, in response to the changing needs of the industry, the Singapore Film Commission revamped the existing feature film investment programmes, merging the FFIP and CPIP to create the SFC Co-Investment Scheme (SCS). Under the new scheme, the investment quantum was raised to a maximum of S$1 million. At the same time, in addition to the SCS, the Film Commission also launched the Project Development Scheme (PDS). This scheme was aimed at encouraging filmmakers to devote more time to the proper development of a film, including raising full financing for the project.

In addition to production and development funding, the Film Commission takes care of many other aspects. It provides overseas travel grants for film-

Fann Wong in *The Truth about Jane and Sam* by Derek Yee, 1999.

related activities, such as attending international festivals for film screenings. About 50 grants are given every year. Creating greater awareness and appreciation of the art form of film is also part of its mission. It encourages general film culture in Singapore through support given to conferences, seminars, workshops or festivals.

The year 2005 witnessed Jack Neo's fifth movie, confirming his prolific talent. That same year, the promising young filmmaker, Djinn, won numerous awards at the Lyon Asian Festival in France. It was also the year Kelvin Tong returned to directing, and the Singapore Film Commission had a major upgrading of its programmes. The stage was set for the future.

THE HONG KONG CONNECTION II

Foreign directors were a major feature of the Singapore's golden age of film. Many of those directors were Indians and Filipinos. Hardly any were mainland Chinese, except for a few early Shaw productions in the late 1930s. And almost none came from Hong Kong, but for a few almost-forgotten Cathay, Kong Ngee and Chongay movies in the 1950s, 1960s and mid-1970s.

The 1990s and 2000s did not bring back any Indian and Filipino directors. Instead, Hong Kong filmmakers were prominent. This was due to three factors. First, the Singapore film industry was slowly but surely becoming Chinese-driven, as well as Chinese-targeted. Second, Singapore looked up to Hong Kong producers, directors and actors for their international appeal.

Phyllis Quek in *2000 AD* by Gordon Chan, 2000.

Third, Hong Kong's film industry was slowing down after its handover from Great Britain to China, and Hong Kong filmmakers, seeing fewer opportunities in their homeland, started searching for new partners and markets. Singapore producers were ready to pour in money and host them on local soil.

However, unlike in the old days of the Studio Era, none of them remained in Singapore for more than one movie. They just passed through. This flow of talent from Hong Kong to Singapore never had a lasting impact on the local film industry, and its regional and international outreach. It also slowed down slightly after the early 2000s when the handover to China did not shatter Hong Kong's film industry, and it started to recover.

The first of these Singapore-produced and Hong Kong-directed movies was as early as 1995. *Bugis Street* was produced by Jaytex Productions (headed by the Yew family), and directed by Yon Fan (a.k.a. Yueng Fan, who also cowrote the script with Yuo Chan). It was shot in English, Mandarin and Cantonese, making it a regional product with potentially some international appeal. To better position the movie in the international scene, the lead role was given to Vietnamese-American actress Hiep Thi Le who had made her debut two years before in the 1993 Oliver Stone movie *Heaven and Earth*. *Bugis Street*'s story and setting were enough to make it a commercially interesting product. It capitalised on three key elements: exoticism, nostalgia and eroticism (not to mention sex). *Bugis Street* is the name of a street in Singapore which, in the 1960s, was famous for prostitutes, drag queens, outdoor eateries and shops. It has since been cleaned up by the authorities.

Surprisingly, *Bugis Street* was passed by the country's board of censors even though it definitely walked in the steps of *Saint Jack*. Its casual nudity and focus on lurid details of a seemingly deviant subculture, and its sympathetic treatment of a red-light district, drew a picture that modern Singapore officially preferred to forget.

Set in the mid-1960s, the film revolves around the Sin Sin Hotel at *Bugis Street*, where a group of transsexuals and transvestites solicit for 'clients'. Shot in 1995, Yon Fan's film showed rather high production standards that remained unmatched for many years.

In 1999, Singapore company Act Venture Films produced its first feature, *Street Angels* (a.k.a. *Shao Nu Dang*), and asked Hong Kong filmmaker David Lam to direct it. Since his 1985 debut in Hong Kong, Lam had shot numerous movies, including *Girls Without Tomorrow* (a.k.a. *Xian Dai Ying Zhao Nu Lang*) in 1992, which tells the story of five women coping with prostitution.

In *Street Angels*, he features five young girls, aged between 14 and 17, who find it difficult going through their teenage years and encounter family problems. They end up forming a mini gang of fearless chickadees, giving the director many opportunities to shoot a bunch of sexy young girls. It was almost a soft porn movie, were it not produced in Singapore.

This costly production proved to be a rather poorly directed and acted teenage movie, and failed at the box office. It was David Lam's first and last movie in Singapore. In an attempt to make it regionally marketable, *Street Angels* cast a mishmash of up-and-coming actors. From Hong Kong were Grace Yip and Nicholas Tse, the son of Patrick Tse (who had acted in a number of Kong Ngee productions). From Singapore was Melody Chen, who had played the year before in *The Teenage Textbook Movie*. Unfortunately, she was given no other chance to act after David Lam's movie even though she proved to be a rather talented young actress.

Street Angels' critical and commercial failure did not encourage Singapore producers to venture into this kind of partnership in which a Hong Kong filmmaker would take charge of directing a local movie. Things remained at a standstill for a few years, while producers explored coproduction deals focused on truly Hong Kong movies.

A last attempt was made in 2003, with Hong Kong director Ken Bi, to shoot a movie set in Singapore. It was titled *Hainanese Chicken Rice* (a.k.a. *Hainan Ji Fan*) after one of Singapore's famous dishes. Initially coproduced by both Hong Kong and Singapore, it ended up being a solely Hong Kong-driven project when Singapore's Ground Glass Images pulled out. The film became less and less in tune with the Singapore lifestyle. It was finally released as a Hong Kong production under a different international title, *Rice Rhapsody*. This experience proved how difficult and unfruitful working with Hong Kong directors could be. Singapore might have been following the wrong path.

THE HONG KONG CONNECTION III

Another avenue that Singapore explored in the late 1990s and early 2000s was the pursuit of joint ventures between local and Hong Kong producers. This strategy, favoured by the local authorities, was taken up mostly by Raintree Pictures, which was then trying to find ways to expand its market regionally, if not internationally. It proved to be rather fruitless and unsuccessful.

Such coproductions would generally have a multinational cast, though mainly with actors of Chinese origin (from Singapore, Hong Kong, Taiwan or China). The Hong Kong and Singapore film industries were then both predominantly Chinese, and thus had a common Chinese culture. The shooting locations were partly in Hong Kong and partly in Singapore. The directors would invariably be from Hong Kong — such as Derek Yee for *The Truth about Jane and Sam*, Raymond Wong for *The Mirror*, Gao Lin Pao for *Lucky Number* and Gordon Chan for *2000 AD*.

Hong Kong's versatile actor-cum-director-cum-producer, Raymond Wong Pak Ming, started out as cofounder of Cinema City studio with Mak Kar and Dean Shek Tien in 1980. When this Hong Kong studio closed down in 1991, Raymond Wong incorporated a new company, Mandarin Films. It started operations in Singapore as early as 1993 because of the lucrative tax break which the Singapore government offered to film joint ventures, and because of the uncertainty created by Hong Kong's impending handover to China in 1997.

Having invested in Singapore for the purpose of making films, Mandarin Films produced the 1999 box-office-hit wannabe, *The Mirror* (a.k.a. *Guai Tan Zhi Mo Jing*, a.k.a. *Wuye Xionjing*). The movie is a portmanteau of four horror stories variously set in Ming China, 1920s Shanghai, contemporary Singapore, and modern-day Hong Kong. Jack Neo appeared in the third story, as a Singapore lawyer. *The Mirror* was a major box-office and artistic failure, and soon forgotten.

In tune with Singapore's strategy to become a regional platform, Raintree Pictures coproduced *The Truth about Jane and Sam* (a.k.a. *Zhen Xin Hua*, a.k.a. *Zun Sum Wah*) with Hong Kong partner, Film Unlimited. It was directed by the in-vogue Derek Yee who was a success in the 1990s with his 1993 *C'est la vie mon chéri* (a.k.a. *Xin Buliao Qing*), and his 1996 *Viva Erotica* (a.k.a. *Se Qing Nan Niu*).

The Truth about Jane and Sam starred Singapore actress Fann Wong, and Hong Kong's Peter Ho. The story revolves around Sam (Peter Ho), a fresh graduate from Singapore, who works as a journalist in Hong Kong to gain wider exposure to life. There, he chances upon Jane (Fann Wong), a streetwise

Hong Kong girl who captures his interest for a cover story. What starts out as fascination develops into a heartwarming love story. Together, the two young lovers discover hope, happiness and the truth about love.

In working with Derek Yee, who had proven himself to be an excellent talent scout, shooting actresses like Shu Qi and Anita Yuen to stardom, Raintree Pictures certainly hoped to boost Fann Wong's career. But in trying too hard to be what Faye Wong was in Wong Kar-wai's 1994 *Chungking Express*, she appeared to be nothing more than a copycat, unable to match her model.

The Truth about Jane and Sam was itself an attempt to do something à la Wong Kar-wai, to whom it naively paid a very explicit homage. It was shot mainly in Hong Kong, but also in mainland China, and partly in Singapore. The original version was in Cantonese, but it was later dubbed in Mandarin to reach out to various Chinese markets, including Singapore. Even though it was rather well-received locally, almost breaking even in financial terms, it was not the international and critical success that had been hoped for, and that it had been designed for.

Raintree Pictures' next venture into coproduction with Hong Kong, the year after, was *2000 AD* (a.k.a. *Gongyuan 2000 Nian*). It was directed by Gordon Chan (a.k.a. Chan Kar Sheung), known for his cops and robbers stories, and other action movies such as *Beast Cops*. With *2000 AD*, Chan was asked to put together a regional spy actioner, once again shot partly in

Hong Kong and partly in Singapore. It starred mainly Hong Kong actors like pop idol Aaron Kwok, up-and-coming Daniel Wu, and Francis Ng, who all delivered excellent performances. The Singapore cast included James Lye, Phyllis Quek (who proved to have high potential) and Lim Yu Beng.

Although a rather mid-range production according to Hong Kong standards, *2000 AD* stood out for its action scenes which were shot in Singapore. This was an unusual movie for the city-state; it was as if it were trying to be Hong Kong, or trying to beat Hong Kong at its own game.

Most of these coproduced films tended to have sensibilities more in tune with the Hong Kong way of life than to the Singapore one. This was not surprising since they were predominantly based on screenplays written by Hong Kong scriptwriters, with a cast of mainly Hong Kong actors, who were always directed by Hong Kong filmmakers. On the whole, the input of Singapore talent was minimal. Most of them were also joint ventures that proved to be artistic and commercial failures.

SHORT FILMS ERA

Far more interesting and fruitful for Singapore was the mushrooming of numerous locally made short films. This was a new phenomenon since the Studio Era did not produce any short films, and the forgotten decade of the 1980s had only a handful of videos.

Promising talents were Dzulkifli Sungit, Nisar and Nazir Hussain (their 1993 *Ragged* won them the Special Jury Prize at the Singapore International Film Festival) and Christine Lim. Unfortunately, they have not gone on to make any full-length films.

A major wave of young directors followed in the mid-1990s, with the likes of Cheek, Meng Ong, Kelvin Tong, Jasmine Ng and Lim Suat Yen. They all shot their maiden short films before 1996 and moved on to feature films.

New talent blossomed. At the turn of 1997, short movies were made by students graduating from newly-created film departments at various learning institutions in Singapore (film studies had been progressively introduced from 1992 onwards). The Singapore International Film Festival thus saw a major increase in the number of applications for its short film competition. The Festival, having to remain selective, was unable to accommodate them all.

This second wave of short film makers were fortunate in being able to benefit from the support of the Singapore Film Commission that was established one year later, in 1998. With film studies churning out many aspiring artists, short film grants being given away in growing numbers, and a renowned international film festival offering first

Moveable Feast by Sandi Tan, Jasmine Ng and Kelvin Tong, 1996.

Adrian Pang in *Holiday* by Wee Li Lin, 2002.

exposure, the young up-and-coming Singaporean cinema was ready to grow.

This expanding pool, like everywhere else in the world, had quite a few one-timers, those who would disappear in pursuit of other paths. However, there was also emerging talent which would be more long-lasting, and interestingly enough, many of them were women.

Sandi Tan, one of the most promising, started slightly ahead of the others. She was one of the first to attend training courses provided by the Substation in the early 1990s. In 1996, together with Kelvin Tong as scriptwriter, and Jasmine Ng as editor, she directed her first short movie, *Moveable Feast*. This short film, focusing on the different varieties of food in Singapore, was indirectly addressing multiculturalism in the nation-city.

When one knows the importance of food in Singapore life, its use as a metaphor for this multilayered society was intelligent and appropriate.

Moveable Feast won the Best Short Film award at the Singapore International Film Festival, and went on to compete at festivals like Clermont-Ferrand in France. It was screened at the Museum of Modern Art in New York and was acquired by Europe's ARTE channel. It was an achievement and a breakthrough for a local work.

In 1997, Sandi Tan won the top arts grant from the National Arts Council, which included film in its portfolio. This enabled her to attend Columbia University's film school. In 2001, she came back with a new short movie, *Gourmet Baby*, which premiered at the New York Film Festival. Although

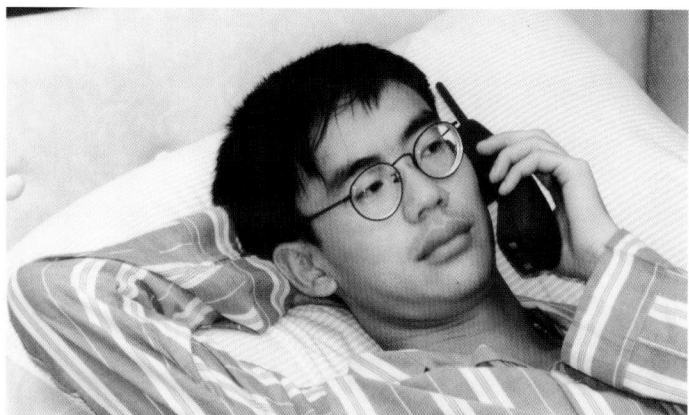

Norman on the Air by Wee Li Lin, 1997.

produced without the support of the Singapore Film Commission, it opened the 2002 Singapore International Film Festival, and put Tan in the limelight.

Gourmet Baby starred veteran actor Lim Kay Tong, and young teen actress Carla Dunareanu, and was a very mature and masterful work. Once again, it went far beyond its obvious reference to food. This tutelage tale is about an older man trying to educate a young girl on the delights of fine dining. He imposes his tastes and views on her, metaphorically portraying political power in Singapore. Sandi Tan was silent and unproductive for many years after, though remaining one of the most promising young talents.

Far more prolific, but less controversial, was another woman director, Wee Li Lin. She had a very different style, less aggressive, less political, and more personal and intimate. Her first short film, *Norman on the Air*, made in 1997, won her an award at the Singapore International Film Festival. It features a frustrated young man calling a radio station to tell everyone about his failed love life during a live broadcast.

It was followed by *Another Guy* in 1999 (in which a young man seems unable to mature and accept life as it is), *Lunch Time* in 2000 (once again a work about frustration, showing a coffeeshop waitress who fantasises about a customer who does not even seem to notice her, but she still goes on daydreaming about him), and *Home Maker* in 2002 (about an idle and rich lady of leisure, a Singaporean bourgeoise, who is dying of boredom).

Wee directed two more very interesting short movies the same year. In *All My Presents*, featuring Denise Tan in the lead role, a young woman invites a few friends over on Christmas Eve. But her evening turns out to be highly frustrating, full of disillusionment, and unhappiness. In *Holiday*, its ironic title hides the story of Boon's retrenchment, and how he deals with it in the few hours that follow. It was excellently underplayed by the talented Adrian Pang, whose most interesting role before that had been *Forever Fever*. Wee Li Lin's movie displayed high sensitivity in the way it examines a social issue through a very individual and personalised case.

In 2003, Wee directed one more short movie, *Autograph Book*, about two 12-year-old girls stuck in a love-hate relationship. It was carefully and skillfully filmed, edited and acted. She then went on to try her first feature.

Rather similar to Wee Li Lin's style, particularly in *Autograph Book*, two other female directors delivered very sensitive and emotional works. Sun Koh filmed *The Secret Heaven* in 2003, which focuses on a mischievous 10-year-old girl who tries as hard as she can to skip the piano classes imposed on her by her mother. As for June Chua, she made *The Usher* in 2004, which revolves around 10-year-old Xiao Ming, who is obsessed with old kung fu movies. He sneaks into cinema halls, getting into trouble with the usher. The usher, in the end, befriends young Xiao Ming and helps him out. The movie celebrates the nostalgia for the old cinema magic. Both June Chua and Sun Koh's movies capture the life of children in a very tender and caring manner, similar to the movies of Wee Li Lin and, on another scale, Jack Neo. They had little in common with Sandi Tan's gritty and merciless *Gourmet Baby*, which had different aims.

Tania Sng, who appeared on the filmmaking scene at around the same time, offered a slightly different approach. She successively directed *No Woman, No Love, No One, No Home* in 1998, *Singapore... Dream* in 1999, *One Track Vision* in 2002, and *Voice of a Stranger* in 2003. These four movies explored the fringes of experimentalism, with a very formal approach either during the shooting or during the editing, each of them driven by an overarching voiceover.

Lunch Time by Wee Li Lin, 2000.

Singapore... Dream immediately stood out for the way it vividly addresses and questions Singapore identity. It blends footage, monologue from the director on the main issue, and patriotic songs learnt in school, so as to give young Singaporeans a sense of belonging to the nation. Sng's experimental short movie aptly puts into perspective the fast pace of nation-building in

G-23 by Anthony Chen, 2004.

explores the life of Indian immigrants who come to Singapore as construction workers, an aspect of Singapore society little attention is paid to.

In *G-23*, debut director Anthony Chen also gives some insight into the Indian community. The story is about a young girl who has difficulty coming to terms with her cultural roots, embodied in her mother and grandmother. In a larger mosaic-like picture of Singapore's multiculturalism, her story intertwines subtly with that of an elderly man who has lost all purpose in life, and a middle-aged lady who is deprived of sex and love.

One of the most outstanding works was Bertrand Lee's 2004 *Birthday*. It was an accomplished 30-minute film displaying all the qualities of a feature. Intimate, yet universal, it tells the story of a young couple having a hard time keeping their relationship going, even during their son's birthday. Masterfully shot, and supported with excellent art direction, it starred two very good young amateur actors who delivered emotionally strong, underplayed performances.

Singapore over the last 30 to 40 years.

In *One Track Vision* and *Voice of a Stranger*, Sng adapted two different texts written by local poet Cyril Wong. They are suffused with melancholia, frustration and ambiguity, thus speaking up for a segment of the new generation of young Singaporeans, those who are misfits in their own society. Based on literary works, and incorporating little-known classical music like Marin Marais (as in *Voice of a Stranger*), Sng's works prefigured the potential birth of intellectualised filmmaking, something not easily grown in Singapore.

Yet, Sng herself slowly moved away from the experimental ground she sowed. First, she made two short movies in the more traditional way, then became producer of a conventional and marketable feature film, *Cages*, shot in Singapore but directed by American Graham Streeter.

Many young apprentice directors of that generation went straight for more conventionally made movies, in which they learnt the art of well-crafted filming and storytelling. A number of them skilfully delivered very moving and unexpected stories about modern-day Singapore. One of them was Han Yew Kwang with his 2001 movie *The Call Home*. In this 29-minute movie shot in Tamil and English, Han

The Usher by June Chua, 2004.

EXPERIMENTAL SHORTS Two filmmakers stand apart for fully exploring experimental moviemaking, far more than Tania Sng with some of her early works. Victric Thng actively made numerous very intimate and personal movies, of very short duration, sometimes of no more than three or four minutes. These were often lyrical vignettes; a kind of cinematic haiku. *Locust*, made in 2003, about the once fond and now bitter memory of a momentary encounter, is generally focused on evanescent thoughts and recollections. In *Bliss*, shot in 2004, a man simply reminisces about his wedding day.

Ho Tzu Nyen's 23-minute *Utama — Every Name in History is I*, made in 2003, borders between film and contemporary art — an uncommon position in Singapore cinema. *Utama* revisits the mythical foundations of Singapore in a series of painting tableaux, and even tableaux vivants. It confronts both Sir Stamford Raffles, the British founding father who came in the 19th century, and his long-time but forgotten predecessor, the Malay prince Sang Nila Utama, who supposedly gave the island-state its name.

Locust by Victric Thng, 2003.

Standing against the amnesiac modernity of today's Singapore, Ho's film resurrects the questions of national identity and history. Yet, in a very irreverent and subversive manner, Ho goes on to reportray Prince Utama in the guise of Christopher Columbus, Vasco da Gama, and Captain Cook. What if Singapore had been discovered by one of these other explorers? With its three-part structure, its postmodern re-enactment of history, its critical and intellectual intertextuality recalling the likes of Friedrich Nietzsche or Michel Foucault, its Fellinian scene, and its original display as part of a visual exhibition, *Utama — Every Name in History is I* was to remain difficult to identify in new Singaporean cinema. It was, for once, something aimed at being a totally non-commercial piece of art.

Singapore, a land founded twice, found and lost, founded again

Sang Nila Utama's discovery of Singapore in *Utama — Every Name in History is I* by Ho Tzu Nyen, 2003.

UNIDENTIFIED FILMIC OBJECTS On the one side, the majority of the new film directors were exploring the most conventional and potentially most profitable avenues, and on the other, a few took on the less travelled road of experimental cinema. Others resolutely adopted a different approach, going for a very unconventional form of cinema, belonging to no specific genre. Their works fell somewhere between the amateurish B-grade social satire and the mockumentary. Though they remain unidentified filmic objects, three films greatly contributed to the unabashed portrayal of Singapore at the turn of the 21st century, albeit in their individual and peculiar ways.

In 2002, Colin Goh directed *Talking Cock — The Movie*. It was a 90-minute line-up of short but satirical sketches of Singapore society with a strong focus on Singlish, the local lingo dear to all Singaporeans but not so dear to the government. Though lacking in any form of production value or cinematic expertise, Goh's movie was a breath of fresh air. It had no shame, no complex, no taboo. It spoke about Singapore the way most Singaporeans speak about it, thus also having great documentary value.

Two years later, Eric Khoo and Chew Tze Chuan produced a very odd movie comprising as much fiction as documentary, transcending the genre of the mockumentary. *Zombie Dogs*, also known as *Eat Shit, Fuck and Die*, was officially directed by Toh Hai Leong (even though Khoo himself was in charge), locally known as a very outspoken and merciless film critic. Toh stars as himself, in the role of a cult filmmaker looking for actors to shoot a worse-than-porn movie (something highly improbable in Singapore).

Sunny Pang in *Perth* by Djinn, 2004.

He rattles off endless, long-winded monologues that are sometimes a bit hard to follow, but nevertheless captivating, about film, life, death, and Singapore. And sex. Toh is just as much the object of the film as he is the subject of it. Through him, a very unexpected and unofficial picture of Singapore is unveiled — though nothing very much unknown to Singaporeans. The title refers to the fact that all human beings in general, particularly in Singapore, turn into zombies, obedient like dogs, left with nothing much else to do than eat shit, fuck and die.

A short film that has much in common with *Zombie Dogs* was made a few months later by Lee Wong. It was titled *Lim Poh Huat*, after the eponymous character that it follows, and focuses on. Lim Poh Huat is a familiar face in the local film industry. A very strange man who does not really fit into society, he does not have a car, a washing machine, a refrigerator, or a girlfriend. He has nothing but one passion: cinema. The passion of his life. To satisfy it, he has for many years dedicated all his spare time to appearing

as an extra on film sets, and can once in a while be seen for a few seconds in a film. The link with *Zombie Dogs* is very direct, since he also appears in it as an over-eager extra who tends to push himself in. As for *Lim Poh Huat*, the movie, it is a documentary about the fringe of society. A documentary that draws on fiction, since fiction is never far with Lim Poh Huat, the man.

DJINN, FROM *PONTIANAK* TO *PERTH*

Out of the many makers of short films who appeared in the late 1990s and early 2000s, a young director, Djinn, moved at a much faster pace than the others. He delivered features that remain landmarks in the field of arthouse filmmaking in Singapore. Coming way after the beginning of the revival era in 1995, they signalled that the movie industry was slowly maturing. It was on the verge of reaching a new stage.

Djinn, also known by his real name, Djinn Ong (or Ong Lay Jinn) started in 1998, when he made a successful debut directing *By Dawn's Early Rise*. It was a rather long 31-minute short film, so well put together that it won him the Best Film Award at the Singapore International Film Festival. It portrays Charles Woodrow Wilson as an old widowed landlord living out his last years in Los Angeles. His growing senility begins to get the better of him as he starts imagining that his new Asian tenant is a terrorist with dangerous biochemical weapons. It is a very unexpected story coming from a Singaporean, yet less surprising when one knows that Djinn has, for a long time, been living in the US.

Three years later, in 2001, Djinn made his first feature film, *Return to Pontianak* (a.k.a. *Voodoo Nightmare* in the US). Independently produced by Vacant Films, it starred Djinn's wife, Hiep Thi Le, the Vietnamese-American actress who had earlier acted in *Bugis Street* (after debuting in Oliver Stone's *Heaven and Earth*).

Return to Pontianak is about a young Asian-American girl leading a group of friends on a two-day trek deep into the Malaysian jungle in search of a village she is inexplicably drawn to. The film aptly explores the horror genre, and revisits the pontianak series of the old Malay days. It is a noteworthy movie, so rare are the tributes paid to the past in Singapore cinema. Shot on DV, with a small crew, *Return to Pontianak* is like a Singapore *Blair Witch Project*. Unfortunately, it failed commercially and was also artistically unsatisfying, even though it had come up with very interesting ideas of *mise-en-scène*.

Far more interesting was Djinn's second feature, *Perth*, completed in 2004. He proved to be one of the few new independent directors able to make, not only a first feature, but also a second. With *Perth*, produced by Ground Glass Images and Working Man Films, Djinn made a gritty movie about the limits of the Singapore dream. The movie was also partly inspired by Martin Scorsese's 1976 *Taxi Driver*. There are worse mentors than Scorsese to look up to, and no one can blame Djinn for attempting it; even if following the path of such a seminal and essential movie may prove to be difficult.

Perth tells the story of Harry Lee, a security supervisor at a shipyard who loses his job due to brutal downsizing. To make a living, he becomes a taxi driver. He is on his own. His wife has left him, and he has not seen his son for

many years. Harry Lee has just one dream, to make enough money to retire to Perth, Australia, where life is said to be so good.

Once again, as with many movies made in the late 1990s and early 2000s, *Perth* was about escapism. Through its play on the Harry Lee name (which just happens to be the English name of Lee Kuan Yew, Singapore's former Prime Minister, then Senior Minister), and by giving that name to a loser, the movie conveyed the irony of the Singapore dream, that it was a two-sided medal, one side not as golden and shiny as the other. Tania Sng herself ironically titled her seminal short film *Singapore... Dream*. Almost all the filmmakers of the new generation were speaking about the same thing.

Perth starred, in the lead role of Harry Lee, veteran actor Lim Kay Tong, who delivered a strong performance, even though he overacted his part on occasion. As for Catherine Tan, a local part-time actress also seen in short movies, she excellently played her supporting role as a bar girl. The rest of the cast delivered rather good performances, especially up-and-coming Sunny Pang (as Angry Boy Lee), and Ivy Cheng (as Mai, the prostitute). *Perth* was one of the most promising movies made in the mid-2000s, for its cinematic qualities, good art direction and production value, and it deservedly went on to garner festival awards, including four prizes at the 2005 Lyon Asian Festival in France.

Ivy Cheng in *Perth* by Djinn, 2004.

ROYSTON TAN Coming onto the movie scene slightly after Djinn, Royston Tan was immediately noticed for his remarkable mastery of the art of filming. He won many awards, and ventured, in less than four years, from short film to feature. Starting with *Sons* in 2000, he went on to make *Mother* and *24 Hours* in 2001, as well as *Hock Hiap Leong* and *15* in 2002. The latter was a short film he swiftly expanded into the form of a feature bearing the same title in 2003. He moved almost as fast as Djinn.

A very gifted director, Tan also displayed a refined and acute sensitivity, enabling him to deal with emotionally loaded issues. His five short films, shot in different artistic styles, yet showing coherence and consistency, all approached Singapore society in a very melancholic manner. Tan immediately had much in common with the long-time pioneer of melancholia, Eric Khoo.

Tan's movies, in one way or another, dealt with the loneliness and isolation of people not in tune with Singapore's fast-moving modernisation. *Sons*, for instance, featured the almost impossible relationship between an ageing father and his son. It portrays the growing gap between generations, and shows how all sons are somewhat in the same position.

Hock Hiap Leong is in a more nostalgic vein. A boy is so upset with the closure of an old coffeeshop, he starts dreaming about it. His reverie takes the whole coffeeshop back in time to the swinging 1960s, with a flamboyant musical number performed in platforms, beehives and flares. *Hock Hiap Leong* displays great empathy for the places and faces lost in the shadow of the neverending modernisation of Singapore. This short film bears the strong influence of both Wong Kar-wai (for his camera angles, voiceovers, slow motion and retrostyle) and Tsai Ming-liang (for his sense of humour, and tributes paid to Tsai's *Hole* and Grace Chang's cha cha cha number in *Mambo Girl*).

Yet, it was *15*, shot the same year, in 2002, that fully revealed Royston Tan's own style. Influenced by both MTV and video games, the movie delves into the dark corners of Singapore society. It portrayed three 15-year-old boys, Melvin, Vynn and Shaun, as themselves. These boys are on the verge of dropping out of school, and falling into crime drugs and eventually young death.

More a documentary than anything else, it all started with Royston Tan being invited to give a talk about filmmaking in a secondary school, where he soon got to know one of the students. He spent two months with him, talking about the student's life, and being introduced to his circle of friends. Tan realised there was so much that was misunderstood, hidden and unspoken about these youths. He wanted to give them a voice.

Produced by Eric Khoo's Zhao Wei Films, *15* was such a controversial and critical success that it prompted Royston Tan to consider turning it into a feature film. He could give an even bigger voice to the voiceless whom he had befriended. So, in 2003, again with the help of Eric Khoo, that was what

he did, bringing to the screen an intense and graphic exploration of Singapore's unseen underbelly.

15, the feature, charts the uncharted lives of five teenagers (two more had joined, Erick and Melvin) on the fringe of Singaporean society. They are abandoned by the system, and are thus tempted to abandon it in return. They seek answers to their aimless existence among the misfits and outsiders of the island-state's underclass. Acted by five real street boys under their true names, the different vignettes in the movie were based on what they actually went through. The style of the movie was made to be a metaphor of these teenagers' hectic lives: nothing is fully in sequence, much of it hastily packaged, sometimes glamorous, sometimes untidy. The whole thing screams at the audience, desperately trying to grab attention, just like these street boys.

In exposing the gritty side of modern-day Singapore life that many never knew existed, or did not want to see, *15* was seen as a very provocative movie. It generated discussion both about these unfortunate youths, and about the status and role of film in society. Officially selected for the Venice film festival (a first for Singapore), as well as numerous other international film festivals, it was also released locally, a censored version anyway. Scenes revealing the existence of organised gangs, and male nudity, were cut.

In return, and certainly as revenge, Royston Tan went on to shoot a short film precisely titled *Cut*. It was an acid take on censorship in Singapore, although wrapped in the style of a fun musical. The irony was that *Cut* was

15 by Royston Tan, 2003.

Hock Hiap Leong by Royston Tan, 2002.

passed with no cuts. The movie far from amused everybody. However controversial Royston Tan was locally, his success helped to propel the newest generation of Singapore filmmakers to the international movie scene, proving that there was more to new Singapore cinema than Eric Khoo.

SINGAPORE BRINGS IN WESTERN DIRECTORS

There had always been a number of Western directors interested in shooting movies in Singapore. Bruce Beresford made *Paradise Road* in 1997, Peter Bogdanovich *Saint Jack* in 1979, Bernard Toublanc-Michel filmed *Five Ashore in Singapore* in 1967, and Dudley Birch did *Flight from Singapore* in 1960. But Singapore was used as a location, and nothing else.

The year 2005 saw a major change, with Singaporean producers taking the lead by bringing in Western filmmakers to direct for them in Singapore.

Raintree Pictures produced *One Last Dance*, shot mostly in Cantonese, but directed by Brazil-born Max Makowski. It revisited the film noir genre, in a Singapore setting. Aquafire Productions, a company headed by Tania Sng (also a director), produced a very different feature called *Cages* by American filmmaker Graham Streeter. The two movies told very different stories, but both were located in Singapore, thus contributing to the portrayal of the city through a partly foreign eye.

Cages, in particular, showed a lot of empathy for the Singapore lifestyle, offering an interesting picture of the island. It was different from the rather gloomy tales of despair, loneliness and marginalisation told by other local filmmakers. Avoiding the usual touristy clichés that would please a tourism board, and thus not making the same mistakes as *Medium Rare* almost 15 years before, *Cages* managed to capture many aspects of Singapore generally unseen in recent local movies.

Dickson Tan in *Cages* by Graham Streeter, 2005.

SINGAPORE DOCUMENTED

Singapore filmmaking has seen a new trend in recent years, with the coming-of-age of a new generation of documentary filmmakers. The leading figures, Tan Pin Pin and Martyn See, stand out for their unique, refreshing takes on Singapore's history, society and political life.

The pioneer of this genre, Tan Pin Pin, born in 1969, started off in television, before she decided to explore new avenues. *Lurve Me Now*, an early short film in which she speculates on the fantasies of Barbie dolls, was banned in Singapore due to its sexual overtones.

Her first real documentary, the 2001 *Moving House*, shows the shutting down of a graveyard due to urban redevelopment. It explores the consequences for a family who, like 55,000 other families in Singapore, has to exhume the remains of their relatives and move them to a columbarium. It immediately won her not only local but also international recognition. In a related project, Tan contributed to *Afterlife*, a 6-part documentary series about death and notions of life beyond death in Asia. In her half-hour episode, titled *Gravedigger's Luck*, she documents the work of Ah Kow, who exhumes graves and relocates bodies.

Her next major work, *80km/h*, made in 2004, was based on a simple idea. A journey by car from Changi Airport in eastern Singapore to the Tuas Checkpoint (one of two entry points into Malaysia) located at the western end of Singapore. The car scrupulously keeps to a speed of *80km/h* while the camera shoots out of the side window, thus very mechanically recording the landscape next to the highway. It captures, with almost medical precision, the very indefinable zone between the city and its surroundings, with numerous glimpses of public housing and heavy traffic. Dusk gradually falls, and the car reaches the checkpoint at 7.43 pm, providing a natural closing to both the trip and the movie. With this very simple 38-minute travelling shot, Tan Pin Pin cuts a slice out of Singapore's multilayered society, revealing a cross-section of the entire country. It was conceptualised as a record with close to cartographical value. A cinematic trip which could be retaken year after year so as to capture the changes in the urban landscape.

With *Singapore GaGa* in 2005, she went one step further, cementing her place as the leading documentary filmmaker. The 55-minute *Singapore GaGa*, clearly intent on finding hints of a cultural identity, or cultural identities, other than city's official presentation, searches out people living on the fringes of society. A poor woman in a wheelchair sits in front of an underground train station. She sells handkerchiefs for a dollar each, singing about Jesus to console herself. Inside the underground station, an old man in shorts plays his music to whoever passes by. When asked by the police if he has a busker's licence, he replies that he is registered as a national treasure. At the major radio stations, people read the news in Chinese dialects which have gradually fallen into disuse (in an increasingly Mandarin-speaking Singapore). Veiled Muslim girls at a sports competition yell encouragement in Arabic. *Singapore GaGa* thus draws a fascinating, multifaceted portrait of an unseen Singapore.

Martyn See, born in 1968, spent many years editing other people's films, such as Jack Neo's *That One No Enough* and Tan Pin Pin's *Singapore GaGa*. He ventured into directing his own films in 2005. *Singapore Rebel*, a 26-minute documentary shot on video, scrutinises the life of Singapore's opposition leader Dr Chee Soon Juan. It was banned on the basis that it contravened the Film Act which forbids films on political parties.

Martyn See's next documentary followed just a few months later. Aptly titled *Zahari's 17 Years*, this 49-minute film addresses the 17-year detention without trial of left-

Zahari's 17 Years by Martyn See, 2005.

wing journalist and political activist Said Zahari. He was accused of being a communist in 1963 and arrested. Before his detention, Said Zahari had been a major figure in Singapore's struggle for independence, hence See's interest in documenting his life.

The works of these two filmmakers reveal a need, directly and openly assumed, to document the ongoing history of Singapore, a young nation still in the making. They represent the first breakthroughs by the local industry in the documentary genre, and offer a glimpse of what may yet be a new and significant direction in local filmmaking.

CON CLUSION

LOST IN TRANSMISSION After over 80 years, filmmaking in Singapore has undergone just as many changes as the island-city-state itself, reflecting some of the different aspects of a growing nation. Yet, due to the ethnic structure of the population, and to historical accidents, it is very heterogeneous; and does not have the consistency and coherence that we generally expect from a "national" cinema.

The collapse of film production from the late 1970s to the early 1990s introduced a rupture, which could be seen in the movies themselves, and the people making them. Faces changed, and so did the social issues and cultural references. Movies from the Studio Era were mostly features shot back-to-back, in black-and-white. They were in Malay, starring Malay people, and were strongly rooted both in local Malay mythology and the village lifestyle.

On the other hand, the revived cinema from the 1990s onwards is characterised by its mix of short and feature films, shot predominantly in Chinese, and occasionally in English. These films star Chinese people, plus a few minorities, as well as a bunch of expatriates (since Singapore has opened up so much to foreigners since the 1980s). They are deeply rooted in the urban lifestyle, with a strong focus on life in public housing.

There is no easy answer when we speak about the language of Singapore movies, or the language it should speak. In the past, up to 1972, homegrown films produced by the local studios were mostly in Malay (Chinese movies shot in Singapore were rare). Since they starred Malay actors, and featured Malay characters, they gave the somewhat false impression that Singapore was a predominantly Malay society. In contrast, none of the full-length films of the new era, made between 1995 and 2005, have used Malay.

What Singapore cinema now speaks is mainly Mandarin. Or, you may find a combination of English, Mandarin, local Chinese dialects and Singlish (a local variant of English), in a constant permutation game. Sometimes, there are as many as three different languages in the same sentence, reflecting the country's multiracial and multicultural character. Yet, however sophisticated the linguistic code-switching in these movies, there is a noticeable lack of Malay and Indian languages, with these languages being relegated to only a few short movies. An odd situation when one remembers the role that both the Malay and Indian communities had played in the past movie industry.

Very little brings together the golden age of the studios and the new era of Singapore filmmaking. Everything from the past seems to be buried somewhere, but nobody remembers where. Or, nobody cares. Worse still, few are even aware that something has been lost. It is as if Singapore has so drastically changed that it has retained little of what it was 40 or 50 years ago. Of course, this is not true, but that is what one might infer from the movies; first, due to the differences between the films made in the old days and those made recently; and second, due to the fact that very few movies of the new era seem to draw inspiration from the past. The truth is that, with such a long stagnation from the late 1970s to the early 1990s, filmmaking in Singapore had to start from scratch.

In the early 2000s, some sense of history, mixed with a bit of nostalgia, surged in a few movies made by young Singapore directors. In 2001, with his *Return to Pontianak*, Djinn paid tribute to the old horror genre rooted in Malay folklore, revisiting it and giving it a facelift. But, so far, he is the only one to capitalise, in a feature film, on the legacy of Malay movies made by Shaw and Cathay. Many movie industries elsewhere leverage on their glorious past, producing remakes, and actively revisiting genres that were once popular. In Singapore, it just does not happen.

Nevertheless, nostalgia for the good old days seems to be slowly spreading among the newer generation of filmmakers, particularly in short films, like June Chua's sensitive *Usher*, made in 2003. It portrays 10-year-old Xiao Ming, who is obsessed with old kung fu movies, but cannot afford to go to the cinema, unless the old usher lets him in. Chua drew on the nostalgia for the kung fu craze that stormed Asia and the world some 30 years before. *G-23*, Anthony Chen's movie shot in 2004, did not explicitly celebrate films of the past. But it takes place mostly in the old cinema in Woodlands, which has seen generations of moviegoers, and is irresistibly suffused with nostalgia.

Singapore had a cinema industry long before it became an independent nation-state. Its peak years, in terms of production, preceded independence, from 1953 to 1965. From that point on, it gradually declined, to the extent that

Birthday by Bertrand Lee, 2004.

production came to a halt by the end of 1978. Resuming production more than a decade later was not easy, and if there was a revival, it came slowly.

Film production reached an average of five feature films a year in the early 2000s, a steady pace, but not yet the critical mass required for the industry to grow. Filmmakers, directors of photography, technicians and actors cannot easily learn and improve with just those few movies every year. The pool of talent also cannot grow.

In a number of countries, actors work in three to five movies a year, and sometimes more. In Singapore they hardly have the opportunity to make more than three movies over a decade. Even veteran actor Lim Kay Tong has appeared in only eight to nine feature films in his long career. As for film-makers, seldom did they make more than two to three full-length movies.

All in all, the industry is still too small, revolving around a handful of active leading figures. There is at most a three-degree separation among leading players like Daniel Yun and Jack Neo for almost every movie made in the last few years.

Beyond reaching a critical mass that would enable it to explore new avenues, and provide opportunities for more talents, Singapore cinema also has to accept being truly… Singaporean. Many attempts at making internationally marketable "products" have failed, the product sounding and looking forced and synthetic.

Locally made cinema should not fear being too locally rooted. Many cinemas elsewhere in the world have been successful by being truly themselves, and having a strong identity. Attempts at artificial blends so as to be internationally marketable have been, and are still, even in a globalised world, failures. No one wants to see a Spanish movie that does not look Spanish. No one likes a Japanese film trying to look Hollywoodian. Better to watch a real Hollywood production. And, whatever one may think, Hollywood is very American, and has never given up on its Americanness. And, that is precisely why we like it. As for Singapore cinema, the more Singaporean it is, the better, I guess…

FILMO**GRAPHY**

The original title, whether in Malay, Chinese or English, comes first, followed by other title(s) under which the movie was also known at the time of its release, for example: **SHI ZI CHENG (a.k.a. Lion City, a.k.a. Bandar Raya Singapura).**

Where an English title was not provided at the time of release, a literal translation is proposed (unless it is the name of a person or a place, etc.) , for example: **ANAK-KU SAZALI [lit. My Son Sazali].**

A literal translation is also provided when the English title (under which the movie was also known) is not a direct translation of the original title, as is often the case in the cinema industry, for example: **CHINTA GADIS RIMBA (a.k.a. The Virgin of Borneo) [lit. Love of the Jungle Girl]**

The names of directors, actors or crew members are given in the exact spelling as shown on the movie credits. Over the years, a number of spellings may have evolved either due to changes in the language policy or variations in the way the person wanted to have his or her name spelt. This is particularly true of the Malay names. Here are a few examples to show how frequent these variations can be: B.S. Rajans / B.S. Rajhans; Siput Serawak / Siput Sarawak / Sipot Serawak; Hussain Haniff / Hussein Haniff; B. Yusuff / Yusoff B. / Yusof B.; Ramlee / P. Ramli / P. Ramlee; Roomai Noor / S. Roomai Noor; Ja'afar Wiryo / Jaffar Wiryo / Jaafar Wiryo; Mustapha Marof / Mustapha Maarof; Umi Kalsum / Umi Kalsom / Ummi Kaltoum; Aziz Satar / Aziz Sattar; Ralph Moder / Ralph Modder; Wahid Satay / Wahid Sateh; Mahmud June / Mahmud Jun / Mahmood June; Amat Sentol / Mat Sentol; Rose Yatimah / Ros Yatimah; etc.

The country of origin of either the director or the production company, when it is not Singapore or Malaysia, and when known, is indicated within brackets, for example: **[India]**.

Countries which are partners in coproduction on a Singapore movie are indicated as in the example that follows: **Film Unlimited [Hong Kong]**.

Movies which were produced by the Hong Kong branches of Singapore companies (Shaw, Cathay, Kong Ngee, Eng Wah, etc.) but which were shot partly or entirely in Singapore, are listed in the filmography specially dedicated to foreign movies shot in Singapore (refer to section starting on page 143). The same rule applies to the Hong Kong coproductions of Raintree Pictures, if they are partly shot in Singapore.

Cathay Organisation's productions made in Hong Kong by its sister company MP&GI between 1956 and 1970, as well as Shaw Brothers' movies made in Hong Kong from 1958 onwards, and Kong Ngee's films produced by its Hong Kong branch between 1955 and 1970 which were not shot in Singapore are not listed since they belong more to the history of the Hong Kong film industry and very rarely reflect Singapore's own history, society, culture or identity.

Similarly, the strictly financial coproductions of MediaCorp Raintree Pictures in the early 2000s (such as *The Eye, Turn Left Turn Right, Infernal Affairs II*, etc.), are not included. They have very little to do with Singapore, and do not take from, nor do they contribute to, the Singaporean identity.

Feature films produced by Singapore

1926

XIN KE
[lit. The Immigrant]
B&W – Silent
Directed by (unknown).
Produced by Liu Peh Jing.
Very little is known about the movie. But the title suggests that it might have been targeted at the immigrant population of Chinese workers coming in droves to Singapore at the beginning of the 20th century. If that movie was shot in Singapore with some Singaporean actors, then it means the first Singapore-made movie was not a Malay talkie with Malay stage actors, but a silent movie with Chinese actors. It also means the history of Singapore cinema may not be that clearcut.

1933

LEILA MAJNUN
B&W – Malay
Directed by B. S. Rajhans [India].
Produced by Rai Bahadur Seth and Hurdutroy Motilall (sometimes spelt Motilal) Chamria (a.k.a. Motilall Chemical Co.) [India].
With Suki Ben Noordin, Fatimah Benti Jasman (Leila), Syed Ali bin Mansoor Al-Attas, Cik Tijah, Yem, Sharif Medan, Khairuddin.
The seminal movie. All copies of this movie seem to have been lost long ago. It laid the foundation for all the love stories that would follow — a story about a beautiful, young woman and her *majnun* lover, i.e. a lover unable to cope with the situation and his feelings. The film is adapted from an Arabic story, and also loosely based on Romeo and Juliet. It was advertised in the newspapers as "the first spectacular colonial Malay talkie", "entirely produced in Singapore", with "numerous and beautiful Arabian and Egyptian dances", "songs and dialogues in classical Malay", and was released for Hari Raya Haji (Muslim Festival of the Haj). *Leila Majnun* (often mispelled as "Laila") has long been regarded as the very first movie truly made in Singapore.

1938-1941

BERMADU
[lit. Polygamy]
B&W – Malay
Directed by Hau Yaw (a.k.a. Hou Yao) and Wan Hai Ling (a.k.a. Wan Hoi Ling).
Produced by Shaw Brothers Ltd.
With Yem, Tinah, Habsah, Haji Gong, Puteh Lawak.
A rich man has two wives and two brothers-in-law, each of them related to one of the wives. When he decides to go to England, he takes his first wife's brother with him. During his absence, his second wife, with the help of her brother, treats the first wife badly, eventually trying to get rid of her after she gives birth to a baby boy. The first wife, to save herself and her baby from being burnt, is forced to leave the house.

HANCHOR HATI
[lit. Crushed Heart]
B&W – Malay
Directed by Hau Yaw (a.k.a. Hou Yao) and
Wan Hai LIng (a.k.a. Wan Hoi Ling).
Produced by Shaw Brothers Ltd.
With Habsah.

IBU TIRI
[lit. Stepmother]
B&W – Malay
Directed by Hau Yaw (a.k.a. Hou Yao) and
Wan Hai LIng (a.k.a. Wan Hoi Ling).
Produced by Shaw Brothers Ltd.

MATA HANTU
[lit. Ghost Eyes]
B&W – Malay
Directed by Hau Yaw (a.k.a. Hou Yao) and
Wan Hai LIng (a.k.a. Wan Hoi Ling).
Produced by Shaw Brothers Ltd.

MUTIARA
[lit. Pearl]
B&W – Malay
Directed by Hau Yaw (a.k.a. Hou Yao) and
Wan Hai LIng (a.k.a. Wan Hoi Ling).
Produced by Shaw Brothers Ltd.
With Habsah.

TERANG BULAN DI MALAYA
[lit. Bright Moon (also meaning Full Moon) over Malaya]
B&W – Malay
Directed by Hau Yaw (a.k.a. Hou Yao) and
Wan Hai LIng (a.k.a. Wan Hoi Ling).
Produced by Shaw Brothers Ltd.
With Yem, Habsah, Roekiah, Haji Gong, Puteh Lawak.

TIGA KEKASIH
[lit. Three Lovers]
B&W – Malay
Directed by Hau Yaw (a.k.a. Hou Yao) and
Wan Hai LIng (a.k.a. Wan Hoi Ling).
Produced by Shaw Brothers Ltd.

TOPING SHAITAN
[lit. The Devil's Mask]
B&W – Malay
Directed by Hau Yaw (a.k.a. Hou Yao) and
Wan Hai LIng (a.k.a. Wan Hoi Ling).
Produced by Shaw Brothers Ltd.
With Habsah.

1942

MENANTU DERHAKA
[lit. The Rebellious Daughter-in-Law]
B&W – Malay
Directed by B. S. Rajhans [India].
Produced by Tan and Wong Film Co (a.k.a. Tan Weng Film).
With Mokhtar Wijaya, Tarmina, Haras,
Yusuf Banjar, Juriah, S. Kadarisman.

1946

HUA JIAO SHUE LIU
[lit. The Overseas Chinese Blood Story]
B&W – Chinese
Directed by (unknown).
Produced by Zhong Hua Film Company.

SERUAN MERDEKA
(a.k.a. The Call for Freedom)
B&W – Malay
Directed by B. S. Rajhans [India].
Produced by Malayan Arts Prod
(a.k.a. Malayan Art Production).
With Salleh Ghani, Rokiah Hanafi,
Johar, Siti Tanjung Perak.

1947

CHEMPAKA
[lit. Magnolia Tree]
B&W – Malay
Directed by B. S. Rajhans [India].
Produced by Malay Film Productions.
With Salleh Ghani, Kasma Booty,
Yem, Maroeti, Suhara Effendi,
Jaafar Wiryo.
This movie is about the life of a native island girl, who encounters love for the first time.

SINGAPURA DI WAKTU MALAM
(a.k.a. Singapore Night)
[lit. Singapore by Night]
B&W – Malay
Directed by B. S. Rajhans [India].
Produced by Malay Film Productions.
With Siput Sarawak,
Bachtiar Effendi.

1948

CHINTA
[lit. Love]
B&W – Malay
Directed by B. S. Rajhans [India].
Produced by Malay Film Productions.
With Siput Serawak (Chinta),
Roomai Noor (King Kanchi and Sanchi),
Ja'afar Wiryo (Camban),
Harris (Vidush),
P. Ramlee (Putar),
Suhara Effendi (Ruchi).
A boat is caught in a huge tempest and sinks. Only King Kanchi survives. A few fishermen find him on the shore and rescue him. Chinta, a young village girl, takes care of him.

PISAU BERACHUN
[lit. Poisoned Knife]
B&W – Malay
Directed by B. S. Rajhans [India].
Produced by Malay Film Productions.
With Bachtiar Effendi, Kasma Booty,
Jaafar Wiryo, Johar.

1949

NASIB
[lit. Fate]
B&W – Malay
Directed by B. S. Rajhans [India].
Produced by Malay Film Productions.
Music and songs by Osman Ahmad.
With S. Roomai Noor (Kassim), Siput Sarawak (Puteri Rohana),
Haji Gong (Kalam), Tina (Zainah), Daeng Harris (Puteh),
P. Ramlee (Baki), Jaafar Wiryo (Bujang).
Kassim is living with his brother and sister-in-law when he finds out he is about to inherit all his family's wealth. Kassim, a young man who prefers to sing and play, is thrown out of his home by his brother and deprived of his wealth. He starts to lead a wandering life with two friends. One day, Kassim discovers pirate treasure.

NILAM
[lit. Sapphire]
B&W – Malay
Directed by B. S. Rajhans [India].
Produced by Malay Film Productions.
Story by A. R. Iyer.
Music and songs by Osman Ahmad.
With Siput Serawak (Puteri Nilam), S. Roomai Noor (Ahmad),
Ramlee (Rashid), Siti Tanjung Perak (Suratna),
Neng Yatimah (Penari), Daeng Harris, Jaafar Wiryo.
A young Javanese man, Ahmad, leaves his village with a magic protective dagger given to him by his mother. He takes to the seas, eager to discover the world. He reaches the exotic Arabian coast, and travels all the way to Egypt, encountering belly dancers, harem women, etc. He meets Princess Nilam and falls in love. Nilam's father will allow Ahmad to marry her only if he brings back a blue diamond guarded by monsters at a faraway location.

NOOR ASMARA
[lit. Light of Love]
B&W – Malay
Directed by B. S. Rajhans [India].
Produced by Malay Film Productions.
With S. Roomai Noor (Omar), Kasma Booty (Zaharah),
Daeng Harris (Baba), Siti Tanjung Perak, Jaafar Wiryo,
P. Ramlee, Norsiah B.
Omar, a music teacher, is training Rokiah to play the violin, but soon falls in love with her sister, Zaharah.

1950

ALOHA
B&W – Malay
Directed by B. S. Rajhans [India].
Produced by Malay Film Productions.
Assistant director is A. R. Tompel.
Story by A. R. Iyer.
Music by Osman Ahmad.
Dance choreography by Edith Castillo.
With Mariam (Aloha), Osman Gumanti (Mariyo),
P. Ramlee (Banjo), Jaafar Wiryo (Magoya),
Roseminah (Silpi), A. R. Tompel (Moku),
S. Shamsuddin, Siti Tanjung Perak, Daeng Idris.
On the island of Hawaii, a huge festival with dance, song and boat-racing is taking place. A merchant, Magoya, and his assistant, Moku, are among the tourists. They meet a local man, Makali, who has a beautiful daughter, Aloha.

BAKTI

(a.k.a. Faithfulness)
B&W – Malay
Directed by L. Krishnan [India].
Produced by Malay Film Productions.
Screenplay by L. Krishnan.
Music and songs by Osman Ahmad.
With P. Ramlee (Nasir), Kasma Booty (Sa'adiyah),
S. Roomai Noor (Hassan), Siput Sarawak (Edah).

Ibrahim, a rich man, has a spoilt son, Hassan, who is a thief and a liar. When the family adopts Nasir, a poor orphan, Hassan does not welcome him. But Sa'adiyah, the daughter of the family becomes Nasir's devoted friend and ally.

DEWI MURNI

[lit. Goddess of Purity]
B&W – Malay
Directed by B. S. Rajhans [India].
Produced by Malay Film Productions.
With Osman Gumanti, Kasma Booty, A.R. Tompel,
M. Amin, Daeng Harris.

KEMBAR

[lit. Twins]
B&W – Malay
Directed by S. Ramanathan [India].
Produced by Malay Film Productions.
With M. Amin, Mariam, Daeng Harris,
Siti Tanjung Perak.

PELANGI

[lit. Rainbow]
B&W – Malay
Directed by Naz Achnas [Indonesia].
Produced by Nusantara Film.
With Ismail Kasim, Nona Asiah, Saloma,
Eloni Hayat, Mustarjo, S. Naning.

PENGHIDUPAN

[lit. Life]
B&W – Malay
Directed by L. Krishnan [India].
Produced by Malay Film Productions.
Story by L. Krishnan.
Dialogue by Haji Mahadi.
Music by Ahmad Jaafar.
With P. Ramlee (Salim), Rokiah Jaafar (Salbiah),
Maria Menado (Halima), Daeng Harris (Bakar),
Ulong Jawa (Jaafar), Siti Tanjung Perak, Saamah.

In the Katong area, in eastern Singapore, lives Jaafar, a rich man, together with his wife Rubiah and her brother, the charming but badly-behaved Salim. One day, Salim visits his grandfather in Johor, where he meets a young and attractive girl, Salbiah. Salbiah's family is deeply in debt to a man, and unable to pay him back. The only solution is for Salbiah to marry that man. Salim, after sympathising with Salbiah, promises to help raise the money. Ecstatic and thankful, Salbiah gives her chastity to Salim. Back in Singapore, Salim, after a long silence, writes to her that he in fact cannot help her and that he will not see her again. Heartbroken, Salbiah leaves her family and starts wandering through Singapore in search of the treacherous Salim.

RACUN DUNIA

[lit. Poison World]
B&W – Malay
Directed by B. S. Rajhans [India].
Produced by Malay Film Productions.
Story by A. R. Iyer.
Screenplay by S. Roomai Noor.
Music by Doding Soliano.
With Osman Gumanti (Jamal), Kasma Booty (Aminah),
Siput Sarawak (Aishah), Jaafar Wiryo (Kamal), P. Ramlee (Harun),
A. R. Tompel (Karman), Siti Tanjung Perak (Mariam),
Neng Yatimah (Penari).

Jamal, the eldest son of a rich lumber businessman named Kamal, marries Aminah who delivers a baby girl. But the couple's life changes for the worse when Jamal comes under the influence of Harun and his wicked friends who introduce him to a seductive woman, Aishah.

SESAL TAK SUDAH

[lit. Neverending Regret]
B&W – Malay
Directed by A. R. Tompel.
Produced by Nusantara Film.
With Ratna Si, Daeng Idris, Saloma, R. Suriani, A. R. Tompel.

TAKDIR ILAHI

(a.k.a. The Will of God)
B&W – Malay
Directed by L. Krishnan [India].
Produced by Malay Film Productions.
Dialogue by A. R. Tompel.
Music by Osman Ahmad.
With P. Ramlee (Arshad), Neng Yatimah (Fatimah), Yusuf Banjar
(Village Chief Abdullah), Daeng Idris (Village Chief Ismail),
Siti Tanjung Perak (Khatijah), Salmah (Minah).

Khatijah is a greedy and insecure stepmother who hates her stepdaughter, Fatimah. While her husband is away, she hires an assassin to murder Fatimah. But the assassin sympathises with Fatimah and, instead of killing her, cuts off one of her hands which he shows to Khatijah as a proof of her death.

1951

ANGIN BERPESAN

[lit. Message in the Wind]
B&W – Malay
Directed by Naz Achnas [Indonesia].
Produced by United Malay Film Company.
With S. Kadarisman, Daeng Idris, Suki,
Zeera Agus, Norani Moarti, Saloma, Hamidar.

BAPA SAYA

[lit. My Father]
B&W – Malay
Directed by B. S. Rajhans [India].
Produced by Malay Film Productions.

BERDOSA

[lit. The Sinner]
B&W – Malay
Directed by B. S. Rajhans (and S. Ramanathan,
although this remains unclear) [India].
Produced by Malay Film Productions.
With S. Roomai Noor, Rokiah Jaafar, Siput Sarawak, Yem.

JUWITA

B&W – Malay
Directed by S. Ramanathan [India].
Produced by Malay Film Productions.
Story by S. Ramanathan.
Songs and music by B. Yusuff.
Art direction by P. Ramlee.
With P. Ramlee (as himself), Kasma Booty (Juwita),
A. Rahim (Hassan), Salmah (Rohani), Ulong Jawa (Salim),
Sa'adiah, Daeng Harris, Siti Tanjung Perak.

A young man succeeds in becoming the leader of a big band in Singapore. After signing a five-year contract to perform in Bangkok, he goes back to his *kampong* (village) to bid farewell to Juwita, the love of his youth. But Rohani, the dancer and singer who accompanies him, is secretly in love with him. This movie seems to have been one of the first opportunities for P. Ramlee to try his hand at something more than acting, singing or playing music.

MANUSIA

[lit. Human or Humankind]
B&W – Malay
Directed by S. Ramanathan [India].
Produced by Malay Film Productions.
With Omar Rojik, Kasma Booty, Jaafar Wiryo,
Jaafar Shah, Zainab, Zubaidah.

PEMBALASAN

(a.k.a. Revenge)
B&W – Malay
Directed by L. Krishnan [India].
Produced by Malay Film Productions.
With S. Roomai Noor, Siput Sarawak,
Rokiah Jaafar, M. Amin.

PULAU MUTIARA

[lit. Pearl Island]
B&W – Malay
Directed by S. Ramanathan [India].
Produced by Malay Film Productions.
With Osman Gumanti, Maria Menado,
A. R. Tompel, Siti Rohani.

RAYUAN SUKMA

[lit. The Longing of the Soul]
B&W – Malay
Directed by L. Krishnan [India].
Produced by Malay Film Productions.
Story by Jaafar Abdullah.
Music and songs by P. Ramlee.
With Ali Rahman (Mahadi), Zubaidah (Marliah),
A. Rahim (Musa), Omar Rojik, Junaidah,
Ulong Jawa, Saamah, Rosli,
Yusuf Banjar.

Mahadi and Marliah have known each other since they were kids. As adults, they are still in love, and intend to get married as soon as Mahadi finds a good job. Luckily, he is offered a position as a clerk in Singapore, a big city nearby. Thus, Mahadi and Marliah are able to become officially engaged. However, the marriage itself is postponed when Mahadi is promoted to a higher position in Penang, and has to be away for two months. Musa, a man who has never been his friend, not even when they were young, tries to take advantage of the situation in order to marry Marliah.

SEJOLI

[lit. Lovebirds]
B&W – Malay
Directed by B. S. Rajhans [India].
Produced by Malay Film Productions.
Story by A. R. Iyer.
Dialogue by Jaafar Wiryo.
Music by Sumardi and Yusof B.
With Kasma Booty (Mariam), Rokiah Jaafar (Halimah),
Neng Yatimah (Zubaidah), P. Ramlee (Jamil),
Jaafar Wiryo (Mustar), Daeng Harris (Bakri),
S. Shamsuddin (Bakar), Siti Tanjung Perak,
M. Amin.

Zubaidah marries Ismail, an irresponsible man who abandons her when she becomes pregnant. After Ismail's sudden departure, one of his friends, Mustar, starts harrassing her. When she rejects him, Mustar instigates her landlord to throw her out of her home. The unfortunate Zubaidah is left to wander the streets. She gives birth to a baby girl that she names Mariam, but she is forced to abandon her in the garden of a rich family, hoping that they will take care of her.

1952

ALADDIN

B&W – Malay
Directed by B. S. Rajhans [India].
Produced by Malay Film Productions.
Songs by Ahmad Jaafar.
With Ali Rahman, Mariam,
Jaafar Shah, Jaffar Wiryo,
Mohd. Amin, S. Shamsuddin.

An old storyteller tells the story of Aladdin to a group of children.

ANJURAN NASIB

[lit. Fate's Hand]
B&W – Malay
Directed by B. S. Rajhans [India].
Produced by Malay Film Productions.
Music by Yusof B.
Dance choreography by Edith Castillo.
With P. Ramlee (Inspektor Bahar),
Mariam (Maimun), Harun Omar (Haji Salleh),
Daeng Harris, Sa'diah (Ramlah),
Musalmah, Omar Rojik (Sidek),
R. Azmi, Salleh Kamil.

Young Inspector Bahar is in love with Maimun the singer, and wants to marry her. Ramlah, his young sister, is placed under the custody of Razak, their uncle, who mistreats her physically and mentally. Uncle Razak also happens to be Maimun's boss. Bahar and Ramlah's father (Uncle Razak's elder brother) had left them to grow up in Singapore while he went to live in Java, where he became a millionaire. Just before he dies of old age, he receives a letter from Bahar inviting him to his marriage. He also gets a letter from Ramlah begging him to go back and asking him to protect her from her uncle, Razak. He makes Sidek, his personal secretary, promise that he will look after both his children's interests. This Shaw production displays many shots of the brothers' exhibition circuit at that time: Great World, Atlantic, Rex, etc.

ANTARA SENYUM DAN TANGIS

[lit. Between Smiles and Tears]
B&W – Malay
Directed by L. Krishnan [India].
Assistant director is Omar Rojik.
Produced by Malay Film Productions.
Dialogue by P. Ramlee.
Music by Yusof B. and P. Ramlee.
Dance choreography by Edith Castillo.
With P. Ramlee, Rokiah, Musalma, M. Amin,
Harun Omar, Siti Tanjung Perak

Abidin is an engineer at a mine owned by stingy Hamid, whose daughter, Maimun, is secretly in love with... Abidin. But after Hamid refuses to pay out the insurance to the family of a worker who has just died, Abidin quits and goes to work at another mine. Soon, this mine is taken over by Hamid. Maimun is thus able to work on seducing Abidin, even though he is already married to Faridah.

BUNGA PERCINTAAN

[lit. Love Flower]
B&W – Malay
Directed by L. Krishnan [India].
Produced by Rimau Film Production.
With Mustapha Maarof, Mislia, Nursiah K.

CHEMBURU

[lit. Jealousy]
B&W – Malay
Directed by S. Ramanathan [India].
Produced by Malay Film Productions.
Music and songs by P. Ramlee.
With Yusof Latiff, Rosnani Jamil, Mariani, Nordin Ahmad,
Siti Tanjung Perak, Haji Mahadi.

DERITA

[lit. Suffering]
B&W – Malay
Directed by L. Krishnan [India].
Produced by Malay Film Productions.
Music and songs by P. Ramlee.
With Ali Rahman, Neng Yatimah, Mariam, A. Rahim.

DIAN

[lit. Candle]
B&W – Malay
Directed by Naz Achnas [Indonesia].
Produced by Nusantara Film.
With S. Kadarisman, Normadiah, Junaidah,
Osman Gumanti, Daeng Idris, Mardiana.

GADIS PELADANG

[lit. The Farmer Girl]
B&W – Malay
Directed by B. S. Rajhans [India].
Produced by Malay Film Productions.
With Yusof Latiff, Neng Yatimah, Maria Menado,
Daeng Harris, Omar Rojik, Salleh Kamil, Marliah.

JIWA LARA

[lit. A Heartbroken Soul]
B&W – Malay
Directed by S. Ramanathan [India].
Produced by Malay Film Productions.
With Osman Gumanti, Rokiah Jaafar, Neng Yatimah.

LUPA DARATAN

[lit. Forgetting the Land, meaning forgetting your roots]
B&W – Malay
Directed by L. Krishnan [India].
Produced by Malay Film Productions.
With Omar Rojik, Rosnani Jamil, Jamil Sulong, Haron Omar.

MISKIN

[lit. The Poor]
B&W – Malay
Directed by K. M. Basker [India].
Produced by Malay Film Productions.
Music by P. Ramlee and Yusof B.
With P. Ramlee (Kamil), Rosnani Jamil (Jamilah),
Haron Omar (Yusof), Omar Rojik (Zakaria),
Saemah (Rokiah), Jamil Sulong (Guru Besar).

Yusof is a materialistic rich man. His daughter, Jamilah, falls in love with Kamil, a car washer who works for her father. Kamil being poor, Jamilah decides to help him. She gives him her jewellery to be pawned. Unfortunately, Yusof accuses Kamil of extorting money from his daughter.

NORMA

B&W – Malay
Directed by A. R. Tompel.
Produced by Nusantara Film.
With S. Kadarisman, Salbiah Harun,
Saloma, S. Naning, Hamidar,
Daeng Idris, A.R. Tompel.

PACAR PUTIH

[lit. White Lover]
B&W – Malay
Directed by Naz Achnas [Indonesia].
Produced by Nusantara Film.
With S. Kadarisman, Normadiah,
Junaidah, A. Rahim,
Daeng Idris, Hamidar.

PATAH HATI

[lit. Brokenhearted]
B&W – Malay
Directed by K. M. Basker [India].
Produced by Malay Film Productions.
Screenplay by K. M. Basker.
Dialogue by Jamil Sulong.
Music by Yusof B.
Dance choreography by Edith Castillo.
With P. Ramlee (Kasim), Neng Yatimah (Rahimah),
Musalmah (Salmah), Mohamed Hamid (Yusof),
Ulong Jawa (Hassan), Jamil Sulong,
Hashim Nor.

Kassim, a hardworking young man, has done very well in school, and receives an offer to further his studies overseas. However, his father Hassan cannot afford to send him. Hassan's old friend, Sidek, a rich farmowner, wants Kassim to become his son-in-law, and thus agrees to pay for his overseas studies. When he comes back a few years later from Cambridge University, Sidek is eagerly waiting for him, having made plans to get him engaged to his daughter Salmah. But, in the meanwhile, Kassim has fallen in love with a salesgirl, Rahimah.

PERMATA DI PERLIMBAHAN
[lit. The Jewel in the Valley]
B&W – Malay
Directed by Haji Mahadi.
Produced by Malay Film Productions.
With Nordin Ahmad, Maria Menado,
Salmah Ibrahim, Rokiah Jaafar.

PERWIRA LAUTAN TEDUH
[lit. Warrior of the Calm Seas]
Colour – Malay
Directed by Jaafar Wiryo.
Produced by Keris Film Productions.
This was Keris' first film. It is said to have been shot in colour.

RAMLI RAMLAH
B&W – Malay
Directed by Jaafar Wiryo.
Produced by Keris Film Productions.
Screenplay by A. Razak.
With Rosini, Ahmad Shah,
Tuminah.

SEDARAH
[lit. Kin or Family]
B&W – Malay
Directed by S. Ramanathan [India].
Produced by Malay Film Productions.
Story by S. Ramanathan.
Dialogue by W. H. Barat.
Dance choreography by Edith Castillo.
With P. Ramlee (Harun), Rosnani Jamil (Asiah),
A. Rahim (Hashim), Haji Mahadi (Hassan),
Siti Tanjung Perak (Rubiah), Saadiah,
S. Shamsuddin, Saamah.
When he is offered a job on a boat, Hassan is forced to leave his pregnant wife, Rubiah. In Hassan's absence, Rubiah's house suddenly catches fire and burns down. When he returns, Hassan is told that his wife has perished in the fire. Devastated, Hassan leaves again, and goes to Singapore, where he tries to build a new life, getting married to a Javanese woman. But his first wife had not died in the fire. She had been saved by a man who had later taken her to Penang, where she gave birth to a boy, Harun.

SENIYATI
[lit. Film Star]
B&W – Malay
Directed by A. R. Tompel and Chow Wing Kok.
Produced by Nusantara Film.
With A. Bakarruddin, Normadiah, S. Kadarisman,
Junaidah, Daeng Idris, A. R. Tompel, A. Rahim.

SETIA
[lit. Faithful]
B&W – Malay
Directed by A. S. Simons (a.k.a. A. C. Simmons) and,
according to certain accounts, Jaafar Wiryo.
Produced by Keris Film Productions.
With Rosini, Ahmad Mahmud,
M. Amin, S. Alton.

SHORGA DUNIA
(a.k.a. Syurga Dunia)
[lit. Paradise on Earth]
B&W – Malay
Directed by B. S. Rajhans [India].
Produced by Malay Film Productions.
With Jaafar Shah, Rokiah Jaafar, Musalmah, M. Shariff.

TAS TANGAN WANITA
[lit. A Woman's Handbag]
B&W – Malay
Directed by L. Krishnan [India].
Produced by Malay Film Productions.
With Osman Gumanti, Maria Menado, Neng Yatimah.
Mardiana falls in love with a young man who had saved her father's life. However, her family does not accept this romance.

YATIM PIATU
[lit. Orphan]
B&W – Malay
Directed by B. S. Rajhans [India].
Produced by Malay Film Productions.
With Yusof Latiff (Anuar), Rokiah Jaafar (Rohana),
Saadiah (Aminah), Harun Omar, Mariani.
Aminah, an orphan with behavioural problems, meets Rohana at a party. Rohana befriends her and, trying to help her, asks her parents to look after Aminah too.

1953

AYER MATA
[lit. Tears]
B&W – Malay
Directed by K. M. Basker [India].
Produced by Malay Film Productions.
With Ahmad Mahmud (Rashid), Rosnani Jamil (Hasnah),
Siti Tanjong Perak, Hashim Noor, Mustarjo.
Rashid has not seen his son for ages. He only finds out about him and his whereabouts when he meets Hasnah and falls for her.

BERBAHAGIA DI SINGAPURA
[lit. Happy in Singapore]
B&W – Malay
Directed by Jaafar Wiryo.
Produced by Keris Film Productions.
With Siti Hanim, Rohaya, M. Amin.

BUDI MULIA
[lit. Noble Character]
B&W – Malay
Directed by (unknown).
Produced by (unknown).
With (unknown).

BULOH PERINDU
(a.k.a. Magic Flute)
[lit. Bamboo Grove, alluding to a sweet voice]
Colour – Malay
Directed by B. S. Rajhans [India].
Produced by Cathay-Keris.
With Rosini, Shariff Medan,
Bakarudin, M. Amin.

DAHLIA
B&W – Malay
Directed by B. S. Rajhans [India].
Produced by Cathay-Keris.
With Shariff Medan, Bakaruddin, Norsiah, Yem, Rosini.

HATI IBLIS
[lit. Devil's Heart]
B&W – Malay
Directed by K. M. Basker [India].
Produced by Malay Film Productions.
With Ali Rahman, Aini Hayati, Jamil Sulong,
Salmah Ibrahim, Daeng Harris, Annie Jasmin.

HUJAN PANAS
[lit. Hot Rain]
B&W – Malay
Directed by B. N. Rau (a.k.a. B. N. Rao) [India].
Produced by Malay Film Productions.
Story and screenplay by B. N. Rau.
Music by P. Ramlee.
Lyrics by Jamil Sulong.
Dance choreography by Edith Castello.
With P. Ramlee (Hamid), Siput Serawak (Aminah),
Aini Hayati, Baby Zarinah, Haji Mahadi, Hashim Nor,
Mustarjo, Fatimah A., Malik Sutan Muda.
Hamid and Aminah are musical artists who fall for each other, get married and have a child. But Aminah is having an affair with Hassan, Hamid's friend. The opening shots, before the credits start, show numerous locations in Singapore.

IBU
[lit. Mother]
B&W – Malay
Directed by S. Ramanathan [India].
Produced by Malay Film Productions.
Songs and pantuns by Ahmad Jaafar.
Dance choreography by Edith Castillo.
Mambo dances by Lena Marcello.
With P. Ramlee (Raimy), Neng Yatimah (Raiha),
Aini Hayati (Ratna), Rosnani Jamil (Hamidah), Haji Mahadi (Zulkifli), Nordin Ahmad, Salleh Kamil, Mustarjo, Johnny Tan.
In a village near Kuala Lumpur, a poor blind mother lives with her son Raimy who passionately loves music. Raimy vows to become a famous trumpeter one day after hearing the renowned musician Zulkifli. Raimy meets Zulkifli accidentally, and becomes his student, making his dream come true.

ISTANA IMPIAN
[lit. Palace of Dreams]
B&W – Malay
Directed by V. Girimali [India].
Produced by Malay Film Productions.
With Ahmad Mahmud (Salim), Saadiah (Sapiah), S. Shamsudin (Sulung), Neng Yatimah, Mariani, Omar Rojik, Salleh Kamil.
Salim and Sapiah are attracted to one another, but are too shy to express their feelings.

KASEH MENUMPANG
(a.k.a. Transition of Love)
B&W – Malay
Directed by L. Krishnan [India].
Produced by Shah Film Productions
(apparently in association with Keris Film Productions).

KERANA KAU

[lit. Because of You]
B&W – Malay
Directed by K. R. S. Shastry (a.k.a. Sastry) [India].
Produced by Malay Film Productions.
With Mohamed Hamid, Mariam, Saadiah,
Ahmad Mahmud, Omar Rojik,
Daeng Harris.

MANGSA

[lit. Casualty]
B&W – Malay
Directed by K. M. Basker [India].
Produced by Malay Film Productions.
With Yusof Latiff, Siput Sarawak,
Mariani, Ahmad Mahmud,
Salleh Kamil, Salleh Melan.

NELAYAN

[lit. Fisherman]
B&W – Malay
Directed by Jaafar Wiryo.
Produced by Cathay-Keris.
With Salleh Ghani, Umi Kalsum,
Jaafar Wiryo.

PUTUS HARAPAN

[lit. Broken Hope]
B&W – Malay
Directed by B. N. Rao [India].
Produced by Malay Film Productions.
Music by Osman Ahmad.
With P. Ramlee (Yusof), Rokiah Jaafar (Fatimah),
Musalmah (Hashim), Salleh Kamil (Ismail),
Nordin Ahmad (Osman), Mariani (Kasma),
Aziz Satar, Aini Jasmin.

Hashim, the owner of a huge factory, has two children, Fatimah and Osman. He also has an adopted son, Yusof, whom Hashim's wife hates to the extent that she has forbidden her own children to play or mingle with him. However, Fatimah has inherited her father's good nature and constantly tries to cheer Yusof up. However, when Hashim dies, Yusof's situation immediately worsens, with his adoptive mother starting to treat him like a servant.

RAJA SEHARI

[lit. King for a Day, meaning the bride or the groom]
B&W – Malay
Directed by B. S. Rajhans [India].
Produced by Malay Film Productions.
With Ali Rahman, Mariani, Daeng Harris, Saadiah.

SENGSARA

[lit. Agony]
B&W – Malay
Directed by S. Ramanathan [India].
Produced by Malay Film Productions.
With Yusof Latiff, Neng Yatimah, Siput Sarawak,
Daeng Idris, Normadiah, S. Kadarisman, Daeng Harris.

SIAPA SALAH

[lit. Who is in the Wrong]
B&W – Malay
Directed by B. N. Rao [India].
Produced by Malay Film Productions.
Story by B. N. Rao.
Dialogue by S. Hassan Sahab.
Art direction by Jamil Sulong.
Songs by P. Ramlee.
Music by Yusof B.
With P. Ramlee (Jamil), Daeng Idris (Salim),
Siti Tanjung Perak (Aminah), Neng Yatimah (Yatimah),
Normadiah (Noorma), Salleh Kamil (Salleh),
Haji Mahadi (Aziz).

Salim and his wife Aminah live luxuriously in their huge house in Kuala Lumpur with their son Jamil, who is in love with their maid's daughter, Noorma. When Salim objects to his son marrying a maid's daughter, Jamil is forced to run away with Noorma and becomes a painter. Unfortunately, he loses his eyesight, and Noorma has to take on a waitressing job to support the both of them.

UNTUK SESUAP NASI

[lit. For a Mouthful of Rice]
B&W – Malay
Directed by L. Krishnan [India].
Produced by Rimau Film Production.
With S. Roomai Noor, R. Suriani,
Mustapha Marof, Raden Tuminah.

1954

ARJUNA

B&W – Malay
Directed by V. Girimaji [India].
Produced by Malay Film Productions.
Story by V. Girimaji.
With Ahmad Mahmud, Rokiah Jaafar,
Nordin Ahmad, Aziz Satar, Aini Hayati,
Daeng Harris, Mustarjo,
Raja Hamidah.

CINTA ABADI

(a.k.a. Kembali ke Desa,
meaning return to the village)
[lit. Endless Love]
B&W – Malay
Directed by S. Roomai Noor,
Sho Wee Gok and Jaafar Wiryo.
Produced by Keris Film Productions.
With Mislia, Salleh Ghani.

GELORA HIDUP

[lit. Life's Storms]
B&W – Malay
Directed by B. N. Rao [India].
Produced by Malay Film Productions.
With Yusof Latiff, Rosnani Jamil,
Musalmah, S. Kadarisman,
Nordin Ahmad.

IMAN

[lit. Piety]
B&W – Malay
Directed by K. R. S. Shastry (a.k.a. Sastry) [India].
Produced by Malay Film Productions.
With Ahmad Mahmud, Saadiah,
Haji Mahadi, Neng Yatimah,
Jins Shamsuddin, Ibrahim Pendek.

INSAF

[lit. Repentance]
B&W – Malay
Directed by B. S. Rajhans [India].
Produced by Cathay-Keris.
With Rosini, M. Nor Lambak,
Osman Gumanti, Mala Ratina.

JASA

[lit. Good Deeds]
B&W – Malay
Directed by S. Ramanathan [India].
Produced by Malay Film Productions.
With Yusof Latiff, Mariam, S. Kadarisman,
Salmah Ibrahim, Ali Rahman, A. Rahim,
Saadiah, Aziz Satar, Ibrahim Pendek.

KECHEWA

[lit. Disappointment]
B&W – Malay
Directed by S. Ramanathan [India].
Produced by Malay Film Productions.
With Yusof Latiff (Yusof), Saadiah (Rabiah),
S. Kadarisman (Mokhtar), Mariam,
Salmah Ibrahim, Salleh Kamil.

MERANA

[lit. Languish]
B&W – Malay
Directed by B. N. Rao [India].
Produced by Malay Film Productions.
With P. Ramlee (Amir), Latifah Omar (Aminah),
Siti Tanjung Perak (Amir's mother),
Mariani (Rosini), Aini Hayati (Faridah),
Daeng Idris, Mustarjo,
Omar Suwita.

Amir and Faridah live with their mother, in a house near Ipoh (Malaysia). One day, Amir is sent to visit his rich uncle in Taiping, for the purpose of seducing his cousin Rosini, who is quickly smitten by his charm. But Amir is already in love with Aminah, a village girl.

NAFSU

[lit. Desire]
B&W – Malay
Directed by L. Krishnan [India].
Produced by Cathay-Keris.
With S. Roomai Noor, Maria Menado,
Osman Gumanti, Rosini,
M. Amin.

PANGGILAN PULAU
[lit. Call of the Island]
B&W – Malay
Directed by S. Ramanathan [India].
Produced by Malay Film Productions.
Music by Yusof B.
Dance choreography by Edith Castillo.
Art direction by Jamil Sulong.
P. Ramlee (Zulkifli), Normadiah (Jelita),
Yusof Latiff (Husin), A. Rahim (Musa),
S. Kadarisman (Omar), Salleh Kamil (Shukur),
Latifah Omar (Melati), Ibrahim Pendek (Ramli).
Loosely adapted from *Wuthering Heights*, this is the story of
Zulkifli, who works for Johan and takes care of his horses. Zulkifli
falls in love with Jelita, his boss's daughter.

PAWANG
[lit. Medicine Man]
B&W – Malay
Directed by K. M. Basker [India].
Produced by Malay Film Productions.
With Haji Mahadi, Rosnani Jamil,
Daeng Idris, Omar Rojik,
Musalmah, Jamil Sulong.

PERJODOHAN
[lit. Matchmade]
B&W – Malay
Directed by B. N. Rao [India].
Produced by Malay Film Productions.
With P. Ramlee (Rashid), Normadiah (Habibah),
Nordin Ahmad (Yaakob), Mariani (Salmah),
Aini Hayati (Fatimah), Mustarjo (Kadi).
Rashid and Habibah have been married for seven years and have
a son named Johan. Unfortunately, their marriage is rather unhappy
and they fight all the time.

PERTARUHAN
[lit. The Gamble]
B&W – Malay
Directed by L. Krishnan [India].
Produced by Cathay-Keris.
With S. Roomai Noor, Maria Menado,
Salleh Ghani.

TANGISAN IBU
(a.k.a. The Heartaches of a Mother)
[lit. Mother's Tears]
B&W – Malay
Directed by L. Krishnan [India].
Produced by Cathay-Keris.
With S. Roomai Noor, Mislia,
M. Amin, Tuminah.

TERANG BULAN DI MALAYA
(a.k.a. Moon over Malaya)
[lit. Bright Moon (also meaning full moon) over Malaya]
B&W – Malay
Directed by B. S. Rajhans [India].
Produced by Cathay-Keris.
With Raden Mokhtar, Rosini,
Sukarseh, Bakarudin.

1955

ABU HASAN PENCHURI
[lit. Abu Hassan The Thief]
B&W – Malay
Directed by B. N. Rao [India].
Produced by Malay Film Productions.
Songs by P. Ramlee.
Dance choreography by Edith Castillo.
With P. Ramlee (Abu Hassan), Mariam (Princess Faridah),
Nordin Ahmad (Prince Tartar), Mohd Hamid (Kassim),
Daeng Idris, S. Shamsuddin, Ali Rahman, Wan Hazim.
Abu Hassan, a wanderer, has to steal to survive. One day, at a
marketplace, he sees Princess Faridah and falls in love with her
immediately. Wanting to meet her at whatever cost, he manages
to sneak into the palace after having stolen a wizard's magical
walking stick.

Mutiara dari Malaya, 1955

BERNODA
[lit. Stained]
B&W – Malay
Directed by S. Ramanathan [India].
Produced by Malay Film Productions.
With Yusof Latiff, Normadiah, Latifah Omar,
S. Kadarisman, Nordin Ahmad, Siti Tanjung Perak.

DUKA NESTAPA
[lit. Extreme Sorrow]
B&W – Malay
Directed by L. Krishnan [India].
Produced by Cathay-Keris.
With S. Roomai Noor, Mislia, Nursiah K.

EMPAT ISTERI
[lit. Four Wives]
B&W – Malay
Directed by B. S. Rajhans [India].
Produced by Malay Film Productions.
With Daeng Idris, Normadiah, Saloma,
Latifah Omar, Mariani,
A. Rahim, Salleh Kamil.

GADIS LAYAR
[lit. The Elephant Girl]
B&W – Malay
Directed by Eddy Infante [Philippines].
Produced by Malay Film Productions.

INSAN
[lit. Human Being]
B&W – Malay
Directed by K. M. Basker [India].
Produced by Malay Film Productions.
With Omar Rojik, Siput Sarawak,
Ahmad Mahmud, Saadiah, Latifah Omar.

IRAMA KASIH
(a.k.a. Irama Kaseh Setia,
a.k.a. Melody of Love,
a.k.a. Egyptian)
[lit. The Rhythm of Love]
B&W – Malay
Directed by Lourey Friedman (a.k.a. Laurie Friedman).
Produced by Cathay-Keris.
With Nety Herwaty, Rosini, M. Lor Lambak,
S. Roomai Noor, M. Amin.

JUBAH HITAM
[lit. Black Robe]
B&W – Malay
Directed by S. Ramanathan [India].
Produced by Malay Film Productions.
With Yusof Latiff, Zaiton, S. Kadarisman,
Daeng Idris, A. Rahim.

KELUARGA TOLOL
[lit. The Tolol Family]
B&W – Malay
Directed by S. Ramanathan [India].
Produced by Malay Film Productions.
With Aziz Satar, Siti Tanjung Perak,
Normadiah, S. Shamsuddin, Ibrahim Pendek.

KIPAS HIKMAT
[lit. Magic Fan]
B&W – Malay
Directed by S. Ramanathan [India].
Produced by Malay Film Productions.
With Yusof Latiff, Mariam,
S. Kadarisman, Ibrahim Pendek,
A. Rahim, Omar Rojik.

MENYERAH
[lit. Surrender]
B&W – Malay
Directed by K. M. Basker [India].
Produced by Malay Film Productions.
With Yusof Latiff, Latiffah Omar,
S. Kadarisman, P. Ramlee,
Siput Sarawak.

MUTIARA DARI MALAYA
(a.k.a. Mutiara Malaya, a.k.a. Pearl of Malaya)
B&W – Malay
Directed by Lourey Friedman (a.k.a. Laurie Friedman).
Produced by Cathay-Keris.
With S. Roomai Noor, Mislia,
Sri A. Unety, M. Amin,
Dollah Sarawak.

PENAREK BECHA

(a.k.a. Trishaw Puller)
B&W – Malay
Directed by P. Ramlee.
Produced by Malay Film Productions.
Story and screenplay by P. Ramlee.
Edited by H. R. Narayanan.
Music by P. Ramlee.
Lyrics by Jamil Sulong.
Orchestration by Fred Libio and Lionel B. Ventura.
With P. Ramlee (Amran), Sa'adiah (Azizah), Salleh Kamil (Ghazali), Fatimah Osman, Udo Omar (Marzuki), Saamah (Amran's mother), Habsah, Omar Suwita, Hashimah Yon, Kemat Hassan.

Amran, a poor trishaw puller, meets a rich young lady, Azizah. They fall in love, but Azizah's father, the rich Marzuki, does not approve of their relationship. Instead, he intends to marry her to Ghazali, a young gangster who puts up an act and pretends to be a nice man. Azizah runs away and finds shelter at Amran's place while he is away. When Ghazali comes to take back Azizah, Amran's mother is unfortunately stabbed in the shoulder. This is the first movie directed by P. Ramlee.

RIBUT

[lit. Storm]
Colour – Malay
Directed by K. M. Basker [India].
Produced by Malay Film Productions.
Dance choreography by Edith Castillo.
With Ahmad Mahmud, Saadiah, Haji Majadi, Rosnani Jamil, Habsah, Salbiah, Aziz Sattar.
This colour movie displays many dance and song scenes, showing *kampong* life in the 1950s.

ROH MEMBELA

[lit. The Vengeful Soul]
B&W – Malay
Directed by B. N. Rao [India].
Produced by Malay Film Productions.
With Nordin Ahmad, Neng Yatimah, Daeng Idris, Normadiah, Haji Mahadi, Salleh Kamil, Aziz Satar.

SAUDARAKU

(a.k.a. My Family)
B&W – Malay
Directed by Lourey Friedman (a.k.a. Laurie Friedman).
Produced by Cathay-Keris.
With S. Roomai Noor, Mislia, Ahmad Shah, Maria Menado, Marsita.

SELAMAT HARI RAYA

[lit. Festive Day Greeting]
B&W – Malay
Directed by L. Krishnan [India].
Produced by Cathay-Keris.
With S. Roomai Noor, Maria Menado, Salleh Ghani, Umi Kalsom, M. Amin.

SELAMAT TINGGAL KEKASIHKU

[lit. Goodbye My Dear Lover]
B&W – Malay
Directed by L. Krishnan [India].
Produced by Cathay-Keris.
With S. Roomai Noor, Kasma Booty, M. Amin, Noly Lim, Cheng Li Li, Shariff Medan, Dollah Sarawak.

1956

ADAM

B&W – Malay
Directed by S. Roomai Noor.
Produced by Cathay-Keris.
With S. Roomai Noor, Hasnah Rahman, Nursiah Yem, M. Amin, Umi Kalsom.

ADEKKU

[lit. My Little Brother]
B&W – Malay
Directed by B. N. Rao [India].
Produced by Malay Film Productions.
With Ahmad Mahmud, Rosnani Jamil, Saloma, Haji Mahadi, Siti Tanjung Perak, Malik Sutan Muda, Omar Suwita.

ANAK-KU SAZALI

[lit. My Son Sazali]
B&W – Malay
Directed by Phani Majumdar [India].
Produced by Malay Film Productions.
Songs by P. Ramlee.
Orchestration and background music by L. B. Ventura and Fred Libio.
Playback singing by Saloma and Normadiah.
Dance choreography by Normadiah.
Art direction by Jamil Sulong.
With P. Ramlee (Hassan and Sazali), Zaiton (Mahali), Rosnani Jamil (Rubiah), Nordin Ahmad (Mansor), Hashima Yon (Rokiah), Daeng Idris, Ibrahim Pendek, Salbiah, Tony Castello.

Knowing that their parents will never approve of their marriage, Hassan and Ani run away to Singapore. There, Hassan who has a passion for music, soon makes a name for himself as a musician and composer. Unfortunately, Ani dies while giving birth to Sazali. Hassan's sorrow is great and he showers all his love on Sazali, who grows up to be a spoilt kid. As an adult, Sazali becomes a gangster. During a burglary, he is wounded by the police, but manages to escape. He finds shelter at his father's home.

AZAN

[lit. The Call to Prayer]
B&W – Malay
Directed by L. Krishnan [India].
Produced by Cathay-Keris.
With S. Roomai Noor, Nursiah K., Shariff Medan, Salleh Ghani, Umi Kalsom, M. Amin.

BUNGA PESTA

[lit. Party Flower]
B&W – Malay
Directed by B. N. Rao [India].
Produced by Cathay-Keris.

DONDANG SAYANG

[Note: This is a type of Malay song]
B&W – Malay
Directed by L. Krishnan [India].
Produced by Cathay-Keris.
With Nusiah Yem, Mustapha Maarof, Hasnah Rahman, M. Amin.

HANG TUAH

Colour – Malay
Directed by Phani Majumdar [India].
Produced by Malay Film Productions.
Music and songs by P. Ramlee.
Art direction by Jamil Sulong.
With P. Ramlee (Hang Tuah), Saadiah (Melor), Ahmad Mahmud (Hang Jebat), Zaiton (Tun Teja), Haji Mahadi (Sultan of Malacca), Daeng Idris (Dato Bendahara), Nordin Ahmad (Hang Kasturi), S. Shamsuddin (Hang Lekir), Aziz Satar, Hashim Nur, Siti Tanjung Perak.

Hang Tuah and his four sworn brothers, Hang Jebat, Hang Kasturi, Hang Lekir and Hang Lekiu, pledges to protect the Sultan of Malacca. When Hang Tuah persuades the beautiful Tun Teja to marry the Sultan, the latter rewards Hang Tuah with full honours. But Hang Tuah is soon framed by the old guard of the sultanate, who plots against him and accuse him of treason. The Sultan is then compelled to order that Hang Tuah be killed. One of his sworn brothers, Hang Jebat, feels betrayed and rebels against the Sultan, not knowing that Hang Tuah has in fact been kept alive by one of his secret allies. One of the first of Shaw's superproductions, "in radiant Eastmancolor", as it was advertised at the time of its release.

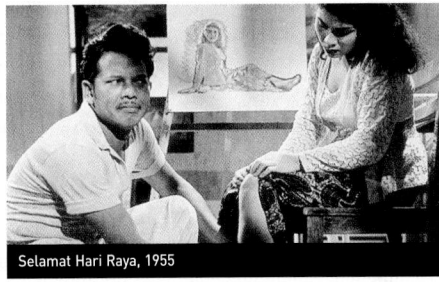

Selamat Hari Raya, 1955

KEADILAN ILAHI

[lit. Divine Justice]
B&W – Malay
Directed by K. M. Basker [India].
Produced by Malay Film Productions.
With Yusof Latiff, Saadiah, S. Kadarisman, Daeng Idris.

MEGA MENDUNG

[lit. Cloudy]
B&W – Malay
Directed by L. Krishnan [India].
Produced by Cathay-Keris.
With S. Roomai Noor, Supatri, Mustapha Maarof, R. Suriani.

PENCHURI

[lit. Thief]
B&W – Malay
Directed by K. M. Basker [India].
Produced by Malay Film Productions.
With Yusof Latiff (Umar), Siput Sarawak (Jamilah),
S. Kadarisman, Siti Tanjung Perak.

While trying to break into a house, Umar bumps into Jamilah, the owner. Coincidentally, a friend of Jamilah is around to witness Umar's attempt at breaking in. In desperation, Umar claims to be Jamilah's husband. Jamilah's friend, believing him, goes around telling the entire neighbourhood the news. Soon, all Jamilah's friends want to meet the husband she has been hiding from them.

SEMERAH PADI

B&W – Malay
Directed by P. Ramlee.
Produced by Malay Film Productions.
Story by Omar Rojik.
Screenplay by P. Ramlee.
Dialogue by S. Sudamarji.
Music by P. Ramlee.
Lyrics by Jamil Sulong.
Dance choreography by Normadiah.
Silat fight scenes by Malik Sutan Muda (a.k.a. Malik S.M.).
Art direction by Jamil Sulong.
With Nordin Ahmad (Teruna), P. Ramlee (Aduka),
Sa'adiah (Dara), Daeng Idris (chief Hitam),
Normadiah (Galak), Salleh Kamil (Borek),
Omar Suwita (Kachiwa), Musalmah.

Aduka and Teruna are two sworn brothers who have been given the responsibility of maintaining law and order in the village of Semerah Padi. But Dara, the village chief's daughter, is secretly in love with Aduka. Not knowing this secret relationship, her father intends to marry her to Teruna. Although they are heartbroken, the two lovers, Dara and Aduka, decide to keep their feelings to themselves — Dara, not wanting to go against her father's will, and Aduka, not wanting to hurt his brother. This is P. Ramlee's second feature as a director, and it is strongly influenced both by Italian neorealism and the then world-famous Akira Kurosawa.

1957

BAJAU ANAK LAUT

(a.k.a. Bajao, the Sea Gypsies)
[lit. The Badjaos Children of the Sea]
B&W – Malay
Directed by Lamberto V. Avellana [Philippines].
Produced by Cathay-Keris and
Dona Narcisa Benvenida de Leon.
Story and screenplay by Rolf Bayer.
Music by Francisco Buencamino Jr.
With Rosa Rosal, Tony Santos,
Leroy Salvador, Joseph de Cordova,
Vic Silayan, Oscar Keesee,
Pedro Faustino.

The Badjaos are a pagan tribe roaming the seas south of the Philippines, whereas the Taosugs live on the land. A beautifully-shot movie. Filmed entirely in the Philippines by a Filipino director, with a Filipino cast and crew. One of Cathay-Keris's international productions. Even though it is a Singaporean production, this movie pertains more to the history of Filipino film.

BELANTARA

[lit. Forest]
B&W – Malay
Directed by S. Ramanathan [India].
Produced by Malay Film Productions.
With Nordin Ahmad, Normadiah, Salleh Kamil, S. Shamsuddin,
Daeng Idris, A. Rhaman, Musalmah.

BUJANG LAPOK

(a.k.a. Confirmed Bachelor)
B&W – Malay
Directed by P. Ramlee.
Produced by Malay Film Productions.
Story by B.H. Chua.
Screenplay by P. Ramlee.
Music by Yusof B.
With P. Ramlee (Ramli), S. Shamsuddin (Sudin),
Aziz Sattar (Aziz), Normadiah (Normah),
Zaiton (Zaiton), Dayang Sofia (Sapiah),
Siti Tanjung Perak, Rahaya Madji, Shariff Dol,
Malik Sutan Muda, Sa'amah.

The movie centres on the lives of three bachelors, Ramli, Aziz and Sudin. Sudin falls for the girl next door, the rich, young Zaiton. But her mother disapproves of this relationship. Sudin, in dismay, asks his friends to help. But, at the same time, Aziz falls in love with Sapiah. As for Ramli, he stays alone, not knowing that his landlady secretly loves him but is too shy to say anything.

DENDAM PONTIANAK

[lit. The Pontianak's Revenge]
B&W – Malay
Directed by B. N. Rao [India].
Produced by Cathay-Keris.
With Maria Menado, Salmah Ahmad,
Mustapha Maarof.

After being murdered, the pontianak (or female vampire) returns to exact revenge.

HANTU JERANGKONG

[lit. The Skeletal Ghost]
B&W – Malay
Directed by K. M. Basker [India].
Produced by Malay Film Productions.
With Aziz Jaafar, Hashimah Yon, Habsah,
Omar Suwita, Zainon, Aziz Satar, S. Shamsuddin.

KASI SAYANG

[lit. Dear Love]
B&W – Malay
Directed by Phani Majumdar [India].
Produced by Malay Film Productions.
With Haji Mahadi, Neng Yatimah,
Saadiah, Hashimah Yon,
Jins Shamsuddin.

Kartini and her husband, Sudanto, leave Singapore to escape the war; entrusting their baby girl, Sukartini, to her maid. Halimah, the maid, takes great care of the baby despite her poverty and the hard times she has to cope with. After the war is over, Kartini returns to Singapore, but Halimah, who has grown to love the child very much, does not want to give her back and decides to run away with her.

KEMBALI SEORANG

[lit. A Man is Back]
B&W – Malay
Directed by Ramon Estella [Philippines].
Produced by Malay Film Productions.
With Ahmad Mahmud, Saadiah, Daeng Idris,
Sunatri, Salleh Kamil.

Dendam Pontianak, 1957

MOGOK

[lit. Strike]
B&W – Malay
Directed by K. M. Basker [India].
Produced by Malay Film Productions.
With Ahmad Mahmud (Ismail), Saadiah (Fatimah),
S. Kadarisman (Hamzah), Mariani, Daeng Idris, Siti Tanjung Perak.

Hamzah, a factory manager having an affair with his boss's wife, is also planning a strike in the factory. Two of his colleagues, who had initially supported him, decide to put an end to his plan.

PANCHA DELIMA

(a.k.a. Five Rubies)
B&W – Malay
Directed by P. Ramlee.
Produced by Malay Film Productions.
Story by Run Run Shaw.
Screenplay by P. Ramlee.
Dialogue by S. Sudarmaji.
With Jins Shamsuddin (Prince Suria Kencana),
Hashimah Yon (Teratai), Udo Omar (Karma), Haji Mahadi (King Kukila Kencana), Aini Hayati, R. Suriani, Shariff Dol.

A young prince, Suria Kencana, is cursed by his stepmother who turns him into a cobra. He becomes a snake by day, and human by night. The terrible spell can be broken only by a red necklace, the Pancha Delima, worn by the beautiful Teratai.

PONTIANAK

B&W – Malay
Directed by B. N. Rao [India].
Produced by Cathay-Keris.
With Maria Menado, M. Amin, Wahid Satay,
Salmah Ahmad, Karim Latiff.

A young female hunchback is transformed into a beautiful woman through magic, but after sucking out snake venom from a bite received by her husband, she becomes a vampiric pontianak. The pontianak tries to transform her daughter into one of the undead. She is eventually destroyed when a nail is driven into her skull. The first in a series of Malay pontianak films. The movie was initially released both in a Malay and a Chinese version. Unfortunately, both prints have been lost.

PUTERA BERTOPENG
[lit. The Masked Prince]
B&W – Malay
Directed by K. M. Basker [India].
Produced by Malay Film Productions.
With Ahmad Mahmud, Normadiah, Daeng Idris,
A. Rahim, S. Kadarisman, Haji Mahadi, Aziz Satar.

RUMAH PANJANG
(a.k.a. Long House)
B&W – Malay
Directed by Phani Majumdar [India].
Produced by Malay Film Productions.
With Kenny Bickaner, Lulu.
Fully shot in Dayak country, the movie was advertised as showing "genuine head hunters".

SALAH SANGKA
[lit. Misunderstanding]
B&W – Malay
Directed by B. S. Rajhans [India].
Produced by Cathay-Keris.
With S. Roomai Noor, Shariff Medan.

Mahsuri, 1958

SERUAN DARAH
[lit. Call of the Blood]
B&W – Malay
Directed by Chew Cheng Kok.
Produced by Malay Film Productions.
With Ahmad Mahmud, Neng Yatimah, Yusoff Latiff.

TAUFAN
(a.k.a. Typhoon)
B&W – Malay
Directed by T. C. Santos [Philippines].
Produced by Malay Film Productions.
Original story by B. H. Chua.
Screenplay by T. C. Santos.
Dialogue by S. Sudarmadji.
Music by Osman Ahmad and Fred Libio.
Lyrics by S. Sudarmadji.
With Ahmad Mahmud (Amir), Zaiton (Fatimah),
Salleh Kamil (Hamid), Mariani,
Omar Suwita, Aziz Sattar,
Shariff Dol, Ali Fijee,
Mustarjo, Nyak Osman.
Hamid, the village shopowner, falls in love with Fatimah, who is engaged to Amir. Torn with jealousy, Hamid tries to separate them.

1958

ANAK PONTIANAK
(a.k.a. Son of Pontianak)
B&W – Malay
Directed by Ramon Estella [Philippines].
Produced by Malay Film Productions.
With Jins Shamsuddin, Hashima Yon,
Dayang Sofia, S. Kadarisman.
A gallery of scary creatures like the son of the infamous vampire, a bodiless monster called the *polong*, and *hantu* the snake-devil. At the time of its release, it was advertised in the newspapers as "the most horrific thriller ever filmed! Stronger than the strongest!". And it introduced Sang Kanchil as the talking mousedeer.

AZIMAT
[lit. Talisman]
B&W – Malay
Directed by Rolf Bayer [Philippines].
Produced by Malay Film Productions.
With Pancho Magalona, Saloma, Jins Shamsuddin,
Salleh Kamil, Tita Doran.
The son of a rich man wastes his life away, flirting with women, listening to music and drinking wine. After an argument with his father, he considers committing suicide, but meets an old bearded Chinese man who gives him a talisman. The lead role is played by Filipino movie star Pancho Magalona. The overall feel is very jazzy and Hollywoodian. It presents a very different picture of Singapore from what was usually seen in movies of that time.

CHE MAMAT PARANG TAJAM
[lit. Che Mamat's Sharp Parang or Machete)]
B&W – Malay
Directed by S. Roomai Noor.
Produced by Cathay-Keris.
With Wahid Satay, Salmah Ahmad, M. Amin, Latiffah Omar.

CHINTA GADIS RIMBA
(a.k.a. The Virgin of Borneo)
[lit. Love of the Jungle Girl]
Colour – Malay
Directed by L. Krishnan [India].
Presented by Cathay Organisation.
Produced by Keris Film Productions.
Original story by Harun Hamid Rashid.
Screenplay by L. Krishnan and Ho Ah Loke.
Edited by Hussain Haniff.
Photography by Arthur C. Symons.
Music by Zubir Said.
With Roomai Noor, Narang, M. Amin,
Mohamed Zain, Dollah Sarawak.
A young man from the Dayak jungle tribe ventures out of the forest and gets lost. He is rescued by Malay villagers, and befriends one of their sons. Years go by, and the two of them remain friends. The Malay man, by now the head of his village, sets off on a long jungle trip with his Dayak friend. Unfortunately, they are attacked by Iban warriors, who capture the Malay man and take him to their village, where they intend to cut his head off during a sacrificial ritual. Shot in colour, entirely on location in Sarawak. It features real indigenous people from the Dayak and Iban tribes, giving this movie very high anthropological value. It visually documents, perhaps for the first time, their lifestyle. It also contains a few amazing scenes, including one of a man being strangled by a real python, and a few traditional war dances.

DOKTOR
[lit. Doctor]
B&W – Malay
Directed by Phani Majumdar [India].
Produced by Malay Film Productions.
With Aziz Jaafar, Zaiton,
S. Kadarisman, Haji Mahadi.

GERGASI
[lit. Giant]
B&W – Malay
Directed by Dhiresh Ghosh [India].
Produced by Malay Film Productions.
With Aziz Jaafar, Hashimah Yon,
Rokiah Jaafar, Aziz Satar.

HANTU KUBUR
[lit. Ghost of the Grave]
B&W – Malay
Directed by Chew Cheng Kok.
Produced by Malay Film Productions.
With Aziz Jaafar, Hashimah Yon,
S. Kadarisman, S. Shamsuddin,
Aziz Satar.

IKAN DUYUNG
[lit. Mermaid]
B&W – Malay
Directed by (unknown).
Produced by (unknown).

KAKI KUDA
[lit. Horse Leg]
B&W – Malay
Directed by Kidar Sharma [India].
Produced by Malay Film Productions.
With Aziz Satar, S. Shamsuddin,
Normadiah, Saloma, Mustarjo,
Ani Jasmin.

MAHSURI
(a.k.a. The Maid of Langkawi)
Colour – Malay
Directed by B. N. Rao [India].
Produced by Cathay-Keris.
With Kasma Booty (Mahsuri),
Nordin Ahmad, S. Roomai Noor.

MASYARAKAT PINCANG
(a.k.a. Masharakat Pinchang)
[lit. Imperfect Society]
B&W – Malay
Directed by Phani Majumdar [India].
Produced by Malay Film Productions.
With S. Kadarisman, Salleh Kamil,
Tony Castello, Rosnani Jamil,
Neng Yatimah, Daeng Idris,
Haji Mahadi.

MATA HARI
(a.k.a. Matahari,
a.k.a. The Rape of Malaya)
[lit. The Sun]
B&W – Malay
Directed by Ramon Estella [Philippines].
Produced by Malay Film Productions.
With Maria Menado (Matahari), Ahmad Mahmud (Ahmad),
Salleh Kamil (Umai), Omar Rojik (Jepun), Daeng Idris,
Alice Ma, Jins Shamsuddin.

Matahari's village is turned into a camp by the invading Japanese army. Bravely, the young Matahari leads a war for the freedom of her country. Umai, however, betrays his people and starts working for the Japanese. At the time of its release, it was billed as "the first authentic film about the Japanese occupation in Malaya".

ORANG LICHIN
[lit. Slippery Man]
B&W – Malay
Directed by L. Krishnan [India].
Produced by Cathay-Keris.
With S. Roomai Noor, Maria Menado, Mahmood June, M. Amin.

Sumpah Orang Minyak, 1958

ORANG MINYAK
(a.k.a. The Oily Man)
B&W – Malay
Directed by L. Krishnan [India].
Produced by Cathay-Keris.
With S. Roomai Noor, Salmah Ahmad, Nordin Ahmad,
Mahmud June, M. Amin.

SATAY
B&W – Malay
Directed by K. M. Basker [India].
Produced by Keris Film Productions.
Presented by Cathay Organisation.
Music by Yusoff B.
With Wahid Satay (Kamil), Aiddie Ali (Satay),
Salmah Ahmad, Puteh Lawak, Shariff Medan.

Kamil is a rich man's son who likes to take life easy, driving his convertible and seeing his friends. One day, at a playground, a young boy, Satay, approaches him claiming to be his son. When Kamil tries to run away, passersby accuse him of abandoning his own son. Kamil is thus forced to temporarily adopt the young Satay. As the two of them go through adventure after adventure, a bond starts to grow. The movie shows many aspects of Singapore in the late 1950s with its changing urban landscape. It also has numerous shots of cinema halls such as the Alhambra, the Odeon, the Majestic, etc.

SELENDANG DELIMA
(a.k.a. The Magic Pomegranate)
B&W – Malay
Directed by K. M. Basker [India].
Produced by Cathay-Keris.
With Latifah Omar, Maria Menado,
M. Amin, Abdullah Chik.

On the recommendation of his father, the prince Tengku Bangsegara goes to Mount Ledang to learn martial arts. When he returns home after a long period of training, he is shocked to find that his whole family and all the people in the kingdom have been killed, with the exception of his sister Sri Banian. They both decide to move on. Soon after, Sri Banian marries Dewa Laksana and gives birth to a girl that they call Selendang Delima.

SERANGAN ORANG MINYAK
[lit. Attack of the Oily Man]
B&W – Malay
Directed by L. Krishnan [India].
Produced by Cathay-Keris.
With M. Amin, Noordin Ahmad,
Latiffah Omar.

Inspector Darsuki has to investigate the case of the oily man. This is going to lead to many changes in his life involving his wife and his father.

SERGEANT HASSAN
(a.k.a. Sarjan Hassan)
B&W – Malay
Directed by Lamberto Avellana [Philippines] and P. Ramlee.
Produced by Malay Film Productions.
Story by Ralph Moder.
Screenplay by P. Ramlee.
With P. Ramlee (Sergeant Hassan),
Saadiah (Salmah), Jins Shamsuddin (Aziz),
Salleh Kamil (Buang), Daeng Idris (Lebai),
Aini Jasmin (Minah), John Gray,
David Downe, Omar Rojik, Ali Fiji.

In his early youth, Hassan loses both his mother and his father. His father's employer, taking pity on him, decides to take care of him, thus placing Hassan under his guidance. But the employer's son, Aziz, becomes envious, and grows bitter towards Hassan. The fact that the beautiful Salmah falls in love with Hassan makes Aziz even more envious. At the outbreak of World War II, Aziz and some friends respond to the call for volunteers to fight the Japanese. Hassan, who wants to go as well, is forced to stay in the village to take care of the plantation with his adoptive father. He is called a coward by the villagers. Hassan, unable to take it any longer, runs away and joins the army, where he quickly proves to be a very skilled soldier.

SRI MENANTI
B&W – Malay
Directed by Phani Majumdar [India].
Produced by Malay Film Productions.
With Salleh Kamil, Zaiton,
Chang Chong, Dong Tan,
S. Kadarisman, S. Shamsuddin,
Ibrahim Pendek.

SUMPAH ORANG MINYAK
[lit. The Curse of the Oily Man]
B&W – Malay
Directed by P. Ramlee.
Produced by Malay Film Productions.
Story by Teuku Djaafar.
Screenplay by P. Ramlee.
Dialogue by S. Sudamarji.
Music by P. Ramlee and Yusof B.
With P. Ramlee (Si Bongkok),
Salleh Kamil (Buyong), Shariff Dol,
Sri Dewi, Marion Willis, Daeng Idris,
Haji Mahadi, Ali Rahman.

Bongkok is born a disfigured hunchback. The villagers, and especially Buyong, bully him. Though he is crippled, Bongkok is a gifted artist. He is also secretly in love with the village chief's daughter. One night, he tries to offer her a drawing, but is violently chased away from the village by Buyong and his friends. He later returns to take his revenge.

SUMPAH PONTIANAK
(a.k.a. Curse of the Vampire)
B&W – Malay
Directed by B. N. Rao [India].
Produced by Cathay-Keris.
Story by A. Razak.
Dialogue by Hamza.
Photography by Laurie Friedman.
Edited by Hussain Haniff.
Music by Zubir Said.
With Maria Menado (Chomel, the pontianak),
Mustapha Maarof (Samad),
Salmah Ahmad (Maria),
Shariff Medan, Puteh Lawak,
Wahid Satay, Amat Sentol,
Yem, Aman Belon.

A woman who died young returns to protect her growing but still innocent daughter. The deceased woman who first appears as a poor disfigured hunchback is able to turn into a flying vampire monster with humongous fangs known as the pontianak. She can also turn back into her original form, the one of the lovely Maria Menado, a beautiful woman if any. The pontianak is not that bad, and as a matter of fact, she is the avenging superheroine who gets really upset when bad ugly guys and monsters alike try to harm her daughter or any woman for that matter (yes, there is something of a feminist touch). Shot in Cathayscope (for the first time). This has become a cult Z-grade film, found in all the fanzines and websites dedicated to vampires.

1959

BATU BELAH BATU BERTANGKUP
[lit. Stone Splits Stone Closes]
B&W – Malay
Directed by Jamil Sulong.
Produced by Malay Film Productions.
With Aziz Jaafar, Zaiton,
Neng Yatimah, Salleh Kamil,
S. Kadarisman, Haji Mahadi,
Bat Latiff, Hasnah Hassan.

BAWANG PUTEH BAWANG MERAH

[names of two women,
Bawang Puteh and Bawang Merah,
also lit. Garlic and Onion]
B&W – Malay
Directed by S. Roomai Noor.
Produced by Cathay-Keris.
Story by Salleh Ghani.
With Latifah Omar (Bawang Merah),
Umi Kalsom (Bawang Putih),
Mustapha Maarof,
Siti Tanjung Perak,
Shariff Medan.

After her father dies, Bawang Merah and her mother Labu are forced to live with Bawang Putih and her domineering mother, Kundor. When her mother also dies, Bawang Merah is left alone, enduring more and more hardship from Kundor and Bawang Putih, who bully her. But Bawang Merah is lucky enough to encounter a prince in the woods. He falls in love with her and offers to marry her. This, of course, makes Kundor very jealous and bitter, as she wishes her own daughter were the one to marry the prince.

DANDAN SETIA

[lit. Loyal Dandan]
B&W – Malay
Directed by Dhiresh Ghosh [India].
Produced by Malay Film Productions.
Screenplay and art direction by Omar Rojik.
Music by Osman Ahmad and P. Ramlee.
Dance choreography by Normadiah.
With Jins Shamsuddin, Saadiah,
Aziz Jaafar, Normadiah,
Rahmah Rahmat.

There is war in the spiritual world of Kayangan among its people, the dewa-dewa, for the possession of the beautiful Gemala Dewi, daughter of Indera Betara, King of Kayangan. The King, much aggrieved by the unsettled dispute, finally decides to take away the cause. He transforms his daughter into a mango that he throws down upon the Earth. The fruit floats in the sea and is finally picked up by the maids of King Pardashah and eaten by the Queen. The heirless King is overjoyed when the Queen becomes pregnant. But the Queen dies while giving birth, and adding to the King's sorrow, the offspring is ugly and dark-skinned.

JULA JULI BINTANG TIGA

[name of main character,
also lit. Jula Juli Third Star]
B&W – Malay
Directed by B. N. Rao [India].
Produced by Cathay-Keris.
With Salmah Ahmad (Jula Juli Bintang Tiga),
Abdullah Chik (Raja Dhasyahalan Syah).

Jula Juli Bintang Tiga is a fairy princess who has married a king. But when her secret is revealed, she has to run away, leaving behind a son named Baharum Syah.

KORBAN FITNAH

[lit. Victim of Slander]
B&W – Malay
Directed by P. L. Kapur (a.k.a. P. L. Kapoor) [India].
Produced by Cathay-Keris and Maria Menado Productions.
Screenplay by Ralph Modder.
With Siput Serawak, Sukarno M. Noor, A. N. Alcaff, Maria Menado, Abdul Hadi, Syed Hassan, Yem, Munah, Ahmad Sabri, Julia (singing Saputangan), Murni (singing Bangawan Solo).

With the financial support of his brother Hassan who now lives in Singapore, Hussein is trying to complete his studies in Kuala Lumpur. Unfortunately, his roommate Wahab, a skirt-chaser and troublemaker, is getting more and more difficult to handle, slowly drawing him into a love drama that will, in the end, take Hussein to court. The movie opens with noteworthy shots of modern Singapore, and unveils very interesting aspects of the lifestyle in the late 1950s.

Musang Berjanggut, 1959

MUSANG BERJANGGUT

[lit. The Bearded Fox]
B&W – Malay
Directed by P. Ramlee.
Produced by Malay Film Productions.
Music by P. Ramlee.
Dance choreography by Normadiah.
With P. Ramlee (Tun Nila Utama, a.k.a. Raja Muda Pura Cendana, Prince of Pura Cendana),
Saadiah (Puspawangi),
Ahmad Nisfu (Raja Alam Syahbana),
Udo Omar (Datuk Bendahara),
Malik Sutan Muda (Datuk Bentara Mangku Bumi),
Nyong Ismail (Datuk Pujangga),
Mustarjo (Datuk Nikah Kahwin),
Shariff Dol, Habsah Buang, Zainon Fiji, M. Rafee, Ali Fiji.

Unable to have a child of their own, the king and queen of Pura Cendana have decided to adopt a son. The young Tun Nila is thus chosen from amongst thousands. When he grows up, he is asked to find a partner of his own. Tun Nila therefore undertakes a long journey to far places to find the perfect woman. He meets many, but none who suits him until he finally encounters the young and beautiful Puspawangi. When Tun Nila returns to his kingdom with Puspawangi, the king and all his ministers are mesmerised by her great beauty.

NUJUM PAK BELALANG

[lit. The Clairvoyant Pak Belalang]
B&W – Malay
Directed by P. Ramlee.
Produced by Malay Film Productions.
Music by P. Ramlee.
Dance choreography by Normadiah.
With P. Ramlee (Pak Pelalang),
Hasimah Yon (Princess Bujur Sireh),
Bat A. Latiff (Young Belalang),
Ahmad Nisfu (Sultan Shahrul Nizam),
Aziz Sattar (Badan),
S. Shamsuddin (Nyawa).

One day, as he was returning home from the fields, young Belalang sees two looters. They are arguing with each other as to how to divide the cows and goats they have stolen from a nearby village. Hidden in a tree, young Belalang starts shouting that he is the son of the jungle ghoul in lust for human blood, hence scaring the thieves. He herds the animals to his home. Together with his father, Pak Belalang, he plots how to return them to their rightful owners, at a profit. He hides the animals, then goes to see the head of the village, claiming that his father is an expert astrologer. Of course, when the villagers come to see him, father Belalang has the answer ready and knows where to find the animals. When the Sultan's treasures are stolen, the villagers immediately suggest that the Sultan consult Pak Belalang, not knowing he is a fake. Only through pure luck will Pak Belalang locate the hidden treasure.

PENDEKAR BUJANG LAPOK

[lit. The Bachelor Warrior]
B&W – Malay
Directed by P. Ramlee.
Produced by Malay Film Productions.
Music and songs by P. Ramlee.
With P. Ramlee (Ramli), Aziz Satar (Aziz),
S. Shamsuddin (Sudin), Rose Yatimah (Ros),
Mustarjo (Mustar), Ahmad Nisfu (The rich Nisfu),
Momo (Ros's mother).

Ramli, Aziz and Sudin decide to learn the martial art of *silat* from the village expert, Mustar. They encounter Mustar's daughter, Ros, who is the village teacher. Ros initially takes the three of them for crooks, but soon finds out how wrong she was, and eventually falls in love with Ramli. One of P. Ramlee's silliest comedies, and one of the most successful.

PUTERI GUNUNG BANANG

[lit. The Princess of Mount Banang]
B&W – Malay
Directed by Dhiresh Ghosh [India].
Produced by Malay Film Productions.
With Sri Dewi (Puteri Gunung Banang),
Ahmad Mahmud, Hashimah Yon,
Salleh Kamil, Kemat Hassan,
S. Kadarisman.

RADEN MAS

B&W – Malay
Directed by L. Krishnan [India].
Produced by Cathay-Keris.
With Noordin Ahmad, Latifah Omar, M. Amin,
Siput Sarawak, Mahmud June, Siti Tanjung Perak,
Mustapha Maaraof, Umi Kalsom.

During a palace celebration, Pangeran, the brother of the Sultan of Java, falls in love with a beautiful dancer and immediately decides to marry her. However, the marriage is shortlived when his wife is suddenly killed by enemies. Pangeran then resettles in Singapore with his only daughter, Raden Mas. The Sultan of Singapore, pleased to have someone of royal blood settling on his island, decides to marry his own daughter to the newly-arrived Pangeran. But Pangeran's new and young wife becomes terribly jealous of Raden Mas and tries to get rid of her. Interestingly enough, the film opens with a scene which has, at first glance, nothing to do with the rest of the story, but says "Singapore today" and goes on to show the city's landscape, as if the director was aware of the necessity to recontextualize the whole movie.

RAHSIA HATIKU

[lit. The Secret of My Heart]
B&W – Malay
Directed by Naz Achnas [Indonesia].
Produced by Malay Film Productions.
With M. Amin, Maznah Ahmad, Sharifah Hanim.

RAJA LAKSMANA BINTAN

B&W – Malay
Directed by Jamil Sulong.
Produced by Malay Film Productions.
With Ahmad Mahmud, Normadiah, Aziz Jaafar,
Rosnani Jamil, S. Kadarisman, Salleh Kamil,
Haji Mahadi, Rahmah Rahmat, Aziz Satar.

RASA SAYANG – EH

[lit. The Feeling of Love]
B&W – Malay
Directed by L. Krishnan [India].
Produced by Cathay-Keris.
Photography by N.B. Vasudev.
Edited by Hussain Haniff.
Dialogue by Hamzah and M. Amin.
Music by Yusof B.
Dance choreography by Noorsiah Ali.
With Wahid Satay, Dollah Serawak,
Kasmah Booty, Kuswadi, Sheriff Medan,
Mahmood June, M. Amin.

Wahid, a music hall entertainer, is flying from Penang to Kuala Lumpur, and then to Singapore. On the way, he encounters the charming Doctor Faridah, who owns a clinic in Singapore. But he is also closely followed by some gangsters who have hidden precious documents in his suitcase.

SAMSENG

[lit. Gangster]
B&W – Malay
Directed by Ramon Estella [Philippines].
Produced by Malay Film Productions.
With Jins Shamsuddin, Rosnani Jamil.

Isi Neraka, 1960

SAUDAGAR MINYAK URAT

[lit. The Massage Oil Merchant]
B&W – Malay
Directed by Ramon Estella [Philippines].
Produced by Malay Film Productions.
Music by P. Ramlee.
With S. Kadarisman, Normadiah, S. Shamsuddin, Aziz Satar,
Mariani, Saloma, Leng Hussein, Ibrahim Pendek, Ahmad Nisfu.

1960

ANTARA DUA DARJAT

[lit. Between Two Social Classes]
B&W – Malay
Directed by P. Ramlee.
Produced by Malay Film Productions.
Story and screenplay by Omar Rojik.
Dialogue by P. Ramlee.
Music and songs by P. Ramlee.
With P. Ramlee (Ghazali), Saadiah (Tengku Zaleha),
S. Kadarisman (Tengku Mukri), S. Shamsuddin (Sudin),
Yusof Latiff (Tengku Aziz), Ahmad Nisfu (Tengu Karim),
Kuswadinata (Tengku Hassan), S. Sudarmaji (Maji), Mariam,
Rahmah Rahmat, Kemat Hassan, Ainon Fiji, Ali Fiji,
Rahimah Alias (Yang Chik).

Ghazali, a local musician, and his friends rescue the rich, young and pretty Tengku Zaleha when her car gets stuck in the mud during a heavy rain. He meets her again when his band performs at her birthday party held at her parents' villa near Johore Bahru, and they fall in love. However, Zaleha is from the upper class, whereas Ghazali is merely a commoner. When Zaleha's father catches them cuddling together in the park at night, he strongly opposes their love and has his men beat up Ghazali until he faints. The next morning, when he recovers, the villa is empty, and Zaleha is said to have died during the night. In fact, she has been put to sleep on her father's orders and sent back to Singapore where she is forced to marry Tengku Mukri, someone of her status. Years later, she returns with her husband to the villa in Johore. This is a classic blend of film noir, melodrama and musical, in which P. Ramlee appears to be very critical of Malay feudal class system.

CHE MAMAT PARANG TUMPUL

[lit. Che Mamat's Blunt Parang or Machete]
B&W – Malay
Directed by L. Krishnan [India].
Produced by Cathay-Keris.
With Wahid Satay, Latifah Omar, M. Amin, Siti Tanjung Perak.
Che Mamat is always unlucky in life. After losing his job, he becomes a children's storyteller. His girlfriend, Fatimah, coaxes him to enter a short story competition. Che Mamat suprisingly emerges as the winner. He is soon offered a good job at a newspaper.

HANTU RIMAU

(a.k.a. Pembunuhan dalam Gelap,
meaning murder in the dark)
[lit. Tiger Ghost]
B&W – Malay
Directed by L. Krishnan, B. N. Rao [India]
and S. Roomai Noor.
Produced by Cathay-Keris.
Edited by Hussain Haniff.
With S. Roomai Noor, Mary Lim,
Siput Sarawak, Yem, Safinah,
Puteh Lawak, Aman Belon,
Mahmud June, Darn Singh.

This is a sketch movie comprising three stories: *Mud on her Shoes* by L. Krishnan, *Hantu Rimau* by B. N. Rao and *Double Knock Out* by S. Roomai Noor.

ISI NERAKA

[lit. Contents of Hell]
B&W – Malay
Directed by Jamil Sulong.
Produced by Malay Film Productions.
With Ahmad Mahmud, Saadiah,
Salleh Kamil, Habsah,
Haji Mahadi, S. Kadarisman,
Rahmah Rahmat, A. Rahim,
Shariff Dol.

In 14th-century Malacca, an Arab named Sidi Abdul Aziz starts spreading the teachings of Islam until it becomes accepted as the new official religion by the Sultan himself.

LELA MANJA

[lit. Pampered Lela]
B&W – Malay
Directed by Jamil Sulong.
Produced by Malay Film Productions.
With Ahmad Mahmud, Zaiton,
Jins Shamsuddin, Aziz Satar,
Rosnani Jamil, Normadiah,
A. Rahim, Haji Mahadi,
Bat Latiff, Habibah Harun.

MEGAT TERAWIS

B&W – Malay
Directed by Dhiresh Ghosh [India].
Produced by Malay Film Productions.
With Ahmad Mahmud (Megat Terawis),
Jins Shamsuddin (Megat Sari),
Hashimah Yon, Normadiah (Tengku Kamariah),
Haji Mahadi, A. Rahim,
S. Kadarisman, Kemat Hassan,
Shariff Dol.

Megat Terawis and Megat Sari are the two sons of Paduka Haji, a commoner who happens to be married to Princess Kamariah, the younger sister of the Sultan. Although the Sultan himself has consented to the marriage, his younger brother, Prince Long, who is Prime Minister of the Sultanate, is still not able to accept the idea that his sister is married to a commoner.

NOOR ISLAM

(a.k.a. Nur Islam)
[lit. The Light of Islam]
B&W – Malay
Directed by K. M. Basker [India].
Produced by Cathay-Keris.
Edited by Hussain Haniff.
Music by Zubir Said.
Dance choreography by Rose Eberwein.
With Mahmood June (Panglima Merah Hitam),
Shariff Medan (Murshid),
Salmah Ahmad (Tengku Katna Suri),
Nordin Ahmad (Tengku Bada),
Siput Serawak (Melok),
Mat Sentol, Rahman Ali,
Dollah Serawak, Yem.
In pre-Islamic Malaya, paganism still rules. The first Muslims are forced to hide and worship secretly, until a prince, Tengku Bada, joins them. With his support, the teachings of Islam are brought to the whole population and to the king, who, in the end, adopts it as the official state religion. The story is slightly stereotypical, but the pagan dances are beautifully choreographed, shot and edited.

PAK PANDIR MODERN

B&W – Malay
Directed by J. Cabin Yoo
(a.k.a. J. Cabin Yeo, a.k.a. Kaben Yeo).
Produced by Cathay-Keris.
Original story by H. Asby.
Screenplay by J. Cabin Yoo.
Edited by Hussain Haniff.
Music by J. Dodo Mailinger.
Lyrics by Rahim Hamid.
With Puteh Lawak (Pak Pandir),
Roomai Noor, Mat Sentol,
Wahid Sateh, M. Amin,
Osman Pendek, Ros Yatimah,
Aman Belon, Dollah Sarawak,
Shariff Medan.
Pak Pandir brings up his four children in a strict manner: early to bed, early to rise, no mixing with the opposite sex, no relationship with the commoners, etc. But, behind his back, his grown-up children discreetly befriend people from the neighbouring village.

PERTARUNGAN

[lit. Duel]
B&W – Malay
Directed by Omar Rojik.
Produced by Malay Film Productions.
With Aziz Jaafar, Zaiton, Jins Shamsuddin, Normadiah,
S. Kadarisman, Salleh Kamil.

PUTERA SANGKAR MAUT

[lit. Prince of the Death Trap]
B&W – Malay
Directed by Dhiresh Ghosh [India].
Produced by Malay Film Productions.
With Aziz Jaafar, Saadiah, Zaiton, M. Rafee, Jins Shamsuddin,
A. Rahim, Saamah.

SHI ZI CHENG

(a.k.a. Lion City,
a.k.a. Bandar Raya Singapura,
meaning Singapore City)
106 min – B&W – Mandarin
Directed by Yi Sui (a.k.a. Tang Pak Chee).
Produced by Cathay-Keris.
A young woman from a poor family works in a clothes factory in Singapore. She meets a young man from a wealthy family. Not knowing what to do, and trying not to fall in love too fast, she hesitates and decides to take a few days off to visit her family in Muar. This movie, shot entirely in Malayan-style Mandarin, is Cathay-Keris' attempt to make a movie about and for the Chinese population of Singapore. It is loaded with excellent location shots, giving it great documentary value. There are numerous panoramic and travelling shots, including Mount Faber, the port, the first HDBs, factories, schools, etc. It also documents the modernisation process, including the first jukeboxes, pinballs, convertibles, etc.

SUMPAH WANITA

(a.k.a. A Woman's Vow)
B&W – Malay
Directed by Omar Rojik.
Produced by Malay Film Productions.
With Aziz Jaafar, Hashimah Yon, Jins Shamsuddin,
Normadiah, Aziz Satar, M. Zain.

TUNANG PAK DUKUN

[lit. Pak Dukun's Fiancéée]
B&W – Malay
Directed by S. Roomai Noor.
Produced by Cathay-Keris.
With Abdullah Chik (Karim),
Rose Yatimah (Tijah), Mahmud June.
Two medical students, Karim and Tijah, fall in love at university. Unfortunately, when they go back to their village, Tijah discovers that she has been matchmade to the local medicine man.

1961

ALI BABA BUJANG LAPOK

[lit. Ali Baba, Confirmed Bachelor]
B&W – Malay
Directed by P. Ramlee.
Produced by Malay Film Productions.
Screenply by P. Ramlee.
With Aziz Satar (Ali Baba), P. Ramlee (Chief Abu Hassan),
S. Shamsuddin (Kassim Baba), Normadiah (Siti Aloya),
K. Fatimah (Norsiah), Leng Husein, Ibrahim Pendek, Sarimah.
Ali Baba, the poor brother, and Kassim Baba, his rich brother, live in Baghdad. Ali Baba has to beg for food from his brother. One day, while collecting wood in the forest, Ali Baba sees a group of thieves heading towards a huge stone mountain. Once in front of it, the chief of the thieves mumbles some magic words, and the entrance to a secret cave, where they hide their loot, opens.

ANEKA HIBURAN & RAHSIA KEJADIAN

[lit. All Kinds of Entertainment and Secret Events]
B&W – Malay
Directed by S. Kadarisman and C. C. Kok.
Produced by Malay Film Productions.

GADO GADO

[Note: Name of a famous Malay dish, also means all mixed up]
B&W – Malay
Directed by S. Roomai Noor.
Produced by Cathay-Keris.
With Wahid Satay, Mahmud June,
Aman Belon, Siti Tanjung Perak.
A medium-length film, comprising a series of sketches by Wahid Satay.

HANG JEBAT

B&W – Malay
Directed by Hussain Haniff.
Produced by Cathay-Keris.
With Nordin Ahmad (Hang Jebat), M. Amin (Hang Tuah),
Latifah Omar (Dang Baru), Mahmud June (Pateh Karmawijaya),
Rosnani Jamil (Permaisuri), Siput Sarawak, Abdullah Sani.
Hang Jebat and Hang Tuah are best friends. When the Sultan decides to send Hang Tuah into exile, Hang Jebat feels betrayed. Outraged, he runs amok in the city, killing people and seeking revenge on the Sultan.

INDERA BANGSAWAN

(a.k.a. Twin Princes)
B&W – Malay
Directed by Dhiresh Ghosh [India].
Produced by Malay Film Productions.
With Jins Shamsuddin, Sarimah, Saadiah, Kuswadinata,
Haji Majadi, K. Fatimah, S. Kadarisman, Habsah,
Malik Sutan Muda.

JALAK LENTENG

B&W – Malay
Directed by Salleh Ghani.
Produced by Cathay-Keris.
With Yusof Latiff, Latifah Omar, Mahmud June.

Pak Pandir Modern, 1960

LELA SATRIA

B&W – Malay
Directed by S. Roomai Noor.
Produced by Cathay-Keris.
With Mahmud June, Fatimah Ahmad.

MAS MERAH

[lit. Red Gold]
B&W – Malay
Directed by Dhiresh Ghosh [India].
Produced by Malay Film Productions.
With Ahmad Mahmud, Saadiah, Sri Dewi, A. Rahim, Habsah,
Saamah, Salleh Kamil, Kemat Hassan, Malik Sutan Muda.

PANJI SEMERANG

B&W – Malay
Directed by Omar Rojik.
Produced by Malay Film Productions.
With Saadiah, Aziz Jaafar,
S. Kadarisman, Dayang Sofia,
Normadiah.

PUTERI GUNUNG LEDANG

[lit. The Princess of Mount Ledang]
B&W – Malay
Directed by S. Roomai Noor.
Produced by Cathay-Keris.
Music by Zubir Said.
With Elaine Edley (Puteri Gunung Ledang),
Mazlan Ahmad, Fatimah Ahmad,
Wahid Satay, Puteh Lawak,
Mahmud June, Haji Harshad,
Yem, Abdullah Sani.

Sultan Mahmud Shah wants to marry the Princess Gunung Ledang.
He sends Hang Tuah and Tun Mamat as his representatives to ask
for her hand in marriage. The Princess accepts, but in return makes
several strange requests that she wants to see satisfied prior to
the wedding.

SENIMAN BUJANG LAPOK

(a.k.a. The Nitwit Movie Stars)
[lit. The Bachelor Actors]
B&W – Malay
Directed by P. Ramlee.
Produced by Malay Film Productions.
Story by P. Ramlee.
Screenplay by H. M. Rohaizad.
With P. Ramlee (Ramli), Aziz Satar (Aziz),
S. Shamsuddin (Sudin), Saloma (Salmah),
Zaiton (Zaiton), Ahmad Nisfu (the film director),
Kemat Hassan (the studio head),
Ahmad Mahmud (the doctor),
M. Zain (Jiran India), S. Kadarisman,
Siti Tanjung Perak.

Ramli, Aziz and Sudin are a crazy trio facing daily problems in the
crowded boarding house where they live. Jobless and penniless,
they decide to go for a screen test, hoping to be movie stars.

SI TANGGANG

B&W – Malay
Directed by Jamil Sulong.
Produced by Malay Film Productions.
With Jins Shamsuddin, Sarimah, Haji Mahadi, Zaiton,
Normadiah, Salleh Kamil, S. Kadarisman.

SITI ZUBAIDAH

B&W – Malay
Directed by B. N. Rao [India].
Produced by Cathay-Keris and Maria Menado Production.
With Maria Menado, Nordin Ahmad, Siput Sarawak,
M. Amin, Mahmud June, Rose Yatimah, Mat Sentol.

After landing on an island while on a sea voyage, Sultan Zainal
Abidin encounters a woman who has a mesmerising voice. He
asks her to marry him.

SRI MERSING

B&W – Malay
Directed by Salleh Ghani.
Produced by Cathay-Keris.
With Nordin Ahmad (Damaq), Rosnani Jamil (Sri),
Rose Yatimah, Mahmud June, Mustapha Maarof.

Damaq decides to start a new life in another village, where he
proves to be someone having integrity and honesty. One day, he
rescues Sri, a very beautiful woman from the village, from the
chauvinistic Awang. He is forced to participate in a duel. Awang
loses, but he takes revenge on Damaq, creating a slanderous story
which forces Damaq and his family to leave the village.

SRI TANJUNG

B&W – Malay
Directed by Jamil Sulong.
Produced by Malay Film Productions.
With Ahmad Mahmud, Hashimah Yon,
Bat Latiff, Normadiah, Omar Suwita,
Rahma Rahmat, Haji Mahadi, Malik Sutan Muda.

Two orphans are forced out of their home by their merciless
stepmother. They manage to survive in the village by selling cakes
and doing domestic work.

SULTAN MAHMUD MANGKAT DI-JULANG

[lit. Sultan Mahmud Passed Away and is Carried]
B&W – Malay
Directed by K. M. Basker [India].
Produced by Cathay-Keris.
Story and screenplay by Salleh Ghani.
Music by Zubir Said.
Dance choreography by Siput Sarawak.
With Noordin Ahmad, Maria Menado,
M. Amin, Siput Sarawak, Mustapha Maarof,
Mahmood June, Mariani, Wahid Satay,
Dolah Sarawak, Yem.

In Malacca, during the golden days of the sultanate, Datuk Megat
Seri Rama successfully defeats a gang of pirates. Thrilled by this
victory, Sultan Mahmud promotes him to the title of Datuk Laksmana.
But one of the ministers, Tun Bija Ali, becomes very envious of
Datuk Laksmana Megat. His jealousy becomes even deeper when
Datuk Laksmana Megat is about to marry a beautiful lady from
the Sultan's court.

SUMPITAN RACUN

[lit. The Poisonous Blowpipe]
B&W – Malay
Directed by S. Roomai Noor.
Produced by Cathay-Keris.
With S. Roomai Noor, Latifah Omar, Mary Lim.

TANGGAL

[lit. Take Off]
B&W – Malay
Directed by S. Kadarisman.
Produced by Malay Film Productions.
With Ahmad Mahmud, Noor Azizah,
S. Kadarisman, Mahyon Ismail,
Hussein Abu Hassan, Nor Sabariah.

YATIM MUSTAPHA

[lit. Orphan Mustapha]
B&W – Malay
Directed by B. N. Rao [India].
Produced by Cathay-Keris.
With Nordin Ahmad, Siput Sarawak, Umi Kalsom, Salmah Ahmad,
Abdullah Chik, Mustapha Maarof, Abu Bakar Yem.

In a faraway kingdom, the third queen becomes very envious of
the youngest queen, who is obviously the king's favourite. She
thus plots against her, putting together a scheme in which the
king is poisoned and the youngest queen is accused of the crime.

1962

BADANG

B&W – Malay
Directed by S. Roomai Noor.
Produced by Cathay-Keris.
Screenplay by M. Amin.
Dialogue by S. Roomai Noor.
Music by Zubir Said.
Indian dances by the Bhaskar's Academy of Dance.
With Wahid Satay (Badang), Zainal Gemok (Bakong),
Rose Yatimah (Tengku Manis), Umi Kalthoum (Anak Penghulu),
Shariff Medan (Tengku Bendahara),
Dollah Sarawak (Datuk Penghulu), Yem (The Sultan),
Siti Tanjung Perak (Permaisuri), Mariam, Ani Jasmin, Udo Omar.

Badang, a rather weak man from the village, encounters a monstrous
spirit of the forest who makes him eat his vomit so as to pass on
to him some supernatural force. Badang returns to the village
strong as an elephant, able to uproot a tree with only one hand.
But to retain his strength, he must not marry, or else he will die in
atrocious pain. Hearing about his feats, the Sultan summons him
to his court. There, Badang meets a beautiful girl who falls in love
with him. A rather silly movie, especially the monster scenes, but
beautifully shot, with very interesting jungle locations.

BATU DURHAKA

[lit. Traitorous Stone]
B&W – Malay
Directed by Omar Rojik.
Produced by Malay Film Productions.
With Jins Shamsuddin, Sarimah, Aziz Jaafar, S. Kadarisman,
Kemat Hassan, Kuswadinata, Rahmah Rahmat, Sri Dewi,
Malik Sutan Muda, Suraya, Saamah.

Sri Mersing, 1961

Dang Anom, 1962

BLACK GOLD

Directed by Yi Sui (a.k.a. Tang Pak Chee).
Produced by Cathay-Keris.

CELORONG CELORENG

B&W – Malay
Directed by S. Roomai Noor.
Produced by Cathay-Keris.
With Wahid Satay, Latifah Omar,
Siti Tanjung Perak.

Crown Prince Derma Kesuma refuses to marry a Princess from another country, because her father has been at war against his own father. He then flees the palace and he marries Harum Cendana, a woman that he is attracted to. However, one day, Harum Cendana, now his wife, is captured by pirates. Derma, together with his friends, Celoreng and Celorong, embarks on a quest, searching for her.

DANG ANOM

B&W – Malay
Directed by Hussein Haniff.
Produced by Cathay-Keris.
With Fatimah Ahmad (Dang Anom),
Nordin Ahmad, Mahmud June,
M. Amin, Rose Yatimah,
Yusoff Latiff.

Dang Anom, the daughter of Sang Rajuna Tapa, is engaged to Panglima Malang. However, the Sultan, who is obsessed with women, soon falls in love with her and forces her to becoome one of his numerous concubines. Panglima Malang manages to sneak into the palace for a secret meeting with his beloved Dang Anom. Unfortunately, they are caught meeting each other and sentenced to death by the Sultan. In order to save his daughter from being put to death, Sang Rajuna Tapa opens the gates of the palace and lets in the Majapahit army.

GERHANA

[lit. Eclipse]
B&W – Malay
Directed by Jamil Sulong.
Produced by Malay Film Productions.
With Ahmad Mahmud, Zaiton,
Haji Mahadi, Bat Latiff,
Rahmah Rahmat,
Saamah, Habsah.

IBU MERTUAKU

(a.k.a. My Mother-in-law)
B&W – Malay
Directed by P. Ramlee.
Produced by Malay Film Productions.
Story by Ahmad Nisfu.
Screenplay by P. Ramlee.
With Sarimah (Sabariah Mansoor), P. Ramlee (Kassim Selamat),
Ahmad Mahmud (Doctor Ismadi), Mak Dara (Nyonya Mansoor),
Amhad Nisfu (Mamak Maidin), Zainon Fiji (Mami).

Kassim Selamat is a talented saxophonist and famous singer adored by his female fans. When one fan, Sabariah Mansoor, makes a courageous effort to phone him and then meet him, it is love at first sight. But Sabariah's mother, Nyonya Mansoor, strongly disapproves. She wants her daughter to marry Doctor Ismadi instead of a musician. Sabariah and Kassim get married nevertheless, and leave Singapore to settle down in Penang. When Sabariah becomes pregnant, she is taken back to Singapore by her mother, while Kassim stays on in Penang. Nyonya Mansoor, still unhappy with their marriage, sends a false telegram to Kassim stating that Sabariah passed away while giving birth. Kassim is so devastated that he cries until he loses his vision and becomes blind. Symbolically, the film opens to the sound of a radio saying "Inilah Radio Singapura" (This is Radio Singapore), and contains many interesting location shots of the modernising city in the early 1960s.

JULA JULI BINTANG TUJUH

[name of main character, also lit. Jula Juli Seventh Star]
B&W – Malay
Directed by B. N. Rao [India].
Produced by Cathay-Keris.

KORBAN KASEH

[lit. Sacrifice of love]
B&W – Malay
Directed by Hussain Haniff.
Produced by Cathay-Keris.
With Yusoff Latiff (Ariffin), Fatimah Ahmad (Marhaini),
Sipot Serawak (Zainab), Yem, Dollah Serawak,
Siti Tanjong Perak, Zahara Selamat.

LABU DAN LABI

(a.k.a. Labu and Labi)
B&W – Malay
Directed by P. Ramlee.
Produced by Malay Film Productions.
Story by S. Kadarisman.
Screenplay by S. Sudarmaji.
Dialogue by P. Ramlee.
Music and songs by P. Ramlee.
With Mohamed Zain (Labu, Doktor, Tarzan, Jesse Labu, etc.),
P. Ramlee (Labi, Majistret, Harimau, Sheriff, and also as himself),
Mariani (Manisah), Udo Omar (Haji Bakhil, Pelayan Kelab, Monyet,
Pelayan Bar, etc.), Rahimah Alias (Isteri Haji Bakhil),
Saloma (as herself), Sarimah (as herself), Aziz Satar (as himself).

Haji Bakhil (whose name means "stingy") has two servants, Labu the cook, and Labi the driver. The two of them are secretly in love with Haji Bakhil's daughter, Manisah. Little do they know they are in love with the same woman. At night, Labu and Labi discuss their dreams, wondering what it would be like to be rich and famous. They start fantasising about being Tarzan, a cowboy, a doctor, a magistrate... The opening credits show interesting shots of the Sultan Mosque, the Capitol Theatre, Middle Road, etc.

LAILA MAJNUN

B&W – Malay
Directed by B. N. Rao [India].
Produced by Cathay-Keris.
With Nordin Ahmad (Qais), Latifah Omar (Laila),
Umi Kalthom, Ahmad Nisfu, Abu Bakar, Habibah Harun.

Laila is the daughter of a rich man, Amir, whereas Qais is the son of the poor Amri. Both Laila and Qais are in love, even though it seems impossible for them to fulfil their desires. This is one more adaptation of the traditional *majnun* lover story, mixing both *The One Thousand Nights* and *Romeo and Juliet*, together with strong Indian influences.

LANCHANG KUNING

(a.k.a. Yellow Sailboat)
B&W – Malay
Directed by M. Amin.
Produced by Cathay-Keris.
With Nordin Ahmad, Latifah Omar, Yusof Latiff,
Haji Arshad, Rose Yatimah.

Seeking revenge on a woman who does not reciprocate his love, Dato Ali lies to the Sultan by telling him that misfortune awaits him and his kingdom if the sacrificial ritual of a pregnant woman is not performed soon.

LUBALANG DAIK

B&W – Malay
Directed by Jamil Sulong.
Produced by Malay Film Productions.
With Aziz Jaafar, Sarimah, Jins Shamsuddin, S. Kadarisman,
Rosnani Jamil, Normadiah, A. Rahim, Haji Mahadi, Habsah,
Saamah.

MABOK KEPAYANG

B&W – Malay
Directed by Hussain Haniff.
Produced by Cathay-Keris.
With Wahid Satay (Ahmad), Ani Jasmin (Ahmad's mother),
Siti Tanjung Perak.

Ahmad and Aminah are together against the will of their families. When Ahmad has to leave the village for the city, Aminah is courted by a rich man.

MATA SHAITAN

(a.k.a. Mata Syaitan)
[lit. Eyes of the Devil]
B&W – Malay
Directed by Hussain Haniff.
Produced by Cathay-Keris.
With Yusoff Latiff, Fatimah Ahmad, Sipot Serawak,
Dollah Serawak, Siti Tanjung Perak, Ghazali Sumantri,
Yem B. Jaffar, Rahmah Ali.

NORLELA

B&W – Malay
Directed by Dhiresh Ghosh [India].
Produced by Malay Film Productions.
With Aziz Jaafar, Sarimah, Murni Sarawak,
S. Kadarisman, Salleh Kamil, Kuswadinata,
M. Rafee, Omar Suwita.

SINGAPURA DILANGGAR TODAK

(a.k.a. Swordfish Attack on Singapore)
B&W – Malay
Directed by Omar Rojik.
Produced by Malay Film Productions.
With Aziz Jaafar, Hashimah Yon, S. Kadarisman,
Kuswadinata, Bat Latiff, M. Babjan.
In 13th-century Singapore, mysterious events start occurring,
threatening the island and its people.

SITI MUSLIHAT

Directed by Dhiresh Ghosh [India].
Produced by Malay Film Productions.
With Ahmad Mahmud, Saadiah, Shariff Dol, Ahmad Nisfu,
Aziz Satar, Ibrahim Pendek, Mariani, Kemat Hassan,
Mohamed Zain, S. Shamsuddin.
A maid marries the King of Indera Permai. She is the source of
great support to him throughout his reign.

TUN FATIMAH

B&W – Malay
Directed by Salleh Ghani.
Produced by Cathay-Keris.
Story by Mazah Hussein.
Screenplay by Salleh Ghani.
Music by Zubir Said.
With Maria Menado (Tun Fatimah), Noordin Ahmad, Yusoff Latiff,
Rose Yatimah, Yem, Shariff Medan, Noorzeham, Ghazali Sumantri,
Mat Sentol, Rahmah Ali.
Tun Fatimah is a high-spirited female warrior. She becomes
actively involved in defending the kingdom of Malacca against the
Portuguese (played by poorly disguised Malay actors). Based upon
a historical figure recorded in the 17th-century Malay Annals.

Tun Fatimah, 1962

YOU KOW PIK YING

(a.k.a. Ask and It shall be Given,
potentially a.k.a. To Ask is to Obtain)
B&W – Cantonese
Directed by (unknown).
Said to be produced by Ho Ah Loke on his own, during
his days in between Cathay-Keris and Merdeka Studio.
A movie of which the print has been lost long ago. It is said
to have been entirely shot in Malaysia, in Cantonese. Another
title is sometimes mentioned, i.e. *A Wish Comes True*, but it
is not clear whether it is the same movie or a different one.

1963

BAYANGAN DI WAKTU FAJAR

[lit. A Shadow at Dawn]
B&W – Malay
Directed by Usmar Usmail.
Produced by Cathay-Keris.
With S. Roomai Noor, Latifah Omar.

BUDI DAN DOSA

[lit. Good and Evil]
B&W – Malay
Directed by Jamil Sulong.
Produced by Malay Film Productions.
With Jins Shamsuddin, Zaiton, Hashimah Yon,
Haji Mahadi, Zainon Fiji, Kuswadinata.

BUNGA TANJUNG

B&W – Malay
Directed by Ramon Estella [Philippines].
Produced by Cathay-Keris.

CHEMPAKA BIRU

[lit. Blue Magnolia]
B&W – Malay
Directed by B. N. Rao [India].
Produced by Cathay-Keris.
With Ghazali Sumantri, Suraya Harun, Rose Yatimah, Yem.
A Sultan dies while still looking for his daughter who had been
abducted by pirates many years ago. But the Sultan's body cannot
be buried until the Princess is found. Thus, an army led by Wan
Perkasa is sent to search for her.

CHUCHU DATUK MERAH

(a.k.a. Datuk Merah's Grandson)
B&W – Malay
Directed by M. Amin.
Produced by Cathay-Keris.
Music by Zubir Said.
With Noordin Ahmad (Awang), Latifah Omar, Rose Yatimah,
A. Rahim, Yem Jaafar, Dollah Sarawak, Rahimah Alias.
Awang Janggut has always been proud of being the grandson of
Datuk Merah, a well-known admiral much respected in Terengganu.
He refuses to work as a labourer like others in the village, preferring
to live in poverty with his wife. Awang trains fighting cocks as a
hobby. One day, Awang rescues the lovely Siti while she is being
harrassed by a man from a neighbouring village. Siti then persuades
her rich father to hire Awang as the family bodyguard.

DARAH MUDA

(a.k.a. Young in Heart)
[lit. Young Blood]
B&W – Malay
by Jamil Sulong.
Produced by Malay Film Productions.
With Jins Shamsuddin, Sarimah, Salleh Kamil, Mariani,
S. Kadarisman, Mislia, Omar Suwita.
In Kuala Lumpur, Fauziah is left alone to look after her ageing father.
Her brother Zohari is of no help to her since he is totally controlled by
his selfish, high-maintenance wife, Ramlah. When her father finally
dies, only Yazid, whom she met recently, helps her. Fauziah and
Yazid fall in love and marry. When Yazid is transferred to Singapore,
they move into a beautiful house with all the modern comforts,
making Zohari and Ramlah extremely jealous.

DARAHKU

[lit. My Blood]
B&W – Malay
Directed by Ramon Estella [Philippines].
Produced by Cathay-Keris and
Maria Menado Production.
With Maria Menado, Malik Selamat.

GILA TALAK

[lit. Crazy]
B&W – Malay
Directed by Hussein Haniff.
Produced by Cathay-Keris.
With Wahid Satay, Fatimah Ahmad,
Yusoff Latiff, Dollah Sarawak,
Siti Tanjung Perak, Umi Kalthom.

GUL BAKAWALI

B&W – Malay
Directed by B. N. Rao [India].
Produced by Cathay-Keris.
With Noordin Ahmad,
Latifah Omar.

KASEH TANPA SAYANG

(a.k.a. Love's Dilemma)
[lit. Love without Tenderness]
B&W – Malay
Directed by Omar Rojik.
Produced by Malay Film Productions.
With Ahmad Mahmud, Hashimah Yon,
Normadiah, Aziz Jaafar, Rosnani Jamil,
Mohamed Zain, Habsah, Omar Suwita,
Ibrahim Pendek.
A family that places too much importance on money is unable to
cope with a love issue when it arises.

KORBAN

[lit. Sacrifice]
B&W – Malay
Directed by Dhiresh Ghosh [India].
Produced by Malay Film Productions.
With Ahmad Mahmud, Saadiah,
S. Kadarisman, Mariani, Zaiton,
Kuswadinata, Omar Suwita,
Bat Latiff.

MASUK ANGIN KELUAR ASAP

(a.k.a. Love Crazy)
[lit. Wind Goes in, Smoke Comes out]
B&W – Malay
Directed by Hussein Haniff.
Produced by Cathay-Keris.
With Wahid Satay, Fatimah Ahmad,
Yusoff Latiff, Dollah Sarawak,
Siti Tanjung Perak,
Udo Omar, Mat Sentol.

NASIB SI LABU LABI

[lit. Labu and Labi's Luck]
B&W – Malay
Directed by P. Ramlee.
Produced by Malay Film Productions.
With P. Ramlee (Labi, Joe Labi),
Mohamed Zain (Labu, Rocky Labu),
Udo Omar (Haji Bakhil), Mariani (Manisah),
Ibrahim Pendek (Haji Ibrahim),
Murni Sarawak (Murniyati), S. Sudarmaji.
After Haji Bakhil's wife dies, the whole family grieves, even Labu the driver and Labi the cook. Soon, Murniyati, a teacher at the orphanage nearby, rekindles Haji Bakhil's will to live. When she approaches Haji Bakhil for a donation, he swiftly obliges, even though he is normally famous for his stinginess. He also starts dressing up, and buys a new car. At the same time, Labu and Labi finally find out that all these years they have been secretly in love with the same woman, Manisah, Haji Bakhil's daughter.

NERACHA

(a.k.a. The Scales)
B&W – Malay
Directed by Dhiresh Ghosh [India].
Produced by Malay Film Productions.
With Jins Shamsuddin (Rahman), Sarimah, Aziz Jaafar,
S. Kadarisman, Murni Sarawak, Malik Sutan Muda.
Rahman makes a small living out of his job as a clerk. He has hardly any money to pay for his son's needs. When his sons falls ill, he cannot even afford the doctor. In desperation, he steals from his employer's safety box. Soon, he becomes a runaway, and is chased by the police. Rahman manages to sneak out of Singapore, and ends up in Pahang, where he is mistaken for Hussein, the long missing prodigal son of a wealthy family. Rahman takes on Hussein's identity and gets remarried.

PILIH MENANTU

[lit. Choosing a Daughter-in-law]
Directed by Omar Rojik.
Produced by Malay Film Productions.
With Aziz Jaafar, Sarimah, Mohamed Zain,
Sofia Dayang, Habsah, Ahmad Nisfu, Udo Omar, Mustarjo.

PONTIANAK KEMBALI

(a.k.a. The Vampire Returns)
B&W – Malay
Directed by Ramon Estella [Philippines].
Produced by Cathay-Keris and Maria Menado Productions.
With Malik Selamat, Maria Menado.

RAJA BERSIONG

(a.k.a. The King with the Fangs)
B&W – Malay
Directed by K. M. Basker [India].
Produced by Cathay-Keris and Maria Menado Productions.
Music by Ismadi.
With Maria Menado, Malek Selamat, Eddy Ali,
Marsita, Izat Emir, and the Wai Ki Ki Girl.
Unhappy with his life, a king feels bloodthirsty, and he turns into a monster.

RUMAH ITU DUNIAKU

(a.k.a. My Home, My World)
[lit. That House is My World]
B&W – Malay
Directed by M. Amin.
Produced by Cathay-Keris.
Original story by Hamzah Hussein.
Screenplay and dialogue by M. Amin.
With S. Roomai Noor, Latifah Omar, Malik Selamat,
Rose Yatimah, Tony Kassim.
A young woman works in her father and stepmother's home as a servant.

TAJUL ASHIKIN

B&W – Malay
Directed by M. Amin.
Produced by Cathay-Keris.
With Nordin Ahmad, Rose Yatimah.
Prince Ibrahim wants to see the world with his own eyes. One day, he decides to leave his hometown without his father, the king, knowing. Disguising himself as a merchant named Tajul Ashikin, he meets a young woman in the streets and falls in love with her.

Kalong Kenangan, 1964

1964

AYER MATA DUYONG

(a.k.a. Air Mata Duyung)
[lit. Tears of the Mermaid]
B&W – Malay
Directed by M. Amin.
Produced by Cathay-Keris.
With Nordin Ahmad, Suraya Haron, Malik Selamat,
Neng Yatimah, Salina, Rohani Yusoff.
Awang is a young fighter. When he wins a competition organised by the Sultan, his life changes. Soon, he falls in love with the Sultan's daughter, Intan. But on their wedding day, Intan is cursed, and becomes a mermaid.

DUA PENDEKAR

[lit. Two Warriors]
B&W – Malay
Directed by Hussain Haniff.
Produced by Cathay-Keris.
With Yusoff Latiff, Salleh Melan, Rose Yatimah,
Dollah Serawak, Siti Tanjung Perak.
The new Sultan abuses his own people, taking advantage of them, turning them almost into slaves. Only Adam is wiling to stand up and fight. Beautifully shot (especially the opening scene), it is very carefully edited, showing Hussain Haniff's craft at its best.

DUPA CHENDANA

[lit. The Sandalwood Incense]
B&W – Malay
Directed by Ramon Estella [Philippines].
Produced by Malay Film Productions.
With Ahmad Mahmud, Saadiah, Mariani, Aziz Jaafar, S. Kadarisman.

HUTANG DARAH DIBAYAR DARAH

[lit. A Blood Debt Paid with Blood]
B&W – Malay
Directed by Hussain Haniff.
Produced by Cathay-Keris.
With Nordin Ahmad, Rose Yatimah.

ISTANA BERDARAH

[lit. The Palace of Blood]
B&W – Malay
Directed by Hussain Haniff.
Produced by Cathay-Keris.
With Yusoff Latiff, Fatimah Ahmad, Salleh Melan.
Adapted from Shakespeare's *Macbeth*.

JERITAN BATIN

[lit. The Soul Screams]
B&W – Malay
Directed by Omar Rojik.
Produced by Malay Film Productions.
With Ahmad Mahmud, Saadiah, Aziz Jaafar, Normadiah,
Haji Mahadi, Omar Suwita, Aziz Satar.

KALONG KENANGAN

[lit. The Necklace of Nostalgia]
B&W – Malay
Directed by Hussain Haniff.
Produced by Cathay-Keris.
With Latiffah Omar, Ghazali Sumantri, Haji Arshad, Umi Kalthom,
Rahmah Ali, Tony Kassim, Yem, Dollah Serawak.

MADU TIGA

[lit. Third Wife]
B&W – Malay
Directed by P. Ramlee.
Produced by Malay Film Productions.
Story by S. Kadarisman.
Screenplay and dialogue by P. Ramlee.
Music by P. Ramlee.
Songs by Saloma and P. Ramlee.
With P. Ramlee (Jamil), Sarimah (Rohani, the third wife),
Jah Mahadi (Hasnah, the second wife),
Zahara Agus (Latifah, the first wife), Ahmad Nesfu (Haji Latiff),
M. Rafee (Rafee), Mislia, Zainon Fiji.
Jamil works in a bank as an associate. Already married to Latifah, he decides to get a second wife, Hasnah, without his first wife's permission. When Latifah comes to know about it, she makes a huge fuss, creating chaos. Jamil runs away, spending a few days on his own. When he returns, he pretends to have been badly injured in an accident to gain his wives' sympathy. When everything is calm again, he encounters Rohani and falls in love with her at first sight. Jamil decides to take her as his third wife. The film is loaded with excellent location shots of Singapore: the Standard Chartered Bank building, the Fitzpatrick's chain store with some 1960s chi chi tai tais, the Hotel Ambassador, the Shaw House, and long travelling shots of the city streets.

MAMBANG MODEN

[lit. Modern Partner]
B&W – Malay
Directed by Jamil Sulong.
Produced by Malay Film Productions.
Music by Osman Ahmad and Yusof B.
With Saadiah, Aziz Jaafar, Dayang Sofia, Omar Suwita,
H.M. Busra, M. Rafee, Ali Fiji, Momo Latif, Udo Omar.
A few young people try their luck at singing. It is the 1960s,
the heydays of *pop yeh yeh*, and the guitar, the Converse,
rock 'n' roll music, the convertible car, etc.

MAT TIGA SUKU

(a.k.a. Mat 3/4, a.k.a. Crazy Mat)
B&W – Malay
Directed by Mat Sentol.
Produced by Cathay-Keris.
With Mat Sentol, Noraini, Wahid Satay.

Mat is unlucky in life. He cannot catch a bus, enter a house, drink
water from the tap or make some tea without some mishap or
other. And he has ghosts in his bedroom.

MELANCHONG KE TOKYO

[lit. Going to Tokyo]
B&W – Malay
Directed by Ramon Estella [Philippines].
Produced by Malay Film Productions.
With Aziz Jaafar, Saadiah, S. Kadarisman,
Asao Mutsumoto, Motoko Furakawa, Normadiah.

PANGLIMA BESI

[lit. Commandant of Iron]
B&W – Malay
Directed by M. Amin.
Produced by Cathay-Keris.
With Nordin Ahmad, Rose Yatimah, M. Wari.

PONTIANAK GUA MUSANG

(a.k.a. The Vampire of the Cave,
a.k.a. The Vampire of the Civet-cat Cave)
B&W – Malay
Directed by B. N. Rao [India].
Produced by Cathay-Keris.
Music by Zubir Said.
With Suraya, Malek Selamat, Ghazali Sumantri, Wahid Satay,
Mat Sentol, Alias Congo, Chinta Yem, Siput Sarawak.
One more adventure of the pontianak, and the last shot by B. N.
Rao. The pontianak is a miserable woman turned vampire. She
tries to protect her careless daughter who often goes wandering
in the jungle. However, there are actually very few monsters in
this movie.

SIAPA BESAR

[lit. Who is the Great One]
B&W – Malay
Directed by Omar Rojik.
Produced by Malay Film Productions.
With Aziz Satar, Zaiton, Normadiah, Udo Omar, Ibrahim Pendek,
Ahmad Daud, S. Shamsuddin.

TIGA ABDUL

[lit. The Three Abduls]
B&W – Malay
Directed by P. Ramlee.
Produced by Malay Film Productions.
Screenplay and dialogue by P. Ramlee.
With P. Ramlee (Abdul Wahub),
Haji Mahadi (Abdul Wahab),
S. Kadarisman (Abdul Wahib),
Ahmad Nisfu (Sadiq Segaraga),
Sarimah (Ghasidah),
Mariani (Hamidah),
Dayang Sofia (Rafidah).
Two brothers, Abdul Wahab and Abdul Wahib, conspire to
cheat their youngest brother, Abdul Wahub, out of his share
of the inheritance left to them by their recently-deceased father.
But Abdul Wahab and Abdul Wahib are tricked into marrying
the two daughters of a greedy businessman, Sadiq Segaraga,
who swiftly cheats them out of their wealth. It is then left up
to Abdul Wahub to recover the family's fortune. This movie is
based on a traditional Malay fable.

TUN MANDAN

B&W – Malay
Directed by Salleh Ghani.
Produced by Malay Film Productions.
With Salmah Ahmad, Abdullah Chik,
Rosemawati, Mustapha Maarof.

Aksi Kuching, 1966

WAN PERKASA

B&W – Malay
Directed by Nordin Ahmad.
Produced by Cathay-Keris.
With M. Amin, Latifah Omar,
Malik Selamat, Siput Sarawak,
Tony Kassim, Dollah Sarawak.
Linggi is having an affair with the young village headman. One
day, he is asked to take over Wan Perkasa's position (as Wan
Perkasa has just been promoted to lead the Sultan's army). This
gives Linggi the opportunity to meet Wan Perkasa, and she tries
to seduce him.

1965

BIDASARI

B&W – Malay
Directed by Jamil Sulong.
Produced by Malay Film Productions.
Story by S. Kadarisman.
Screenplay by Jamil Sulong.
Music by Osman Ahmad and Yusoff B.
With Jins Shamsuddin, Sarimah, S. Kadarisman,
Malik Sutan Muda, Habsah, Saamah,
S. Shamsuddin, M. Rafee.
In the ancient Nusantara days, Bidasari, a beautiful young woman
is invited to sing in front of the princess. Her voice is so charming
that the princess becomes very jealous and starts bullying her,
eventually forcing her to be her servant, someone that she can
abuse anytime she likes. Slightly sadistic, this movie is perfect
for those who want to see pretty women fighting and grabbing
each other by the hair.

CHINTA KASEH SAYANG

[lit. My Darling Love]
B&W – Malay
Directed by Hussain Haniff.
Produced by Cathay-Keris.
Story by Hussain Haniff.
Music by Mellowess.
With Latiffah Omar, Fatimah Ahmad,
Ahmad Osman, Ghazali Sumantri,
Tony Kassim, Siti Tanjung Perak.
Normah is married to a painter who is more focused on his art
than on her, and she is bored. When he leaves for a trip abroad,
Jamal, a car dealer, starts courting her, and she does not reject his
advances. However, Jamal is himself married with two kids, a fact
which he keeps from her. When she finds out, she is disappointed,
but goes on flirting with other men. When her husband returns,
she shows disinterest. The movie is a very acute social study of
Singapore at the time of its independence, with all the changes
brought by modernity and Westernisation: phones, Fiat cars,
escalators, sewing machines, etc.

DAYANG SENANDONG

B&W – Malay
Directed by Jamil Sulong.
Produced by Malay Film Productions.
With Ahmad Mahmud, Sarimah, Haji Mahadi, Salleh Kamil,
Habsah, Malik Sutan Muda, Ibrahim Pendek.

IKAN EMAS

[lit. Goldfish]
B&W – Malay
Directed by M. Amin.
Produced by Cathay-Keris.
With Ghazali Sumantri, Latifah Omar, Siput Sarawak.
Kintan is being constantly abused by her stepmother and stepsister.
One day, Kintan accompanies her father on a fishing trip, and he
falls into the water and turns into a goldfish. Kintan brings the
goldfish back home, but her stepmother and stepsister accidentally
kill it. She then buries the goldfish in the garden. Soon, a golden
tree sprouts from that very same spot.

JIRAN SEKAMPONG

[lit. Village Neighbours]
B&W – Malay
Directed by Hussein Haniff.
Produced by Cathay-Keris.
Story by Hussain Haniff.
With Rose Yatimah, Ahmad Osman, Yusoff Latiff,
Siput Serawak, Tony Kassim.

The intertwined stories of the different low and middle-class families in a *kampong* (village) in Singapore in 1965. Rohani's mother, even though she has been sick, must go back to work in the bourgeois family where she serves as a maid. Saloma invites some friends home for a dance session one afternoon while her parents are out. Hassan's parents do not want him to marry Suryani because they find her too "seksi". The movie captures with great sensitivity the changing times of the mid-1960s, the clash between tradition and modernity, the growing gap between generations.

KASEH IBU

[lit. The Love of a Mother]
B&W – Malay
Directed by Nordin Ahmad.
Produced by Cathay-Keris.
With Mustapha Maarof,
Latifah Omar, Bat Latiff.

KUBUR TAK BERTANDA

[lit. An Unmarked Grave]
B&W – Malay
Directed by A. Razak.
Produced by Cathay-Keris.

MATA DAN HATI

[lit. The Eyes and the Heart]
B&W – Malay
Directed by M. Amin.
Produced by Cathay-Keris.
With Tony Kassim, Rose Yatimah,
Siput Sarawak, M. Wari.

MUDA MUDI

[lit. Youths]
B&W – Malay
Directed by M. Amin.
Produced by Cathay-Keris.
Story and screenplay by Hamzah.
Music by the Tornadoes.
With Rose Yatimah, Siput Sarawak,
Malek Selamat, Tony Kassim,
Wahid Satay, Ahmad Sabri,
Anny Jasmin.

Two actresses compete fiercely in the world of show business.

PATONG CHENDANA

[lit. The Sandalwood Doll]
B&W – Malay
Directed by M. Amin.
Produced by Cathay-Keris.
With Nordin Ahmad, Latifah Omar,
Siput Sarawak.

PUSAKA PONTIANAK

(a.k.a. The Accursed Heritage, a.k.a. The Pontianak Legacy)
B&W – Malay
Directed by Ramon Estella [Philippines].
Produced by Malay Film Productions.
Music by Yusoff B and The Swallows.
With Ahmad Mahmud, Sa'adia, Ahmad Daud, Haji Mahadi,
Normadiah, Salleh Kamil, Ibrahim Pendek, Aziz Satar,
Dayang Sofia, Mariam Bahrun.

Some people are gathered in a large mansion to share the legacy of a rich rubber tycoon. But, very soon, mysterious things start happening. The last of the pontianak movies, and also the last movie made by a Filipino director for one of the Singaporean studios.

SAYANG SI BUTA

[lit. For the Love of the Blind One]
B&W – Malay
Directed by Omar Rojik.
Produced by Malay Film Productions.
Music by Yusof B., Kassim Masoor and The Swallows.
With Jins Shamsuddin, Sarimah, Aziz Jaafar, Dayang Sofia,
Saamah, Ahmad Nisfu, Ibrahim Pendek, Ed Osmera.

Asmah, a young woman who has to look after her family, and particularly her blind sister, finds a job as a clerk. She gets to meet doctor Rachid, who specialises in eye surgery.

TAKDIR

[lit. Fate]
B&W – Malay
Directed by Omar Rojik.
Produced by Malay Film Productions.
With Jins Shamsuddin, Saadiah, Zaiton,
S. Kadarisman, Normadiah, Aziz Satar.

TIGA BOTAK

[lit. Three Bald Men]
B&W – Malay
Directed by Mat Sentol.
Produced by Cathay-Keris.
With Suraya, Ismail Boss, Mat Sentol, Wahid Satay,
Ghazali Sumantri, Siti Tanjung Perak.

Three friends live together. During a stormy night, a little girl seeks refuge in their home. Things are going to change.

1966

AKSI KUCHING

[lit. Cat Antics]
B&W – Malay
Directed by Omar Rojik.
Produced by Malay Film Productions.
With Aziz Satar, Zaiton, Ahmad Daud.

ANAK BULUH BETONG

[lit. Bamboo Child]
B&W – Malay
Directed by S. Kadarisman.
Produced by Malay Film Productions.
With Aziz Ja'afar, Saadiah, Ahmad Mahmud, Rosnani, Normadiah.

A baby boy is found in a tree trunk.

ANAK DARA

[lit. The Virgin Girl]
B&W – Malay
Directed by M. Amin.
Produced by Cathay-Keris.
With Mat Sentol, Tony Kassim, Malik Selamat,
Suraya Haron, Jah Lelawati, S. Rosli, Wahid Satay.

DAHAGA

[lit. Thirst]
Directed by Omar Rojik.
Produced by Malay Film Productions.
With Aziz Jaafar, Sarimah, Norma Zainal,
S. Shamsuddin, Malik Sutan Muda.

DUA KALI LIMA

[lit. Two Times Five]
Directed by M. Amin.
Produced by Cathay-Keris.
With Mat Sentol, Wahid Satay, Anita Sarawak, Dewi Asiah,
Ahmad Nesfu, Omar Hitam, Siti Tanjung Perak.

Kulop the Big and Kulop the Small both run their own tailoring businesses. Both are also going around, one in his convertible car, the other on his scooter, trying to look for women.

Gurindam Jiwa, 1966

GURINDAM JIWA

(a.k.a. Sonnet of the Soul)
B&W – Malay
Directed by M. Amin.
Produced by Cathay-Keris.
Music by Rahim Hamid.
Songs by Wandy Yazid.
With Nordin Ahmad, Latifah Omar,
Malek Selamat.

Dahlan is a poet who excels at making *pantuns*, a form of Malay poetry. He is summoned by the Sultan to replace the late court poet. Dahlan is to stay at the Prime Minister's house. Melati, the Prime Minister's daughter, soon falls in love with him. Although he is already married to Dahlia, Dahlan agrees to marry again, without Dahlia's knowledge (since Dahlan is not allowed to mix with commoners anymore due to the strict palace rules). But Dahlan feels terrible when he learns that both his parents have died while he was away. He then has only one thought, to be reunited with his first wife Dahlia.

JEFRI ZAIN — GERAK KILAT

[lit. Jefri Zain — Moves in a Flash]
B&W – Malay
Directed by Jamil Sulong.
Produced by Malay Film Productions.
With Jins Shamsuddin (Jefri Zain), Sarimah (Tina),
Salleh Kamil (Komander Jeeman), Rahmat Rahmat (Ratna),
Ibrahim Bachik (Ed), Sylvia Koh (Jefri's mate),
Shariff Dol, Omar Suwita.
"S'pore's own Bond", as advertised at the time of the release. Aksi aksi... Action action action... and babes.

KACHA PERMATA

[lit. Glass and Gems]
B&W – Malay
Directed by Jamil Sulong.
Produced by Malay Film Productions.
Story by S. Sudamarji.
Screenplay by Jamil Sulong.
Music by Yusof B. and Kassim Masdor.
With Jins Shamsuddin (Hamzah), Rosnani (Laili),
Zaiton, Haji Mahadi.
Hamzah is a young man from a wealthy family who marries Laili, a poor dancer, against his father's will. Soon, the young couple faces financial troubles and is relegated to the low ranks of society.

NAGA TASEK CHINI

[lit. The Dragon of Lake Chini]
B&W – Malay
Directed by Nordin Ahmad.
Produced by Cathay-Keris.
With Latiffah Omar, Mustapha Maarof,
Siput Serawak, Malek Selamat,
Wahid Satay, Dollah Dagang.
The villagers give Mayang the task of building a house by the jungle. She cannot cope until she is visited by the ghost of a mysteriously disfigured woodsman who starts helping her in secret. When she is forced to marry a rich man she does not love, supernatural forces come to her aid again.

SRI ANDALAS

B&W – Malay
Directed by S. Kadarisman.
Produced by Malay Film Productions.
With Ahmad Mahmud, Sarimah, Aziz Jaafar,
Noor Azizah, Salleh Kamil, Malik Sutan Muda,
S. Kadarisman, Ed Osmera, Aziz Satar, Normadiah.

UDANG DISEBALEK BATU

[lit. The Shrimp behind the Stone,
meaning hidden motive]
B&W – Malay
Directed by Hussain Haniff.
Produced by Cathay-Keris.
With Rose Yatimah, Suraya Harun,
Ahmad Osman, Mustapha Maarof,
Rahmah Latiff, Ahmad Sabri, M. Jatirata.
A young carpenter, Man, is hired by a man who wants to have his house restored. While he is working there, Man meets the daughter of the family, Suria. But Suria already has a lover, a skirt-chaser who does not really like her and who secretly heads a band of looters.

1967

A GO GO 67

B&W – Malay
Directed by Omar Rojik.
Produced by Malay Film Productions.
With Aziz Jaafar, Noor Azizah,
Norma Zainal, Kuswadinata,
S. Shamsuddin, Ibrahim Pendek.

DOSA WANITA

[lit. A Woman's Sin]
B&W – Malay
Directed by M. Amin.
Produced by Cathay-Keris.
Music by Wandy Yazid, The Pretenders,
The Rythm Boys.
With Fatimah Ahmad, Malek Selamat,
Salim Bachik, Tony Kassim,
Ummi Kaltoum, Dolla Dagang,
Anie Jasmin, A. Rhyme.
A young woman has just married into a rich family. Unfortunately, her stepmother does not welcome her at all. When she finally has a son, it is the stepmother who chooses his name. As for her husband, he is too busy with his business to even think of her. She allows herself to be courted by another man.

JEBAK MAUT

[lit. Lethal Snare]
B&W – Malay
Directed by Jamil Sulong.
Produced by Malay Film Productions.
With Ahmad Mahmud, Rosy Wong,
Aziz Jaafar, Haji Mahadi, Salleh Kamil,
Mohamed Hamid, Malik Sutan Muda,
Susan Chua.

LAMPONG KARAM

[lit. The Float Sinks]
B&W – Malay
Directed by S. Kadarisman.
Produced by Malay Film Productions.
With S. Rosely, Saadiah, Zaiton, Yusoff Latiff,
Normadiah, S. Kadarisman, Shariff Dol,
Sri Dewi, Kuswadinata.

MAT BOND

B&W – Malay
Directed by M. Amin and Mat Sentol.
Produced by Cathay-Keris.
Story by Mat Sentol.
Music by The Pretenders.
With Mat Sentol, Siti Tanjung Perak,
Dollah Serawak, Dollah Dagang,
Malek Selamat, Dollah Red Indian,
Rahim Hamid, Sherley Koh.
A hilarious parody of James Bond (and Jefri Zain) by Mat Sentol turned "secret secret agent". Witty, silly, funny, with an excellent guitar soundtrack by The Pretenders.

MAT RAJA KAPUR

B&W – Malay
Directed by Mat Sentol and M. Amin.
Produced by Cathay-Keris.
With Mat Sentol, E. Daud.

Jefri Zain – Gerak Kilat, 1966

NORA ZAIN – AJEN WANITA 001

[lit. Nora Zain – Female Agent 001]
Colour – Malay and Mandarin versions
Directed by Low Wei [Hong Kong].
Produced by Malay Film Productions and
Shaw Brothers HK Ltd [Hong Kong].
With Saadiah (Nora Zain), Aziz Jaafar, Sarimah, Nordin Arshad.

PLAY BOY

B&W – Malay
Directed by Noordin Ahmad.
Produced by Cathay-Keris.
Story by Hamzah.
Music by Wandy Yazid and Les Feontones.
With Noordin Ahmad, Rosnani Jamil, Mustapha Maarof,
Tony Kassim, Dollah Dagang, Salmah Ibrahim,
Rokiah Ahmad, Jamilah Ali.
An ex-gangster is trying to settle down and start a new life with the woman he loves. He opens a restaurant, but troubles surface again.

RAJA BERSIONG

(a.k.a. King with the Fangs)
Colour – Malay
Directed by Jamil Sulong.
Produced by Malay Film Productions.
With Ahmad Mahmud, Sarimah, Noor Azizah,
Zaiton, Malik Sutan Muda.
A king in ancient Malaya becomes bloodthirsty and starts killing people. This is the last production initiated by Malay Film Productions, the Singaporean Shaw studio. This superproduction, shot in colour and cinemascope, was a huge commercial failure.

TERLIBAT

[lit. Involved or Implicated]
B&W – Malay
Directed by S. Kadarisman.
Produced by Malay Film Productions.
With S. Rosely, Sharifah Aminah, Shirley Koh,
Aziz Satar, Haji Mahadi, Salleh Kamil,
Ghazali Sumantri, Hussein Abu Hassan.

1968

BAYANGAN AJAL – A JEFRI ZAIN STORY

[lit. Shadow of Death]
Colour – Malay and Mandarin versions
Directed by Low Wei [Hong Kong].
Produced by Malay Film Productions and
Shaw Brothers HK Ltd [Hong Kong].
With Jins Shamsuddin (Jefri Zain), Landi Chang,
Sharifah Aminah, Fanny Fan.

Secret Agent Jefri Zain is involved with the Hong Kong connection. This movie is a perfect panasian production, involving Singapore, Kuala Lumpur and Hong Kong, with a mixed cast and crew. As such, it is difficult to say if it pertains more to Malaysian, Hong Kong or Singaporean film history, and probably lies somewhere in the middle.

JEFRI ZAIN DALAM JURANG BAHAYA

[lit. Jefri Zain Caught in a Dangerous Ravine]
Colour – Malay and Mandarin versions
Directed by Low Wei [Hong Kong].
Produced by Malay Film Productions and
Shaw Brothers HK Ltd [Hong Kong].
With Jins Shamsuddin, Landi Chang, Shen Yi, Lo Wei.

Secret Agent Jefri Zain ("Saya Zain, Jefri Zain" / lit. "My name is Zain, Jefri Zain") is sent on a mission to Hong Kong. This movie, just like the previous one, is a perfect regional or panasian production, involving Singapore, Kuala Lumpur and Hong Kong, with, once again, a mixed cast and crew. As such, it is difficult to say if it pertains more to Malaysian, Hong Kong or Singaporean film history. It probably lies somewhere in the middle, even though this one tends to look more like a Hong Kong production. After all, it was produced by Shaw Run Run in Hong Kong, ten years after he had moved out of Singapore. Interestingly shot in colour and cinemascope (the "SBscope").

Kekaseh, 1968

KEKASEH

[lit. Lover]
B&W – Malay
Directed by Noordin Ahmad.
Produced by Cathay-Keris.
Music by Wandi and Rahim Hamid.
With Fatimah Ahmad, Salim Bachik, Normah Zainal,
Dollah Dagang, Shariff Medan, Dollah Sarawak.

Even though he is engaged to Rose, Salim suddenly disappears without a trace. Six years later, his father and Rose's father finally manage to find him, and he is leading a totally different life. He is married to Kasmini and has a child. In the meantime, Rose has become a very modern young lady, teaching ballet and going out with many men. Yet, when Kasmini finds out that Salim was once engaged to someone else, she decides to leave with the child.

MAT LANUN

[lit. Mat the Pirate]
B&W – Malay
Directed by Mat Sentol.
Produced by Cathay-Keris.
With Mat Sentol.

MIANG MIANG KELADI

B&W – Malay
Directed by Omar Rojik.
Produced by Malay Film Productions.
With Jins Shamsuddin, Sarimah, Yahya Sulong, Zahara Agus.

POP MUDA

[lit. Young Pop]
B&W – Malay
Directed by M. Amin and Toh Wing Kai.
Produced by Cathay-Keris.
With Fatimah Wati, Siput Sarawak, Tony Kassim.

SI MURAI

[lit. Magpie or Robin]
B&W – Malay
Directed by Noordin Ahmad.
Produced by Cathay-Keris.
With Mustapha Maarof, Malik Selamat, Mariam, Mat Sentol.

1969

KERANDA BERDARAH

[lit. Bleeding Coffin]
B&W – Malay
Directed by Noordin Ahmad.
Produced by Cathay-Keris.
With Tony Kassim, S. Noni, Dayang Sofia, Shariff Dol, Salleh Melan.

KERIS EMAS

[lit. Golden Dagger]
B&W – Malay
Directed by M. Amin.
Produced by Cathay-Keris.
Story and screenplay by Hamzah Hussin.
With Kuswadinata, Annie Jaafar, Salleh Melan, Shariff Doll,
Shariff Medan, Dollah Sarawak, Noor As.

A young warrior is thrown out of the family home. With his flute-playing partner, he takes to the roads and explores a world of adventures, from fights to women.

MAS TOYOL

B&W – Malay
Directed by Mat Sentol.
Produced by Cathay-Keris.

NAFSU BELIA

[lit. Youthful Desire]
B&W – Malay
Directed by Noordin Ahmad.
Produced by Cathay-Keris.

SIAL WANITA

[lit. Bad Luck of Women]
B&W – Malay
Directed by M. Amin.
Produced by Cathay-Keris.
With Fatimah Ahmad, Noordin Ahmad, Saadiah.

SRIKANDI

(a.k.a. Serikandi)
[lit. Heroine]
B&W – Malay
Directed by M. Amin.
Produced by Cathay-Keris.
With S. Noni (Sri Mala), Noordin Ahmad,
Malik Selamat.

Sri Mala decides to avenge her father's death after he has been framed and murdered by dignitaries of the sultanate. To do so, she agrees to marry the Sultan, and becomes his closest confidant.

1970

AKU MAHU HIDUP

[lit. I Want to Live]
B&W – Malay
Directed by M. Amin.
Produced by Cathay-Keris.
With Kuswadinata, Malik Selamat.

LUBANG NERAKA

[lit. Hell Hole]
B&W – Malay
Directed by Noordin Ahmad.
Produced by Cathay-Keris.
With Kuswadinata, S. Noni,
Rahmah Rahmat, Malik Selamat.

MAT KARONG GUNI

[lit. Mat the Gunny-Sack Man, meaning rag-and-bone man]
B&W – Malay
Directed by Mat Sentol.
Produced by Cathay-Keris.
With Mat Sentol, Normadiah,
Dollah Sarawak, Hamid Bond,
Ismail Boss.

Mat is a delivery boy, nicknamed Karong Guni because of he makes a living buying used items from the villagers. One day, by pure chance, he picks up a bag full of precious stones belonging to Dollah, a rich man. Many troubles await Mat Karong Guni when Dollah sends his men to hunt him down.

PUAKA

[lit. Spirit]
B&W – Malay
Directed by M. Amin.
Produced by Cathay-Keris.
With Aziz Jaafar, Ed Osmera, Mariati.

1971

JAHANAM

[lit. Destruction]
B&W – Malay
Directed by M. Amin.
Produced by Cathay-Keris.
With Noordin Ahmad, Saadiah.

MAT MAGIC

B&W – Malay
Directed by Mat Sentol.
Produced by Cathay-Keris.
With Mat Sentol.

The last of the "Mat movies" made in Singapore.

SEMUSIM DI NERAKA

[lit. A Season in Hell]
B&W – Malay
Directed by M. Amin.
Produced by Cathay-Keris.
With Tony Kassim, S. Noni,
Mustapha Maarof.

1972

DARA-KULA

B&W – Malay
Directed by Mat Sentol.
Produced by Cathay-Keris.
Screenplay by Mat Sentol.
With Ahmad Jais, Rosnita,
Aziz Manaf, Sue Sarkawi.

A man tries to rape a pregnant woman named Dara. His own wife, Kula, also pregnant, enters the room, discovers them and tries to separate them. In the ensuing fight, he ends up killing both pregnant women and runs away. Dara's husband goes looking for his wife and finds the two corpses. He decides to bury both of them at night, in a field, during a storm. The next day, he goes back to the tomb, as he has a strong feeling that he should dig into it. He discovers that during the night the two women have given birth postmortem to their children. In the following days, the two women are transformed into female vampires that appear only at night. This nonsensical and rather sickening horror Z movie represents one last take on the pontianak genre inherited from the 1950s and 1960s. This film is clearly linked, by the pun in its title, to the Dracula films made in the West. Hardly watchable, yet amazing.

HARIMAU JADIAN

[lit. Tiger Man]
B&W – Malay
Directed by M. Amin.
Produced by Cathay-Keris.
With Malek Selamat,
Rohani Yusoff, S. Azam.

HATI BATU

[lit. Heart of Stone]
B&W – Malay
Directed by M. Amin.
Produced by Cathay-Keris.
With Latiffah Omar, S. Azam, Hasnah Harun,
Fauziah, Faizal, Ahmad Daud, Saleh Melan,
M. Shahdan, Siti Tanjung Perak,
Rahmah Latiff, Hafsah Buang.

After the accidental death of her husband, a young mother is forced by her father-in-law to leave her two children, a little girl and a little boy, under his custody. She is not allowed to see them anymore. Unfortunately, the grandfather mistreats the children, and, frequently losing his temper, beats them up with his cane. One day, having had enough, the children run away in search of their mother. The film contains numerous shots of Singapore, hence capturing the city's landscape at the beginning of the 1970s.

SATU TITIK DI GARISAN

[lit. A Drop at the Line]
B&W – Malay
Directed by M. Amin.
Produced by Cathay-Keris.
With Aziz Jaafar (Kamal), Dayang Sofia (Sofia),
Kuswadinata (Haron), Bat Latiff.

Haron and Kamal are best friends. The latter is in love with Sofia, but has to leave the village to further his studies. While he is away, Haron seduces Sofia and, in the end, marries her. When Kamal returns to the village, he is heartbroken to learn that Sofia has not waited for him. However, she is not happy in her marriage due to Haron's infidelity. One day, while they are fighting, she accidentally murders him. Only Kamal is there to help her.

Satu Titik di Garisan, 1972

SEMANGAT ULAR

[lit. The Spirit of the Snake]
B&W – Malay
Directed by M. Amin.
Produced by Cathay-Keris.
With Mustapha Maarof, Emma Desita.

1973

RING OF FURY

Colour – Mandarin
Directed by Tony Yeow and James Sebastian.
Produced by Center 33.
With Peter Chong.

A hawker refuses to 'protection' money, so gangsters kill his mother. Wishing to avenge her, he learns kung fu from an old master, and comes back and kills them all. The film had almost no actors. The cast, like the hero, Peter Chong, was largely made up of martial arts practitioners in karate, shaolin or tai chi. The fight scenes were not prechoreographed — the director would just let them fight for as long as they liked.

1974

HUANG TANG SHI JIA

(a.k.a. The Hypocrite, a.k.a. Family Degeneration)
Directed by (unknown).
Produced by Chongay Organisation.

YI JIA ZHI ZHU

(a.k.a. Crime does not Pay, a.k.a. Master of the Family)
Directed by (unknown).
Produced by Chongay Organisation.

1976

QIAO DE LIANG AN

(a.k.a. The Two Sides of the Bridge)
Colour – Mandarin
Directed by Lim Ann (a.k.a. Lim Meng Chew).
Produced by Chongay Organisation.

A young man, Yu Fei, from Kelantan in Malaysia, wants to marry a Singaporean girl and work in the city-state. But once in Singapore, he has difficulties coping with the modern world, and is dragged into all sorts of wrongdoings.

1977

BIONIC BOY

95 min – colour – English
Directed by Leody M. Diaz [Philippines].
Produced by B. A. S. Films [Singapore, Malaysia, Philippines].
With Johnson Yap, Susan Beacher.

1978

DYNAMITE JOHNSON

(a.k.a. Bionic Boy Part II)
103 min – colour – English
Directed by Bobby A. Suarez [Philippines].
Produced by B.A.S. Films [Singapore, Malaysia, Philippines].
With Marrie Lee (Cleopatra Wong), Johnson Yap (Bionic Boy),
Susan Beacher, Kerry Chandler, Carole King, David McCoy,
Ken Metcalfe, Steve Nicholson, Clem Persons,
Debra Jean Rogers, Ron Rogers,
Kathleen Scherini, Joseph Zucchero.

Johnson Yap, the world's first bionic boy, teams up with his sexy 19-year-old auntie, Cleopatra Wong, to track down and defeat a nasty Nazi with the dubious name of Kuntz.

THEY CALL HER... CLEOPATRA WONG

110 min – colour – English
Directed by George Richardson [Philippines].
Produced by B. A. S. Films [Singapore, Malaysia, Philippines].
With Marrie Lee (Cleopatra Wong), George Estregan,
Dante Varona, Kerry Chandler, Chito Guerrero,
Alex Pecate, Brian Richmond.

Cleopatra Wong is in charge of smashing a counterfeiting ring spanning Singapore, Manila and Hong Kong. The movie poster said it all: "She purrs like a kitten... Makes love like a siren... Fights like a panther. This side of the Pacific, she is the deadliest, meanest and sexiest secret agent!" Some people were really having fun...

1991

MEDIUM RARE

(a.k.a. The Medium)
Colour – English
Directed by Arthur Smith [UK].
Produced by Errol Pang /
Derrol Stepenny Productions [Singapore].
With Dore Kraus, Margaret Chan, Brenda Bakke.

Entirely shot in Singapore and usually presented as the first movie of the Singaporean movie industry's revival and listed as such. However, it is an international production which has, in many ways, very little to do with Singapore's identity. In many aspects, it is more American than anything else. Although rather inept, it now offers real documentary value for having recorded the Singapore landscape at the beginning of the 1990s, when hardly anyone was shooting anything in the city-state.

1995

BUGIS STREET

(a.k.a. Yao Jie Huang Hou)
100 min – colour – English, Mandarin, Cantonese
Directed by Yon Fan (a.k.a.Yeung Fan) [Hong Kong].
Produced by Jaytex Productions [Singapore].
With Hiep Thi Le (Lian), Michael Lam (Meng),
Greg O (Drago), Benedict Goh (Sing),
Maggie Lye (Maggie), Sim Boon Peng (Ah Kit).

Lian, a young woman becomes a maid at a hotel in the red light district of Singapore in the 1960s. Little does she know that the residents are all transvestites and transsexuals who service young men and are eventually ready to teach the young woman about life. Coquettish yet naive, young Lian learns the lessons of life and love from some of the reigning queens at Sin Sin, including the worldly Drago and the tormented Lola, who's trapped in a codependent relationship with an abusive, philandering boyfriend. Behind the vivid facades put up by the residents also lies pain and self-doubt.

MEE POK MAN

105 min – colour – Cantonese and Hokkien
Directed by Eric Khoo.
Produced by Zhao Wei Films.
Edited by Martyn See.
With Joe Ng (The mee pok man),
Michelle Goh (Bunny, the prostitute),
Lim Kay Tong, David Brazil.

A slightly mentally disabled noodle stand owner, known as the mee pok man after the noodles he prepares, falls for one of his customers, a local prostitute named Bunny. When Bunny is injured in a hit-and-run accident outside his stall, the mee pok man takes her to his home and, even after she dies, he tries to take care of her.

They Call Her... Cleopatra Wong, 1978

1996

ARMY DAZE

Colour – English, Hokkien, Cantonese, Mandarin
Directed by Ong Keng Sen.
Produced by Cathay Asia Films.
Edited by Peter Tan.
With Ahmed Azad, Sheikh Haikel,
Adrian Lim, Kevin Verghese,
Edward Yong.

A group of young Singaporean men from very different backgrounds and with different profiles have to go for national service.

1997

GOD OR DOG

(a.k.a. Dabayao Shatongan, a.k.a. Wo Er Wu Zui)
90 min – colour – English, Hokkien, Cantonese
Directed by Hugo Ng (a.k.a. Ng Doi Yung).
Produced by LS Entertainment & Prod.
With Hugo Ng.

A man uses his aura as a medium to abuse women and commit crimes. Like the 1991 *Medium Rare*, it is adapted from the true story of Adrian Lim.

THE ROAD LESS TRAVELLED

(a.k.a. Gui Dao)
90 min – colour – Mandarin
Directed by Lim Suat Yen.
Produced by Oak3 Films.
With Robin Goh (Ah Jie), Chua Li Lian, Jackie Lui.

A group of four friends struggle to realise their aspirations. Among them is a loving couple. They sing at a music lounge, and dream of making it big one day. They both receive strong suppport from their friends.

12 STOREYS

(a.k.a. Shi Er Lou)
105 min – colour – Mandarin,Cantonese, Hokkien,
Malay, English, Tagalog
Directed by Eric Khoo.
Produced by Zhao Wei Films.
Edited by Jasmine Ng Kin Kia.
With Jack Neo, Koh Boon Pin, Chuang Yi Fong,
Lum May Yee, Lucilla Teoh.

Ah Gu is a chubby, middle-aged man who lures a woman from mainland China with his lies, and marries her. However, he is unprepared for the discovery that she is a gold-digger with a less-than-zero commitment to the marriage. San-San is a single woman so crushed since infancy by her late mother's contempt that she still hears it ringing in her ears, day in, day out, to the extent that she even considers committing suicide. Trixie and her kid brother are not-so-covert rebels against their elder brother Meng, who talks like he's making a public service announcement and has a real problem with his authoritarian impulses and his sexual desires.

1998

FOREVER FEVER

(a.k.a. That's the Way I Like It)
95 min – colour – English
Directed by Glen Goei.
Produced by Tiger Tiger Productions.

Kung fu meets disco in Singapore. Hock is a grocery clerk longing for a motorbike. He lives with his parents and sister, and they idolise his younger brother, Beng, a medical student. Hock loves Bruce Lee — he works out and imitates his moves. When Hock sees a cheesy local version of *Saturday Night Fever*, he gets the disco bug. He takes his pal Mei to lessons in the hope of winning a contest and buying a bike. He is blind to Mei¨'s growing affection for him. Meanwhile, Beng reveals a personal secret to his family and a crisis ensues.

MONEY NO ENOUGH

(a.k.a. Qian Bu Gou Yong)
Colour – Mandarin, Cantonese, Hokkien, English
Directed by Tay Teck Lock.
Produced by JSP Entertainment.
Edited by A. Supramaniam.
With Jack Neo (Chew), Mark Lee (Ong),
Henry Thia (Hui), John Cheng,
Patricia Mok, Zhuo Huiqin.

Three friends, an office worker, a renovation contractor and a coffeeshop assistant, go through hard times. The office worker, Keong, spends more than he earns. However, one day, he has to resign from his job. The contractor, Ong, borrows from a loanshark to import imitation tiles from Taiwan. In the end, he is cheated and has to hide from the loanshark when he is not able to repay the loan. The coffeeshop assistant fancies a girl who patronises the coffeeshop.

THE TEENAGE TEXTBOOK MOVIE

Colour – English
Directed by Phillip Lim.
Produced by Monster Films Prod.
Original story by Adrian Tan.
Screenplay by Haresh Sharma and Edmund Tan.
With Melody Chen (Mui Ee), Lim Hwee Sze (Sissy Wong),
Caleb Goh (Chung Kai), Chong Chee Kin (Kok Sean),
Steven Lim.

In a postsecondary institution, Mui Ee falls in love with a very handsome boy. At the same time, Chung Kai, the typical boy-next-door, falls for her, while his best friend, Kok Sean, is after Sissy Wong (Mui Ee's best friend and a real boy magnet). The boy-girl relationship plot thickens, things get complicated, but in the end everything is happily resolved.

TIGER'S WHIP

Colour – English, Cantonese
Directed by Victor Khoo.
Produced by River Films.
Andrea De Cruz, C.K. Cheong,
Victor Khoo, David Calig.

1999

EATING AIR

(a.k.a. Chi Feng)
100 min – colour – Mandarin, Hokkien, Malay, English
Directed by Kelvin Tong Wen Kia and Jasmine Ng Kin Kia.
Produced by Multi-Story Complex.
Edited by Jasmine Ng.
With Benjamin Heng, Alvina Toh,
Joseph Cheong, Ferris Yeo, Andy Chng,
Mark Lee, Michelle Chong, Debra Png.

For Ah Boy, breaking into bridal shops is as wildly exciting as taking Ah Girl on her first motorcycle spin through the blinding fluorescent tunnels of the Central Expressway. For Ah Girl, hurtling down the highway is as intoxicatingly frightening as wondering where Ah Boy rushes off to every time he receives a page at midnight. *Eating Air* seeks the delirious madness that makes 18 years an age invincible to low fuel, fists and oil puddles on the road. It is about a boy, a girl, a motorbike, and no brakes.

LIANG PO PO — THE MOVIE

(a.k.a. Liang Po Po Chong Chu Jiang Hu)
Colour – Hokkien, Mandarin, Cantonese, English
Directed by Teng Bee Lian.
Produced by MediaCorp Raintree Pictures and
Zhao Wei Films.
With Jack Neo (Liang Po Po), Mark Lee (Ah Beng),
Henry Thia (Ah Seng), Patricia Mok (Ah Lian),
John Cheng (Big Boss), Eric Tsang, Shereen Tang, A-niu.
Liang Po Po, an 85-year-old granny, decides to leave the old folks
home in search of a new life. Left alone and broke after she gets
robbed on her first day out by Ah Lian and her gang, Liang Po Po
seeks employment as a pump attendant, but soon creates chaos.
She then meets a couple of useless gangsters, Ah Beng and Ah
Seng, and gets involved in a secret society. This really funny
comedy is also rich with over 30 shooting locations in Singapore,
giving it great documentary value for the way it shows many
aspects of the urbanscape.

LUCKY NUMBER

(a.k.a. Bailiu Libai)
Directed by Gao Lin Pao / Lam Po Ko.
Produced by D. S. Movies.
With Law Kar Ying.

STREET ANGELS

(a.k.a. Shao Nu Dang)
Colour – English, Mandarin
Directed by David Lam (a.k.a. Tak Luk Lam) [Hong Kong].
Produced by Act Venture Films.
With Grace Yip, Melody Chen, Nicholas Tse.
Five teenage girls, between 14 and 17 years of age, and from very
different family backgrounds, go through a rebellious phase of
their lives, when they seek to assert their independence from
family, school and society. They do so by forming a gang and living
by rules they have set.

THAT ONE NO ENOUGH

(a.k.a. Na Ge Bu Gou)
Colour – Hokkien, Mandarin
Directed by Jack Neo.
Produced by Cathay Asia Films.
Jack Neo (Hong Hao Ren), Mark Lee (Zhu Guo Rong),
Henry Thia (Liu Ah Kua), Hong Huifang (Chow Min Hui),
Patricia Mok (Chen Hui Yu), Tan Kheng Hua, Irene Ong.
Three good male friends have problems with women. Guo Rong's
wife has gotten fat after having his kids, and so he cheats on
her constantly, and spends all his money on karaoke bars. Hao
Ren is married to a beautiful, successful wife but she is too
busy with her career to think about sex or children, despite his
family's demands for grandchildren. He begins having an affair
with his wife's secretary from mainland China. Ah Kua is a 30-
something virgin, who has just fallen for the daughter of
his boss. The men gossip about the women, the women gossip
about the men, and relationships ebb and flow in this comedy
about life and love in Singapore.

WHERE GOT PROBLEM

(a.k.a. Wenti Bu Da)
Colour – Hokkien, Mandarin, Cantonese, English
Directed by J. P. Tan.
Produced by Sunnez.
With Edmund Chen, Lim Kay Siu, Neo Swee Lin, Shery Tan.

2000

CHICKEN RICE WAR

(a.k.a. Jiyuan Qiaohe)
100 min – colour – Cantonese, English
Directed by Cheek (a.k.a. Cheah Chee Kong).
Produced by Oak 3 Films and MediaCorp Raintree Pictures.
Two young lovers are caught in the tangle of an interfamily feud
which has been sparked off by chicken rice! Both families have
been in the chicken rice business for the last two decades which
is how far the rivalry spans. In the midst of bitter rivalry, close
friends and chicken rice, love begins to blossom.

CRAZY PEOPLE

Directed by Lin Ting.
Produced by Wealth Film Production.

Chicken Rice War, 2000

STAMFORD HALL

Colour – English
Directed by Manoharan Ramakrishnan.
Produced by NU(Studios) NUS.

STORIES ABOUT LOVE

Colour – English
Directed by James Toh, Abdul Nizam and
Cheek (a.k.a. Cheah Chee Kong).
Produced by Zhao Wei Films and Cyberflics.
With Mark Richmond, Amy Cheng,
Beatrice Chia, Paul Zach.
Three stories about love.

2001

A SHARP PENCIL

Colour – English
Directed by Gallen Mei.
Produced by Under Pressure Pictures.
With Beatrice Chia (Tania), Mark Richmond (Simon),
Lim Kay Tong (Derek).
A young couple is bored to death and starts committing petty
crime.

HYPE

102 min – colour – DV – English
Directed by Vincent Wong.
Produced by NU(Studios) NUS.
With Walter Thevathasan (David), Adelina Ong (Cassandra),
Alan Anand Johnson (Sean), Stella Chew (Maxine).

MISS WONTON

87 min – colour – English, Mandarin, Cantonese
Directed by Meng Ong.
Produced by Dream Chamber Films [USA].
With Amy Ting (Ah Na), Ben Wang (Chung),
James C. Burns (Jack), Chyna Ng (Ling), Sakura Ting (Sum).
A young woman leaves China to go to the USA. There, she starts
working in a Chinese restaurant.

ONE LEG KICKING

Colour – English
Directed by KhooKoh (Eric Khoo and Wei Koh).
Story by James Toh.
Produced by Zhao Wei Films and MediaCorp Raintree Pictures.
With Mark Lee, Sharon Au, Gurmit Singh, Moe Alkaff, Kumar,
Hossan, Lim Kay Tong, Moses Lim, Fiona Xie.
A group of underdogs form an amateur football team to play in a
local league. The prize is a trip to the 2002 World Cup Finals. The
team includes a common man's hero raising his two children single-
handedly after his wife passes away, an ex-con with major anger
management problems, a lounge singer struggling against his deadly
nemesis, the karaoke machine, and a tender but tough tomboy.

RETURN TO PONTIANAK

(a.k.a. Voodoo Nightmare)
81 min – colour – English
Directed by Djinn (a.k.a. Ong Lay Jinn).
Produced by Vacant Films.
With Hiep Thi Le (Charity), Fadali (Eye),
Eleanor Lee (Uzi), Steve Banks (Luke).
A young Asian-American girl leads a group of friends on a two-day
trek deep into the Malaysian jungle in search of a village she is
inexplicably drawn to. Once there, she and her companions
encounter an evil female vampire, a pontianak, bent on revenge.

THE TREE

(a.k.a. Haizi Shu)
Colour – Mandarin
Directed by Daisy Chan.
Produced by MediaCorp Raintree Pictures.
Francis Ng (Wu Chongzhe), Zoe Tay (Guo Mei Feng),
Phyllis Quek (Jiang Liangxing).
Qingyu's mother, Meifeng, is arrested for the murder of her husband
(Qingyu's stepfather). The pathologist, Chongzhe, who is involved
in the case, gradually befriends the young boy who is the sole
witness in the murder case. He realizes that Qingyu yearns for
paternal love, since his father has mysteriously disappeared years
ago. As Qingyu gets to know Chongzhe better, he starts to explain
what he had seen on the night of the accident.

2002

ANGEL HEART

Directed by Gerald Lee.
Produced by Touch Entertainment / Gateway Entertainment.

CITY SHARKS

90 min – colour – English
Directed by Esan Sivalingam.
Produced by Hoods Inc. Productions.
With Nicholas Lee (Mike), Corinne Adrienne (Sherry), Kher Cheng
Guan (Big Boss), Marcus Chin (Ang), Sheikh Haikel (Jeff), Hans
Isaac (Chief), Keagan Kang (Al), Lim Kay Tong (Samuel),
Moses Lim (Henry), Michelle Saram (Deanna).
A road movie.

I NOT STUPID
(a.k.a. Xiaohai Bu Ben)
105 min – colour – English, Mandarin, Hokkien
Directed by Jack Neo.
Produced by MediaCorp Raintree Pictures.
Edited by Yeung Yiu Chung.
With Jack Neo (Mr Liu), Yun Xiang (Mrs Liu),
Richard Low (Mr Khoo), Selena Tan (Mrs Khoo),
Huang Po Ju (Terry Khoo), Shawn Lee (Liu Kok Pin),
Joshua Ang (Ang Boon Hock), Cheryl Chan (Selena Khoo Jr).
Three 12-year-old classmates, Koh Pin, Boon Hock and Terry, are not academically successful, and hence have been placed in EM3, the slow stream. Koh Pin is a creative, almost a born artist, but his parents want him to focus only on maths. Boon Hock comes from a poor family and has a hard time balancing school and helping out at his parents' restaurant. Terry is a rich kid who has never been left on his own or required to do anything by himself. Their parents are most worried for the kids, but also have problems of their own.

SONG OF THE STORK
(a.k.a. Vu Khuc Con Co)
111 min – colour – Vietnamese
Directed by Jonathan Foo and
Phan Quang Binh Nguyen [Vietnam].
Produced by Mega Media.
With Chi Bao Pham (Lam), Ngoc Bao Ta (Manh),
Quang Hai Ngo (Van), Quang Vinh Luu (Vinh),
Mai Nguyen Trinh (May).
A few young men from Hanoi join the North Vietnamese army during the war against the Americans. This movies includes archival footage shot by the Vietnamese during the war.

TALKING COCK – THE MOVIE
90 min – colour – English, Singlish
Directed by Colin Goh.
Produced by Wu Liao Media.

2003

HOMERUN
108 min – colour – Mandarin
Directed by Jack Neo.
Produced by MediaCorp Raintree Pictures.
With Shawn Lee (Chew Kiat Kun),
Megan Zheng (Chew Seow Fang), Yun Xiang (Kun's mother),
Wenyong Huang (Kun's father), Joshua Ang (Tan Beng Soon),
Sharon Au (Seow Fang's teacher), Po Ju Huang (Fatty),
Patricia Mok (Mrs Ang), Jack Neo (Beng Soon's father).
Set in 1965 Singapore, *Homerun* is a remake of Iranian director Majid Majidi's *Children of Heaven*. It is the story of Ah Kun, a young boy who accidentally loses his sister's school shoes. Their solution is to share Ah Kun''s shoes, with his sister, Seow Fang, wearing them to school in the morning, then running back home to pass the shoes to Ah Kun for his afternoon classes. Singapore won its first-ever Golden Horse Award, the Chinese equivalent of the Oscars, through the film's 10-year-old female lead Megan Zheng in the 2003 'Best New Performer' category.

THE GIFT
Colour
Directed by Gerald Lee.
Produced by Gateway Entertainment.

TWILIGHT KITCHEN
Colour
Directed by Gerald Lee.
Produced by Gateway Entertainment.

15
(a.k.a. Shi Wu)
90 min – colour – Hokkien, Mandarin
Directed by Royston Tan.
Produced by Zhao Wei Films.
With Melvin Chen, Erick Chun, Melvin Lee, Vynn Soh, Shaun Tan.
Five teenagers living on the fringes of Singaporean society are abandoned by the system. They seek answers to their aimless existence among the misfits and outsiders of Singapore's underclass. Estranged from every social reference, except for that of appearance and close friendships, they live their lives distant from their families and school, passing their days in a complete state of indolence. They go in the search of experiences, at times even physically painful (tattoos, piercing, wounds). Their imaginary world is completely colonised by MTV, cartoons, electronic jingles, publicity and comics.

2004

AVATAR
Colour – English
Directed by Kuo Jiang Hong.
Produced by The Theatre Practice.
With Lim Kay Siu, Richard Low,
Gerald Chew, Kumar, Genevieve O'Reilly,
Joan Chen, Wang Luoyong.
In the futuristic city-state Sintawan, a police detective and a bounty hunter are forced to work together in pursuit of a corporate insider on the run. They uncover a deadly plot by powerful megacorp leaders that threatens all of Sintawan. This movie has been pitched as "Singapore's first Sci-fi thriller". It was entirely shot in Singapore, with an interesting mixed cast of Singaporean and international actors.

CLOUDS IN MY COFFEE
Colour – English, Mandarin
Directed by Gallen Mei.
Produced by Under Pressure Pictures.
With Celeste Lim, Cindy Ng, Ase Wang
Three young women try to find love, each in her own way.

OUTSIDERS
Colour – English
Directed by Sam Loh.
Produced by Little Big Films.
With Christian J. Lee, Corinne Adrienne,
Rachel S., Keagan Kang, Garrett Hoo,
Steph Song, Cheryl Chin.
A serial killer is on the loose in an overcrowded city which looks like a lot like Singapore.

Homerun, 2003

PERTH
106 min – colour – English
Directed by Ong Lay Jinn (a.k.a. Djinn).
Produced by Ground Glass Images and Working Man Films.
Edited by Bin Li.
Music by Marcello de Franscici.
With Lim Kay Tong (Harry Lee),
Sunny Pang (Angry Boy Lee),
Ivy Cheng (Mai), Liu Qiu Lian,
A. Panneeirchelvam (a.k.a. Victory Chelvam),
Catherine Tan.
Harry Lee, a long-serving security supervisor at a shipyard, loses his job due to brutal downsizing. To make a living, he becomes a taxi driver. He does not have much else to do, since he is totally on his own. His wife has left him, and he has not seen his son for many years. Harry Lee has just one dream, to make enough money to retire in Perth, Australia, where life is said to be so good.

THE BEST BET
(a.k.a. Tu Ran Fa Cai)
115 min – colour – Mandarin, Hokkien, English
Directed by Jack Neo.
Produced by MediaCorp Raintree Pictures.
With Mark Lee (Huang),
Richard Low (Richard),
Christopher Lee (Shun),
Joanne Peh (Hui Min),
Chen Liping, Jack Neo.
Richard, a white-collar executive, aims to be a good father and a good husband. However, indecisive and wimpy, he is easily influenced by the people around him. Chen Liping plays Richard's wife who is extremely meticulous when it comes to money matters, especially when it comes to anything that has to do with Shun and Huang. Shun works with Richard in the same company. Unlike Richard, Shun is ambitious, outspoken and full of ideas. However, down on his luck, Shun seldom succeeds in what he does. Huang owns a *bak kut teh* (pork bones soup) stall. A 'super gambler', Huang not only places heavy bets on 4D, he also works part-time as a debt collector for the '4D King'. It is his sister, Hui Min (Joanne Peh), who sees to the running of the *bak kut teh* business. Their friendship is put to the test when one of them strikes 4D and decides to keep the winnings all to himself.

ZOMBIE DOGS

(a.k.a. Eat Shit, Fuck and Die)
61 min – colour – English, Singlish
Directed by Toh Hai Leong.
Produced by Hardly Annie Gore.
With Toh Hai Leong (as himself), Lim Poh Huat.

A mockumentary on the making of Singapore's first snuff movie, by Toh Hai Leong himself. The snuff movie's premise tells the story of a boy who rents out a room in his flat to a pornographer. One day, as he comes in, he finds a naked prostitute sleeping in the room. He kills her, makes love to her and finally eats her, living out his necrophelia fantasy. But the shooting of that snuff movie never really takes place, and Toh Hai Leong goes on and on hilariously about the impossibility of making such a movie. One of the most politically incorrect takes on Singapore society, with some excellent insights. Unofficially produced by filmmaker-cum-producer Eric Khoo.

2005

4:30

88 min – colour – English, Mandarin and
Korean with English subtitles
Directed by Royston Tan.
Produced by Zhao Wei Films and NHK [Japan].

A Chinese boy and his Korean tenant are faced with loneliness in the middle of the night.

BE WITH ME

Colour – English
Directed by Eric Khoo.
Produced by Zhao Wei Films.
Story by Eric Khoo and Wong Kim Ho.
Edited by Low Hwee Ling.
With Theresa Chan (as herself), Ezann Lee (Jackie),
Samantha Tan (Sam), Seet Keng Yew (Fatman),
Chiew Sung Ching (the father), Lawrence Yong (the son),
Lynn Poh (Ann).

"Is true love truly there, my love?", says the typewriter that opens the movie. Theresa Chan is a blind and deaf woman who has learned how to cope with life and has become a teacher for blind children. Jackie and Sam are two teenage girls involved in a lesbian relationship. Fatman is a security guard beaten up in his childhood who does not really know where he stands in society and is fascinated by the lovely Ann. The lonely old man who does not even feel like opening his shop anymore cannot overcome the loss of his beloved wife and the guilt that comes with it.

CAGES

Colour – English
Directed by Graham Streeter [USA].
Produced by Aquafire Productions [Singapore].
Music by Roger Bourland.
With Tan Kheng Hua (Ali), Dickson Tan (Jonah),
Makoto Iwamatsu (Tan), Zelda Rubinstein (Liz),
Robert Tonelli (Ethan).

After fighting with her latest boyfriend Ethan, Ali, a single mother, is forced, with her blind seven-year-old son, Jonah, into the streets in the middle of the night. Desperate, and finding all doors closed, she eventually turns to her father, Tan, whom she has not seen for almost 20 years. This Singapore-driven international coproduction carries the vision of its American director, hence making it sometimes more of an American film than a Singaporean one. Yet, being entirely shot in Singapore, it offers a most interesting portrayal of the city-state.

I DO I DO

Colour – Mandarin
Directed by Jack Neo.
Produced by MediaCorp Raintree Pictures.
With Sharon Au (Hui), Adrian Pang (Peng).

Peng, a truck driver, falls deeply in love with Hui, a senior executive at a food company. Hui is a career-minded woman who is of marriageable age. But she feels that there is no suitable guy fitting her requirements. Peng confesses his love for Hui. However, he is adamantly rejected. Hui, a self-proclaimed sophisticated career woman, who does not believe in love at first sight, falls madly in love with Feng. Feng is the talented, charming, gorgeous guy, the eligible bachelor who has it all, and has no lack of female suitors. He accepts Hui and soon, Feng and Hui become an inseparable couple. In the face of such strong competition, Peng becomes disillusioned and despondent.

I Not Stupid Too, 2006

ONE LAST DANCE

95 min – colour – English and Chinese subtitles
Directed by Max Makowski.
Produced by MediaCorp Raintree Pictures and
Ming Productions.
With Vivian Hsu (Mae), Francis Ng (T),
Thomas Lim (Richard), Sunny Pang (Kay Wing),
Harvey Keitel (Terrtano), Ti Lung (The Captain), Joseph Quek.

Someone has made a mistake, a fatal one, and retribution is forthcoming at the hands of the brotherhood's most lethal assassin, the brooding and methodical T who is known for his hard and fast rules — no drinking, no women, no distractions. In his world, the margin for error is thin, and T likes thinking ahead and staying ahead. He is locked in a literal and figurative chess match with the local Police Captain, his only friend and willing opponent. As the body count rises, T realises that he has made a crucial mistake, one that he has never made before. He has allowed himself to become personally involved. His colourful protégé, Ko and the women that surround him — his beautiful sister Mae, and Ko's neighbor, the painfully innocent Gu — drag his emotions into the dangerous mix of death and revenge, forcing him to follow honor and his code, and to take out the most difficult target an Assassin can ever face.

ONE MORE CHANCE

106 min – colour – Chinese
Directed by Jack Neo.
Produced by J Team.
With Mark Lee, Henry Thia, Marcus Chin.

THE MAID

Colour – English
Directed by Kelvin Tong.
Produced by MediaCorp Raintree Pictures.
With Alessandra de Rossi (Rosa), Chen Shu Cheng (Mr Teo),
Hong Hui Fang (Mrs Teo), Benny Soh (Ah Soon).

Coming from a small village in the Philippines, the 18-year-old Rosa arrives in Singapore on the first day of the Seventh Month to work as a domestic maid in the Teo family. She does not know that during the Chinese Seventh Month, the gates of hell open and spirits are let loose for a period of thirty days, during which the dead walk among the living. For Rosa, all that is just a bunch of old wives' tales. She urgently needs money to save her ill brother back home in the Philippines and ghosts are the last things on her mind. Her employers, the elderly and gentle Mr and Mrs Teo, are a godsend, caring for her as if she is their own daughter. Their mentally-handicapped son Ah Soon also takes to Rosa immediately. That is where the trouble is going to come from.

UNARMED COMBAT

94 min – colour – English
Directed by Han Yew Kwang.
Produced by Digital Media Academy and the
Singapore Film Commission,
in association with Mega Media.
With Johnny Ng, Catherine Sng, Marilyn Lee.

A man signs his wife up for an arm-wrestling competition, but soon he regrets it.

2006

I NOT STUPID TOO

129 min – colour – Mandarin
Directed by Jack Neo.
Produced by MediaCorp Raintree Pictures.
With Ashley Leong, Xiang Yun, Jack Neo,
Joshua Ang, Huang Yi Liang.

LOVE STORY

Colour – Mandarin
Directed by Kelvin Tong.
Produced by Boku Films and Focus Films [Hong Kong].
With Lin Yi Yun, Evelyn Tan, Ericia Lee.

While a theatre usher looks for love and finds it in a library book, a cop chases a killer only to wind up at the end of her own gun. Meanwhile, a pulp romance writer confuses fact with fiction and learns that true love only comes after a great loss.

SINGAPORE DREAMING

Colour – English, Mandarin, Hokkien
Directed by Woo Yen Yen and Colin Goh.
Produced by Woo Yen Yen, Colin Goh and Woffles Wu.
With Richard Low, Lim Yu-beng,
Serene Chen, Yeo Yann Yann.

Old Loh strikes the lottery and thinks he can finally attain the "5Cs": car, cash, credit card, condominium and country club membership. When he dies almost immediately, his family has to deal with his loss, the money and the meaning of life.

SMELL OF RAIN

93 min – colour – Mandarin
Directed by Gloria Chee.
Produced by Gloria Chee.

Foreign movies entirely or partly shot in Singapore or referring to Singapore

1913

A DAY AT SINGAPORE
(a.k.a. Un jour à Singapour)
B&W
Directed by (unknown).
Produced by Georges Méliès [France/USA].

1928

ACROSS TO SINGAPORE
(a.k.a. Un soir à Singapour)
B&W
Directed by William Nigh.
Produced by MGM [USA].
Story by Joseph Farnham.
With Joan Crawford (Priscilla),
Ramon Novarro (Joel Shore),
Ernest Torrence (Mark Shore),
Frank Currier (Jeremiah Shore),
Dan Wolheim (Noah Shore),
Anna May Wong (the celestial temptress).
Joel and Priscilla have been in love since childhood. But Mark, Joel's brother, announces his engagement to her without her permission. While they are at sea, Mark is abandoned in Singapore by the ship's mate, who, upon their return, convinces people that it is Joel who has abandoned Mark, due to jealousy. Joel is jailed, but soon escapes and boards a ship to Singapore where he finds his brother drenched in alcohol.

SAL OF SINGAPORE
(a.k.a. La blonde de Singapour)
B&W
Directed by Howard Higgin [USA].
Produced by (unknown).
Story by Elliott J. Clawson and Dale Collins.
With Phyllis Haver, Alan Hale, Fred Kohler,
Noble Johnson, Dan Wolheim, Jules Cowles.

THE CRIMSON CITY
(a.k.a. under its Italian title, La schiava di Singapore)
B&W
Directed by Archie Mayo [USA].
Produced by (unknown).
Story by Anthony Coldeway.
With Conrad Nagel Myrna Loy,
Leila Hyams, Sojin, Anna May Wong,
Richard Tucker, William Russell.

1931

THE ROAD TO SINGAPORE
B&W – English
Directed by Alfred E. Green [USA].
Produced by (unknown).
Original story by Denise Robins.
Screenplay by Roland Pertwee.
With William Powell, Doris Kenyon,
Marian Marsh, Louis Calhern,
Tyrell Davis, A.E. Anson.
On a steamer between Colombo and Singapore, Hugh and Philippa fall in love. Philippa is a former nurse who has come to the colony to join the doctor as his wife.

1932

BRING 'EM BACK ALIVE
65 min – B&W – English
Directed by Clyde D. Elliott [USA].
Story by Frank Buck.
Produced by A. J. Van Beuren.
With Frank Buck.
American animal trapper Frank Buck travels with Ali, his "number one boy", on an expedition into the Malayan jungle. From their jungle headquarters just north of Singapore, Frank, Ali and a team of native helpers roam the area from northern Johore to Perak in search of interesting wild animals, reptiles and birds. Hoping to find a tiger, Buck captures a monitor lizard and a black leopard, while another black leopard narrowly escapes an encounter with a giant python and then battles a bigger and stronger tiger. After trapping a spotted leopard, Frank adopts a baby honey bear and a baby elephant. The team catches an orangutan, but the tiger eludes their camouflaged pit. Meanwhile, Frank visits the "bathing festival" of a local tribe and watches as tribesmen kill an intruding spotted leopard with blow darts. The tiger then meets an enormous regal python, who has just crushed a crocodile, and fights to a draw with it.

OUT OF SINGAPORE
(a.k.a. Gangsters of the Sea)
B&W – English
Directed by Charles Hutchinson [USA].
Produced by (unknown).
With Noah Beery, Dorothy Burgess, Miriam Seegar,
George Walsh, Jimmy Aubrey, Montagu Love, Leon Wong.
While a ship's captain is being poisoned, a gang of pirates try to take over the ship.

SAMARANG
(also known under its working title, Out to the Sea;
and under its 1940s' reissue title, Shark Woman)
62 min – B&W – English
Directed by Ward Wing.
Produced by United Artists Picture [USA].
Story by Lori Bara.
With Ahmang (the pearl diver), Chang Fu (the captain),
Ko Hai (the brother), Mamounah (the mother),
Sai-yu (the sweetheart).
A story of pearl-fishers. At the time of its release, it was promoted as having been "filmed entirely in Singapore with local artists". Indeed, the cast was made of some rather famous bangsawan actors. It premiered in the USA in 1933 and in Singapore in 1934, and was advertised as "Malaya's first sensational thriller". Malaya, but not Malay.

SHADOWS OF SINGAPORE
(a.k.a. Malay Nights)
63 min – B&W – English
Directed by E. Mason Hopper [USA].
Story by Glenn Ellis.
Screenplay by John T. Neville.
Produced by (unknown).
With Lionel Belmore, Johnny Mack Brown, Dorothy Burgess,
Ralph Ince, Carmelita Geraghty.

SINGAPORE SUE

B&W – English
Directed by Casey Robinson [USA].
Produced by (unknown).
With Anna Chang (Singapore Sue), Joe Wong.

Four sailors enter a Singapore dive. They meet a young Asian lady named Singapore Sue who entertains sailors. Some say that Anna Chang is in fact Anna May Wong, using another name.

WHITE PEARL

(a.k.a. Mutiara Putih)
Directed by Russell [UK].
Produced by (unknown).
With Shariff Medan.

1933

WEST OF SINGAPORE

B&W – English
Directed by Albert Ray [USA].
Produced by (unknown).
Story by Adele S. Buffington.
With Betty Compson (Lou), Weldon Heyburn (Dan),
Margaret Lindsay (Shelby), Noel Madison (Degama),
Clyde Cook (Ricky).

1935

CHINA SEAS

(a.k.a. La malle de Singapour)
87 min – B&W – English
Directed by Tay Garnett [USA].
Produced by (unknown) [USA].
With Rosalind Russell, Clark Gable,
Jean Harlow, Wallace Beery.

1938

BOOLOO

B&W – English
Directed by Clyde D. Elliot.
Produced by Paramount [USA].
With Colin Topley (Captain Rogers), Jayne Regan (Kate Jaye),
Lichio Ito (Chief Sakai), Herbert De Souza (Rod De Souza),
Fred Pullen (Nah Laku), Ah Lee (as himself).

NELAYAN

[lit. Fisherman]
Directed by (unknown).
Produced by (unknown).
Apparently with Khairuddin.

1940

ROAD TO SINGAPORE

85 min – B&W – English
Directed by Victor Schertzinger [USA].
Produced by Paramount [USA].
With Bing Crosby, Bob Hope, Dorothy Lamour,
Charles Coburn, Anthony Quinn.

Shot in 1940, it was the first trip (or "road to") in what would become one of Paramount's most profitable film series of the 1940s (sequels were *Road to Morocco, Road to Zanzibar*, etc.). Unfortunately, it has very little to do with Singapore and was definitely not filmed on location, even though Bob Hope and Bing Crosby officially end up sharing a waterfront shack in Singapore and vying for the affection of a sarong-clad Dorothy Lamour.

1941

SINGAPORE WOMAN

64 min – B&W – English
Directed by Jean Negulesco.
Produced by (unknown) [USA].
Screenplay by Coates Webster and Allen Rivkin.
With Brenda Marshall, David Bruce,
Virginia Field, Jerome Cowan,
Rose Hobart, Connie Leon,
Stanley Logan.

Off slumming one night in a dive on the Singapore waterfront, a group of colonials spot a familiar face off in a corner. It is a woman they know, come to alcohol and hard times because of a curse hurled at her by the widow of a man supposedly driven to commit suicide by that charming temptress. One of the colonials, taking pity on her, decides to whisk her off to his plantation, to sober her up and comfort her. They soon fall in love. Rubber plantations, rickshaws, Raffles Hotel and monsoon rain make the exotic backdrop of this typically East-of-Suez romantic melodrama.

THE BLONDE FROM SINGAPORE

(a.k.a. Hot Pearls)
69 min – B&W – English
Directed by Edward Dmytryk [USA].
Produced by (unknown).
With Florence Rice, Leif Erickson, Gordon Jones,
Don Beddoe, Alexander d'Arcy, Aedele Rowland.

A group of adventurous pilots turned pearl-divers encounter a rather helpless woman whose missionary parents have died. They entrust their cache of pearls to her, but soon discover that she is not who she claims to be. She is a treasure hunter, hunted herself by Prince Ali who wants to add her to his harem.

1942

HAWAI MARE OKI KAISEN

(a.k.a. The War at Sea from Haway to Malaya)
Directed by Kajiro Yamamoto [Japan].
Produced by (unknown) [Japan].
With Susumu Fujita, Setsuko Hara,
Fumito Matsuo, Jiro Takano.

1943

SHINGAPORU SOKOGEKI

(a.k.a. All-out Attack on Singapore)
Directed by Koji Shima [Japan].
Produced by (unknown) [Japan].

1947

NEVER WANT TO SEE THE PAST LOVE

B&W – Cantonese
Directed by Chiang Wai Kwong.
Produced by Linglong Film Company [Hong Kong].
With Wong Chiu Mo, Ng Lai Sheung,
Chow Kwan Ling.

Siu Ling, a secretary, is attracted to her colleague, Tak Kwong. They decide to live together, but Tak Kwong is fired by his jealous boss who also desires Siu Ling. Unemployed, Tak Kwong also falls ill. Siu-ling pleads for help from his father who agrees to help his son on the condition that Siu Ling leaves Tak Kwong. Siu Ling thus goes to Singapore where she becomes a songstress while Tak Kwong slowly recovers, consoled by his new girl friend. One day, Siu Ling returns from Singapore.

SINGAPORE

72 min – B&W – English
Directed by John Brahm.
Produced by Universal Studios [USA].
Story by Seton I. Miller.
With Fred MacMurray, Ava Gardner.

Matt Gordon, a World War II veteran sailor returns to British-controlled Singapore five years later to retrieve a smuggled cache of pearls from his prewar days as a pearl smuggler. Once in Singapore, Matt starts reminiscing about the events that led to the death of his fiancee during a Japanese air raid. But Linda did not really die. She miraculously survived the blast, but became amnesiac. She is now the wife of a wealthy plantation owner, and remembers nothing about her past.

Singapore Woman, 1941

1950

KAMPUNG SENTOSA

[lit. Sentosa Village]
Directed by G.Tom.
Produced by American Film Inn [USA].

SORROWS OF A NEGLECTED WIFE

120 min - B&W – Cantonese
Directed by Kwan Man-ching.
Produced by Huanya Film Company [Hong Kong].
With Kwong Shan-siu (as Pak Chiu-man),
Cheung Ying (Wong Man-king), Pak Yin (Yip Chau-sum),
Ma Ying (Anna).

Yip Chau-sum and Pak Chiu-man have been separated because of the war. Chau-sum ends up in Hong Kong while Chiu-man works in Shanghai. When Chiu-man leaves to work for his uncle in Singapore, he stops over in Hong Kong where he happens to meet Chau-sum. Their affair is soon revived.

THE GRAND HOMECOMING

B&W – Cantonese
Directed by Chu Gei (a.k.a. Chu Kei, a.k.a. Zhu Ji).
Produced by Fada Film Company [Hong Kong].
With Pak Yin, Cheung Wood Yau,
Lam Mui-mui, Lee Pang-fei,
Ng Tung.

Choi Pak-fan, from a humble family, is in love with Ching-mei, daughter of rich man Yau Sik-ping. This makes their relationship difficult. To overcome this, Ching-mei encourages Pak-fan to go to Singapore to make a headstart. They pledge to meet two years later.

THE WAR BABY

B&W – Cantonese

Directed by Ng Wui.

Produced by Shanxing Film Company [Hong Kong].

With Wong Man Lei (Lau So-ying), Yu Kai (Law Yat-ming),
Yuen Yuen (Law Wing-nin), Chow Siu-siu (Wing-nin's Mother).

At the outbreak of war, Law Wing-nin, the manager of an opera troupe, goes to Singapore on a performing tour. He leaves behind his mother, wife So-ying and infant son, Yat-ming.

YUAN JIN JIN SHENG

(a.k.a. Dreams of Reunion)

B&W – Cantonese

Directed by Chu Gei (a.k.a. Chu Kei, a.k.a. Zhu Ji).

Produced by Diyi Film Company [Hong Kong].

With Tsi Lo Lin (a.k.a. Tsi Law Lin), Cheung Ying,
Cheung Wood Yau, Lee Pang-fei, Ng Tung.

Chi-keung and Yeuk-lan have just married, but to earn a living, Chi-keung has to go to Singapore. He leaves a pregnant Yeuk-lan behind. In Singapore, the factory where he works unfortunately closes down, forcing him to work as a labourer.

1952

NIAO YUAN

(a.k.a. You Fu Yi Ran Zai, a.k.a. The Mismatched Marriage)

B&W – Cantonese

Directed by Chiang Wai Kwong.

Produced by Tai Seng Film Company [Hong Kong].

With Tsi Lo Lin (a.k.a. Tsi Law Lin),
Wong Chiu Mo, Ho Fei Fan.

Sum and Bik-lin, a married couple, sell desserts for a living. Third Aunt hires thugs to beat Sum up so that she can approach Bik-lin and lend her money on condition that she works for her to pay off the debt. Knowing Third Aunt's ill intentions, Sum goes to Singapore where he works as a coolie in the hope of raising enough money to pay off Bik-lin's debt.

YOUNG MASTER IS A GIRL

(a.k.a. The Girl Who Plays Young Master)

B&W – Cantonese

Directed by Chan Pei.

Produced by Jinfeng Film Company [Hong Kong].

Filming by Nanyang Film Company [Hong Kong].

With Yam Kim-fai, Cheung Ying,
Ng Dan-fung, Au Yeung Kim.

The parents of a young girl born in Singapore have always told the grandfather, back in China, that they had a boy. When the grandfather falls sick and the family has to visit him, the young girl is forced to disguise herself as a boy. The movie was directed by Chan Pei, a veteran who had started in the mid-1920s and had already directed movies for Shaw's Nanyang Film Company in the late 1930s.

1954

MA LAI YA ZHI LIAN

(a.k.a. Malaya Love Affair)

[lit. Love in Malaya]

121 min - B&W – Cantonese

Directed by Tsi Lo Ling (a.k.a. Tsi Law Ling).

Produced by Ziluolian Film Company [Hong Kong].

With Cheung Wood Yau,
Cheung Ying, Ng Cho Fan.

WORLD FOR RANSOM

82 min – B&W – English

Directed by Robert Aldrich.

Produced by (unknown) [USA].

1955

XING DAO HONG CHUAN

(a.k.a. The Opera Boat in Singapore, a.k.a. It's Never Too Late)

B&W – Cantonese

Directed by Ku Wen Chung.

Produced by Shaw and Sons (Cantonese UnitGroup) [Hong Kong].

With Chung Lai-yung (Ying Lai-pak),
Lee Bo-ying (Ying Lai-pak's brother),
Lai Man-soh (Ying Lai-pak's brother),
Wong Chiu-mo (Yeung So), Tam Sau-zhen,
Cheung Suet-fung.

Ying Lai-pak, a famous opera singer, performs in Singapore with her brother and sister. There, she attracts the attention of Ma Sam-shui, whose mistress, To Tsat-gu, soon rages with jealousy and hires thugs to slander Ying. It is sometimes said to have been the first movie in Cantonese fully shot and produced by the Shaws in Singapore. The movie's theme song is "Paradise in Singapore", performed by Chung Lai-yung, Lee Bo-ying and Lai Man-soh.

1956

FU LAN JIE JIE

(a.k.a. Mother Dearest)

[lit. Sister Fu Lan]

B&W – Mandarin

Directed by Mok Hong-si (a.k.a. Mok Hong See).

Produced by Liberty Film Company [Hong Kong].

With Jeanette Lin Tsui (Fu Lan), Lin Jing (Madam Xu),
Yang Wen (Fu Ying), Ting Ying, Dan Ni, Yu Cong.

Madam Xu, a widow, single-handedly brings up her four daughters. To help with the family finances, second daughter Fu Lan seeks work in Singapore.

SEN LIN ZHI NU

(a.k.a. Maiden of the Forest)

B&W – Mandarin

Directed by Lee Tit.

Produced by Zongyi Film Company [Hong Kong].

With Yang Jing (Dong Xiaolan), Wang Hao (Awang),
Wang Yuen-lung, He Bin (aka Ho Pin), Wu Jiaxiang, Kao Pao Shu.

Malaysian Chinese girl Dong Xiaolan is taken by her father to Singapore to work as a song girl, and is thus forced to separate from her lover Awang.

XING ZHOU YAN JI

(a.k.a. Sin Chow Yim Chik, a.k.a. Romance in Singapore)

B&W – Cantonese

Directed by Lam Chuen.

Produced by International Films Distributing Agency [Hong Kong].

Executive producer is Albert Odell.

With Leung Sing Po, Cheung Ching,
Chow Kwun Ling.

A Chinese businessman and his son fly to Singapore to look after their business but also hoping to find a woman for each other. Whilst the father tries to matchmake his son with a young woman, the son tries to pair the father with a pretty widow. Some personnel from Cathay-Keris were involved in the cinematography and sound recording.

YANG LIN

(a.k.a. A Lonely Heart)

B&W – Mandarin

Directed by Qin Tao (a.k.a. Doe Ching) [Hong Kong].

Produced by Shaw and Sons Company [Hong Kong].

With Lucilla Yu Ming (a.k.a. Yau Man),
Chao Lei (a.k.a. Zhao Lei),
Wang Lai.

A young woman from Singapore is doing missionary work in Kuala Lumpur. There, she chances upon her natural mother.

1957

TANG SAN A SHAO

(a.k.a. She Married an Overseas Chinese)

B&W – Cantonese

Directed by Chan Man.

Produced by Kong Ngee Film Production Company [Hong Kong].

With Patrick Tse Yin,
Patsy Kar Ling,
Nam Hung.

Ho Ah-gau, a gambler, is several hundred dollars in debt. Seeing that her son is not getting anywhere in Macau, Gau's mother decides to spend her life savings to send him off to Malaya. She hopes he will start a new life there. After working for a while in a mine in Malaya, Gau then finds a job in Singapore as a waiter in a club.

XUE RAN XIANG SI GU

(a.k.a. Xue Ran Xuan Si Gu,
a.k.a. Blood Stains the Valley of Love,
a.k.a. Bloodshed in the Valley of Love,
a.k.a. Blood Valley)

B&W – Cantonese

Directed by Chun Kim and
Chor Yuen [Hong Kong].

Produced by Kong Ngee Film Production Company [Hong Kong].

With Patrick Tse Yin, Nam Hung,
Patsy Kar Ling, Geung Chung Ping.

A young man from Hong Kong loves a Malay girl, but his mother strongly disapproves of it. The story is based on a famous illustrated novel then. It was shot partly in Singapore and Malaysia, and features the traditional "Mak Inang" folk dance.

YE LIN YUE

(a.k.a. The Whispering Palms)

93 min – B&W – Cantonese

Directed by Chun Kim and
Chor Yuen [Hong Kong].

Produced by Kong Ngee Film Production Company [Hong Kong].

With Patrick Tse Yin, Nam Hung,
Patsy Kar Ling, Geung Chung Ping.

Ngok Ming is a young man devoted to education, and the Ching siblings, Tsi-wo and Suk-ho, are enthusiastic educators. Ming aspires to establish schools for overseas Chinese children in various parts of Malaysia. There, he falls in love at first sight with rich heiress Leung Cho-lin, but her father will only agree to sponsor the establishment of a school if Ming pledges himself to do business after their marriage

1958

KONG ZHONG XIAO JIE
(a.k.a. Air Hostess)
108 min – colour – Mandarin
Directed by Yi Wen (a.k.a. Evan Yang).
Produced by MP&GI [Hong Kong].
With Ge Lan (a.k.a. Grace Chang), Qiao Hong, Julie Yeh Feng.
After having finished air stewardess school, three young women encounter numerous on-the-job adventures, and love. Shot in an era when air travel was becoming popular in Asia, the movie takes us to various Asian locations, including Singapore.

NAN YANG A BA
(a.k.a. Nan Yang Ya Bo,
a.k.a. Naam Yeung A Ang,
a.k.a. Kuala Lumpur Nights,
a.k.a. The Old Man from Southeast Asia)
B&W – Cantonese
Directed by Lam Chuen.
Produced by International Films Distributing Agency [Hong Kong].
Executive producer is Albert Odell.
With Leung Sing Po, Cheung Ching, Chow Kwun Ling.

SHAN XIA FENG WEN BAO ZANG
(a.k.a. The Treasure of General Yamashita)
Colour – Cantonese
Directed by Chapman Ho.
Produced by Zhongguo Film Company [Hong Kong].
With Lola Young, Napoldo Saiceldo, Mito Mitsuko,
Pancho Magalona, Danilo Montes, Lihualuo.
Yip Fung comes into the possession of a Japanese army treasure map and a watch that once belonged to her lost father. She sets off on a treasure hunt with nightclub boss Pak Mau and others but the team faces numerous obstacles. General Yamashita was in command of the Japanese army during the invasion of Southeast Asia in World War II. He was known as "the Tiger of Malaya". Featuring a cast of Chinese, Japanese and Filipino actors, the movie was shot in Singapore and Malaya. A remake of it was made in the Philippines in 2001.

1959

DU LI QIAO ZHI LIAN
(a.k.a. The Merdeka Bridge, a.k.a. Love on Merdeka Bridge,
a.k.a. Chinta di Jambatan Merdeka)
[lit. Love on the Lonely Bridge]
109 min – B&W – Cantonese
Directed by Chow Sze Luk (a.k.a. Chow See Luk).
Produced by Shaw Brothers [Hong Kong].
With Patricia Lam Fung, Cheung Ying Choy, Mak Gei, Lee Pang Fei.
Yim Mui falls in love with a painter, Man Wai. They meet on the Merdeka Bridge, where they have their sweetheart talks. But one day, Man Wai has to leave for studies.

GUO BU XIN NIANG
(a.k.a. Bride from Another Town)
B&W – Cantonese
Directed by Chow Sze Luk (a.k.a. Chow See Luk).
Produced by Shaw Brothers [Hong Kong].
With Patricia Lam Fung, Cheung Ying Choy, Lung Kong, Lee Pang Fei.
Bride-to-be Chun Siu-yin arrives in Singapore only to discover that her fiance has died in a car accident. Cyclo-driver Lee Tim-fuk tends to her meticulously and the two gradually fall in love.

JIA ZHENG JIN
(a.k.a. The Frivolous Professor)
B&W – Amoy dialect
Directed by Chen Yiqing (a.k.a. Chan Yik Ching).
Produced by Huanqiu Film Company [Hong Kong].
With Ding Lan, Chen Lie,
Huang Ying.
Professor Zhao falls for Yan, an actress. When she goes on a tour of Southeast Asia, he follows her all the way to Singapore.

LIU LIAN PIAO XIANG
(a.k.a. When Durians Bloom,
a.k.a. The Fragrance of the Durians)
B&W – Cantonese
Codirected by Chow Sze Luk (a.k.a. Chow See Luk) and Ng Dan (a.k.a. Ng Tin Chi).
Produced by Shaw Brothers [Hong Kong].
With Patricia Lam Fung,
Lung Kong, Mak Gei,
Lee Pang Fei.
At his father's behest, Ko Cheuk Man takes over the rubber plant business from his uncle Kin Shing in Singapore.

MA LAI YA ZHI LIAN
(a.k.a. Love of Malaya)
B&W – Amoy
Directed by Chen Yiqing (a.k.a. Chan Yik Ching).
Produced by Eng Wah Film Production Company [Hong Kong].
With Ding Lan, Chen Lie,
Guan Xinyi.

NAN YANG QING GE
(a.k.a. Love Songs from Southeast Asia)
B&W – Amoy
Directed by (unknown).
Produced by (unknown) [Hong Kong].
With You Juan, Bai Yi.

XING DAO FANG ZONG
(a.k.a. Black Gold)
B&W – Mandarin
Directed by Rolf Bayer [Philippines].
(other sources mention Bai Yi).
Written by Ralf Modder [Philippines].
(other sources mention Laai Foo Mau Tak).
Produced by Shaw Brothers [Hong Kong].
With Shi Ying, Paul Chang Chung,
Hong Bo.
A young woman, Ling Huei, is used by a drug trafficker, Huang De, but she ends up in jail instead of him. Upon her release six years later, she meets a doctor, Du Sen, who asks her to move to Singapore with him. But Huang De tracks her down and asks her to start trafficking again. The movie was shot on location in Singapore and Malaya. The year before, Filipino Rolf Bayer had directed *Azimat* for Shaw's Malay Film Productions.

Kong Zhong Xiao Jie (a.k.a. Air Hostess), 1958

XING YUE ZHENG HUI
(a.k.a. Love for You)
B&W – Mandarin
Directed by Hang Ying-mo.
Produced by Liberty Film Company [Hong Kong].
With Lan Di, Wang Yuen Lung, Chen Yun, Kim Jin-kyu.
Korean musician Li Changmin is stranded in Malaya during the turmoil of war. Believing that Li is dead, his wife Jin Xing'ai single-handedly raises their children. Years later, their son Mingao meets the diva Xia Yuelian, who invites him and his family to form a dance troupe to tour Malaya.

XIN JIA PO XIAO JIE
(a.k.a. Miss Singapore)
B&W – Amoy dialect
Directed by Yan Qiufeng (a.k.a. Yuen Chow Fung).
Produced by Eng Wah Film Production Company [Hong Kong].
With Xiao Juan (a.k.a. Ivy Ling Bo), Huang Ying.

ZHUO GUI ZOU BIE
(a.k.a. He Has Taken Her for Another)
B&W – Amoy dialect
Directed by Ku Wen Chung.
Produced by Huaye Company [Hong Kong].
Adapted from *The Comedy of Errors* by William Shakespeare.
With Yang Peyun, Xiao Juan, Gao Shan.
Two pairs of twin sisters, Yuluan and Yufeng, and Chunxiang and Qiuxiang were separated during the turmoil of war. Fifteen years later, Yufeng and her maid Qiu travel from Singapore to Hong Kong to look for Yuluan and Chunxiang.

1960

FLIGHT FROM SINGAPORE
74 min – B&W – English
Directed by Dudley Birch [UK].
Produced by (unknown).
With William Abney, Patrick Allen, Rosemary Dorken,
Harry Fowler, Denis Holmes, Patrick Holt, Jane Jordan Rogers.

MONDO CANE
(a.k.a. A Dog's World)
105 min – colour – Italian
Directed by Paolo Cavara, Gualtiero Jacopetti and Franco Prosperi [Italy].
Produced by Gualtiero Jacopetti [Italy].
A world-famous shockumentary presenting a series of loosely-knit events of a bizarre and unusual nature shot throughout the world including Malaysia and Singapore (Chinatown, Sago Lane, etc.). Lurid, sensational, eccentric. It certainly has no match nor equivalent in the history of film in Singapore.

SINGAPORE

Directed by Shakti Samanta [India].
Produced by F.C. Mehra / Eagle Films [India].
Music by Shankar Jaikishen.
With Maria Menado (Maria), Shammi Kapoor (Shyam),
Padmini (Lata), Shashikala (Shobha),
Rajen Kapoor (Ramesh), K.N. Singh (Shivdas),
Madan Puri (Chang).

Shyam sends his manager Ramesh to sell off his rubber estate in Singapore. While going through some old papers, Ramesh finds a map revealing that a treasure is hidden in the estate. He immediately writes to Shyam, but Shyam does not respond. Ultimately, Shyam receives a phone call but the line is suddenly cut off. Shyam then decides to fly to Singapore. In the plane, he meets a Malayan beauty, Maria.

1963

A WEALTHY FAMILY

Colour – Cantonese
Directed by Mok Hong-si (a.k.a. Mok Hong See).
Produced by New Tide [Hong Kong].
With Ng Cho Fan (Lo Yau-cheung),
Cheung Ying (Lo Yau-shing),
Sheung Kwun Kwan Wai.

Lo Yau-shing is a married man whose mistress, Tung Wing-fan, gives birth to twin daughters. Shing is too afraid to face the truth and decides to go to Singapore with his wife, leaving Fan and the babies behind.

MADAM GUM

(a.k.a. Madam Jin)
B&W – Cantonese
Directed by Mok Hong-si (a.k.a. Mok Hong See).
Produced by Lan Kwong Film Company [Hong Kong].
With Pak Yin (Madam Gum),
Ting Ying (Tong Yin-fan),
Cheung Yee (Chau Man-fai),
Keung Chung-ping (Ma Bing-chiu).

Madam Gum, a well-known dance hall girl, gave birth to a daughter, Yin-fan, when she was young. As she did not want Fan to live under the pressure of having a dance hall girl for a mother, she gave her to some relatives. Nineteen years later, Madam Gum accidentally runs into Fan's husband, Man-fai, in Singapore.

1964

I PIRATI DELLA MALESIA

(a.k.a. The Pirates of Malaysia)
110 min – colour – Italian
Directed by Umberto Lenzi [Italy].
Produced by (unknown) [Italy].
With Steve Reeves (Sandokan),
Jacqueline Sassard, Mimmo Palmara,
Andrea Bosic, Sujata,
Asoka, George Wang.

This coproduction involving Italy, Spain, Germany and France tells the story of a Malay rebel, Sandokan, who fights against an evil British general. It was apparently shot on location in Singapore, the island being once again used as an exotic setting.

1965

XIN HUA DUO DUO KAI

(a.k.a. Hong Kong Manila Singapore)
Directed by Qin Tao (a.k.a. Doe Ching) [Hong Kong].
Produced by Shaw Brothers [Hong Kong].
With Peter Chen Ho,
Angela Yu Chien,
Chin Feng, Laam Dai.

A rather forgotten comedy by Qin Tao, who had previously become famous with *Our Sister Hedy*, a 1957 Cathay hit made in Hong Kong by MP&GI, and Les Belles, an acclaimed production by Shaw Brothers with Lin Dai and Peter Chen Ho in 1961.

1966

GOLDSNAKE ANONIMA KILLERS

(a.k.a. Suicide Mission to Singapore,
a.k.a. Singapur, hora cero,
a.k.a. Mission suicide à Singapour)
96 min – colour
Directed by Ferdinando Baldi [Italy].
Produced by (unknown) [Italy].
With Stelio Candelli, Juan Cortes,
Annabella Incontrera, Salleh Melan,
Yoko Tani.

American secret agent Kurt Jackson is sent to Singapore to rescue Professor Wang Li and his son who have escaped from China. Professor Wang Li has discovered a way to produce a small atomic bomb. Chang Tu, a villain, is trying to get the atomic power from Professor Wang Li. Kurt Jackson soon finds help in the mysterious and charming Annie Wong. This coproduction involving Italy, France and Spain was largely shot on location in Singapore.

QING CHANG YI GENG CHANG

(a.k.a. Loyalty)
B&W – Cantonese
Directed by Lung To.
Produced by (unknown) [Hong Kong].
With Ng Kwan-lai (Wong Pui-ying),
Cheung Ying-choi (Ko Chi-fung),
Cheng Wai-sum (Wai Tak-yan),
Lui Woon-suen (Ching Lap-man).

Disillusioned with life, Chi Fung leaves the rich To family in Hong Kong and, with the help of a friend, moves to Singapore.

QING QING HE BIAN CAO

(a.k.a. The Rebellion)
[lit. Green is the Grass]
Colour – Cantonese
Directed by Chiang Wai Kwong.
Produced by (unknown) [Hong Kong].
With Ng Kwan Lai, Woo Fung,
Lam Kau.

A young man from Kuala Lumpur who cannot get the approval of his father for his marriage, is forced to leave his family home. He goes to Singapore to look for a job.

XI JIE WEI LIAO YUAN

(a.k.a. Shuang Liao Wei Hun Qi,
a.k.a. Back Together)
B&W – Mandarin
Directed by Ling Wan.
Produced by Aimei Company [Hong Kong].
With Nam Hung (Diana), Lam Kar Sing (Tong Yan-kit),
Lee Hong Kum (Chin Man-ling), Mak Kei (Man Sai-so),
Yu Ming.

Diana, a young overseas graduate, returns to Singapore. Her father then tries to arranges a marriage for her. Discontented with the situation, she tries to find out whom she will be married to. She goes to Hong Kong and meets her pen friend Ching Chung who is a romance writer.

1967

CINQ GARS POUR SINGAPOUR

(a.k.a. Five Ashore in Singapore,
a.k.a. Singapore, Singapore)
95 min – colour – French
Directed by Bernard Toublanc-Michel (a.k.a. Bernard T. Michel) [France].
Produced by Pierre Kalfon, Georges Chappedelaine,
Les Films Number One, Franco Riganti [France / Italy].
Original story by Jean Bruce.
Screenplay by Sergio Amidei, Pierre Kalfon and
Bernard Toublanc-Michel.
Music by Antoine Duhamel.
With Sean Flynn (Captain Art Smith),
Marika Green (Monica), Terry Downes (Sergeant Gruber),
Marc Michel (Captain Kevin Grey), Denis Berry (Dan),
Peter Gayford (Brown), Bernard Meusnier (Angel McLihemy),
Andrew Ray (Tat-chouen), Jessy Greek (Ten-sin),
See Foon (Hsi-houa), William Brix (Captain Kafir),
Lim Hong Chin, Abdullah Ramand,
Ismail Boss.

Some Marines have recently disappeared in Singapore. Captain Art Smith, from the CIA, is sent to investigate. He meets four marines who are willing to assist him in order to avenge their friends who have disappeared. But Art Smith also meets the mysterious Monica. Entirely shot on location, this movie shows a lot of Singapore in the 1960s. Fifty per cent was shot directly in the streets and in 52 different settings (black and white villas, nightclubs, villages, etc.). Beside its documentary value, it is also interesting for its surprisingly mixed cast: Sean Flynn (the son of Errol Flynn, but with a far less successful movie career, who disappeared without a trace in Cambodia in 1970), Marika Green (who had started in 1959 in Robert Bresson's *Pickpocket*, and who will later play in the 1974 French erotica *Emmanuelle* in Bangkok), Marc Michel (who had played in some of the most famous French movies of the early 1960s, including some by Jacques Demy), Denis Berry (the son of film director John Berry), plus some local actors who were given good parts.

PRETTY POLLY
(a.k.a. A Matter of Innocence)
102 min – colour – English
Directed by Guy Green [UK].
Produced by George W. George [UK].
Original story by Noel Coward.
With Hayley Mills, Trevor Howard,
Shashi Kapoor, Brenda De Banzie.
Miss Polly decides to spend a few months with her stern aunt as a travelling companion, visiting Singapore and the surrounding region.

SHINGAPORU NO YORU WA KOKETE
Colour – Japanese
Directed by Hirokazu Ichimura [Japanese]
Produced by Shochicku [Japanese].

1968

YU NU CHI QING
(a.k.a. Opposite Love)
B&W – Cantonese
Directed by Chor Yuen (a.k.a. Chu Yuan).
Produced by Kam Lan [Hong Kong].
With Connie Chan Bo Chu, Cheung Ching, Woo Fung.
Ho Siu-ling was adopted by Ku Chi-ming's father when young. In the course of time, Ku Chi-ming falls in love with Siu-ling without realizing it. However, Siu-ling only treats him as her elder brother. When Siu-ling gets engaged to Yu Keung, Chi-ming sends his heartbroken blessings. However, on the night of the engagement, Yu Keung's father suddenly arrives from Singapore and asks him to cancel the engagement or else he will disown him. Yu Keung gives in and follows his father back to Singapore because he is afraid of losing his money and status. Siu-ling is very sad but she promises to wait for Yu Keung's return for marriage. Three years later, Siu-ling decides to go to Singapore to find Yu Keung.

1969

DREI GOLDENE SCHLANGEN
(a.k.a. Three Golden Serpents, a.k.a. Island of Lost Girls)
88 min – colour – Italian
Directed by Roberto Mauri [Italy].
Produced by Peter Homfeld and Ralph Zucker [Italy / Germany].
With Tony Kendall, Brad Harris, Monica Pardo.
A Kommissar X adventure in Asia, in which Western women tourists are kidnapped by an Asian ring headed by a rich and mysterious Oriental beauty. Kept on a secret island, they serve as prostitutes to rich tourists. Kommissar X and his usual sidekick are sent to rescue the women.

Niang Re Zhi Lian, 1969

LITTLE JUNGLE BOY
(a.k.a. Momman, Little Jungle Boy)
78 min – colour – English
Directed by Mende Brown [Australia].
Produced by (unknown).
With Lesley Berryman, Mike Dorsey, Willie Fennell, Noel Ferrier, Niki Huen, Rahman Rahman.
A kiddie matinee feature about a young boy who, after having lived in the jungle, is brought to the big city where he encounters "civilisation".

MY LOVE IS LIKE A SPRING BREEZE
Colour – Cantonese
Directed by Lui Kei (a.k.a. Lui Kay).
Produced by Kong Ngee and 21st Century Company [Hong Kong].
With Connie Chun Bo Chu, Lui Kei.

NIANG RE ZHI LIAN
(a.k.a. Nyonya Tsi Lung, a.k.a. Romance of a Nyonya, a.k.a. Love with a Malaysian Girl)
[lit. Nyonya Love Story]
93 min – colour – Cantonese
Directed by Lui Kei (a.k.a. Lui Kay).
Produced by Kong Ngee and 21st Century Company [Hong Kong].
With Connie Chun Bo Chu (Siu-wan), Lui Kei (Ting-han), Chan Leung Chung, Leung Bo Chu, Chan Bo Yee.
Ting-han, a writer from Hong Kong, is invited by his friend to visit Singapore. He goes there in search of inspiration. In Singapore, he meets a local Chinese woman, Siu-wan, an adopted child. It happens that her real-life parents are also the parents of the writer.

1974

SHOCKING ASIA
(a.k.a. Asia Perversa)
94 min – colour – English
Directed by Rolf Olsen (sometimes also credited as Emerson Fox) [Germany].
Produced by (unknown) [Hong Kong / Germany].
A documentary in the style of *Mondo Cane*, depicting ultra graphic scenes from Asia, including a sex change operation in Singapore.

1975

G.I. EXECUTIONER
(a.k.a. Dragon Lady)
86 min – colour – English
Directed by Joel M. Reed [USA].
Produced by Marvin Farkas [USA].
With Tom Keena, Victoria Racimo, Anna Ling, Dragon Lee.
An ex-Vietnam War commando living in Singapore is hired to rescue a kidnapped scientist. Shot in Singapore in 1971, this exploitation flick was not released until 1984. Action includes scenes at Bugis Street and Sago Lane.

1976

A NIU JI YU JI
(a.k.a. A Niu Xia Nan Yang, a.k.a. Crazy Bumpkin in Singapore)
Directed by John Law Ma.
Produced by Shaw Brothers [Hong Kong].
With Yau Fung, Ai Ti.

WOMEN DETECTIVE
Directed by Choi Hoon.
Produced by Woo Sung Enterprises [South Korea].
After a woman's body is found in Singapore, three women detectives (from South Korea, Hong Kong and Singapore) investigate.

1979

SAINT JACK
112 min – colour – English
Directed by Peter Bogdanovich [USA].
Produced by Roger Corman / New World Pictures [USA].
Original story by Paul Theroux.
Screenplay by Howard Sackler, Paul Theroux and Peter Bogdanovich.
With Ben Gazzara (Jack Flowers), Denholm Elliott, Joss Ackland, James Villiers, Monika Subramaniam, Judy Lim, Lisa Lu.
Jack Flowers, with his flowery shirts, is a street-savvy American expatriate living in Singapore at the time of the Vietnam war. His plan is to open a whorehouse, and make money from all the American marines stopping by in Singapore on their way to or back from Vietnam. But he encounters many difficulties with the local pimps and gangsters. Entirely shot on location, this controversial movie, banned in Singapore for many years, has great documentary value, having captured the city's landscape at the end of the 1970s, right before some massive changes radically modified it.

1981

UN ECHIPAJ PENTRU SINGAPORE
Colour – Romanian
Directed by Nicu Stan [Romania].
Produced by (unknown) [Romania].
With Ion Besoiu, Gheorghe Cozorici, Mariana Mihut, Victor Rebengiuc, Stefan Sileanu.

1982

THE SOUTHERN CROSS
(a.k.a. Highest Honor, a.k.a. Minami Jujisei)
144 min - colour - English
Directed by Maruyama Seiji [Japan] and Peter Maxwell [Australia].
Produced by Shin Nihon Eiga [Japan] and Southern International Film [Australia].
With Michael Aitkens, Craig Ballard, Vincent Ball, Kinya Kitaoji.
An information officer at the Japanese Embassy in pre-World War II Singapore is imprisoned by the British authorities for spying. Upon his release from prison by the invading Japanese forces, he becomes involved in efforts to prevent mass execution of the Chinese.

1989

RAFFLES HOTEL
90 min – colour – Japanese
Directed by Murakami Ryu [Japan].
Produced by Shochiku-Fuji [Japan].
With Miwako Fujitani, Jinpachi Nezu, Masahiro Moteki, Fann Wong.
A Japanese actress comes to Singapore, looking for an ex-lover who had abandoned her.

1990

SHOU HU FEI LONG
(a.k.a. Skinny Tiger & Fatty Dragon, a.k.a. Nutty Kickbox Cops)
105 min – colour – Cantonese
Directed by Lau Kar-wing.
Produced by Cinema Capital Entertainments Ltd [Hong Kong].
With Sammo Hung, Karl Maka, Carrie Ng Ka-lai, Jessica Yung Wanda, Lung Ming-yan.
Detectives Skinny and Fatty have infuriated their superior by ruining his wedding ceremony during the arrest of an international drug syndicate. To calm him down, they quit their job and leave Hong Kong for Singapore, where they meet two beautiful ladies, and encounter more troubles.

The Truth about Jane and Sam, 1999

1991

JING TIAN SHI ER XIAO SHI

(a.k.a. The Last Blood, a.k.a. 12 Hours of Fear,
a.k.a. 12 Hours to Die, a.k.a. 12 Hours of Terror,
a.k.a. Hard Boiled 2)
99 min – colour – Cantonese
Directed by Jing Wong (a.k.a. Wong Ching).
Produced by Wallace Cheung and Eric Tsang [Hong Kong].
With Alan Tam (Lui Tai), Eric Tsang (Fatty),
Andy Lau (Brother Bee), Pak Cheung Chan (Ferrai),
Ho Chin (the terrorist leader), May Lo Mei-mei (Ling May),
Ka Yan Leung (Stone).

The Japanese Red Army will stop at nothing to assassinate the Lama during his goodwill visit trip to Singapore on national day. On his way there, he meets Ling May, a young woman who shares his horoscope. He tells her that they face a day of danger, and she scoffs at him. Once at Singapore airport, both are seriously wounded by terrorists. They have a rare blood type, so if the Red Army can keep blood donors from the hospital, both the monk and Ling will die. The police and Hong Kong antiterrorist super-agent Lui Tai have one hope — to get a cowardly conman to go to the hospital to give blood before it is too late.

1993

HUA TIAN SHI SHI

(a.k.a. All's Well Ends Well Too)
87 min – colour – Cantonese
Directed by Clifton Ko Chi Sum and
Raymond Wong Pak Ming [Hong Kong].
Produced by Mandarin Films Ltd [Hong Kong].
With Sam Hui, Leslie Cheung, Teresa Mo,
Ricky Hui, Sandra Ng, Stephen Chow,
Raymond Wong, James Wong.

1997

PARADISE ROAD

122 min – colour – English
Directed by Bruce Beresford.
Produced by Village Roadshow Pictures and YTC Pictures [USA].
Story by David Giles and Martin Meader.
With Glenn Close, Frances McDormand,
Pauline Collins, Cate Blanchett,
Julianna Margulies.

Following the Japanese assault on Singapore, the women are sent away on a boat, while the men remain to defend the city. Unfortunately, the women are captured by the Japanese and sent to a camp in Sumatra. The opening scene takes place in Raffles Hotel, in Singapore. The rest of the movie was shot in other locations. Hardly any local cast is involved.

1998

FULLTIME KILLER

102 min – colour – Cantonese, Mandarin,
English, Japanese, Korean
Directed by Johnnie To and
Wai Ka Fai [Hong Kong].
Produced by Milkyway Image Ltd Production and
Teamwork Motion Pictures Ltd [Hong Kong].
Music by Guy Zerafa.
With Andy Lau, Takashi Sorimachi,
Simon Yam, Kelly Lin, Cherrie Ying.

Two lonely killers with very different ideals oppose each other in a duel taking them throughout Asia: Hong Kong, Kuala Lumpur, Seoul, Singapore. Some interesting scenes were shot in Singapore's railway station and along Boat Quay.

1999

GUAI TAN ZHI MO JING

(a.k.a. Wuye Xion Jing,
a.k.a. The Mirror)
87 min – colour – Cantonese
Directed by Siao Wing, Agan and
Raymond Wong (a.k.a. Raymond Wong Bak,
a.k.a. Wong Bak Ming, a.k.a. Wong Pak Ming).
Produced by Golden Mandarin and
Mandarin Films [Hong Kong].
With Jack Neo, John Cheng,
Raymond Wong, Nicholas Tse.

This omnibus movie comprises four horror stories variously set in Ming China, 1920s Shanghai, modern-day Singapore and contemporary Hong Kong. The four stories are linked by an antique chest of drawers carrying a mirror with the strange capacity to exert power over its various owners, forcing them to behave oddly, with tragic and deadly consequences. Jack Neo stars in the third story, as a Singaporean banker.

ROGUE TRADER

101 min – colour – English
Directed by James Dearden [UK].
Produced by James Dearden [UK].
With Ewan McGregor, Anna Friel, Irene Ng, Gerald Chew, Ivan Heng.

THE TRUTH ABOUT JANE AND SAM

(a.k.a. Zhen Xin Hua,
a.k.a. Zun Sum Wah)
100 min – colour – Cantonese, Mandarin, English
Directed by Derek Yee Tong Sheng (a.k.a. Yee
Tung Shin) [Hong Kong].
Produced by MediaCorp Raintree Pictures [Singapore] and
Film Unlimited [Hong Kong].
With Fann Wong (Jane), Peter Ho (Sam), James Lye, Cheng Pei-pei.

Sam, a fresh graduate from Singapore, works as a journalist in Hong Kong to gain wider exposure to life. He chances upon Jane, a streetwise Hong Kong girl who captures his interest for a cover story. What starts out as fascination develops into a heartwarming love story. Together, the two young lovers discover hope, happiness and the truth about love. Directed by a Hong Konger, it was shot almost entirely in Hong Kong and driven largely by a Hong Kong production house. This is a Hong Kong movie with only a few shots of Singapore, a partly Singaporean cast, and a Singaporean financial coproducer (MediaCorp Raintree Pictures).

2000

2000 AD

(a.k.a. Gongyuan 2000 Nian)
99 min – colour – Cantonese, Mandarin, English
Directed by Gordon Chan (a.k.a. Chan Kar
Sheung) [Hong Kong].
Produced by MediaCorp Raintree Pictures [Singapore] and
Media Asia Films [Hong Kong].
Story by Stu Zicherman and Gordon Chan.
Music by Umebayashi Shigeru.
With Aaron Kwok (Peter),
Daniel Wu (Benny),
James Lye (Eric),
Phyllis Quek (Salina),
Andrew Lin (Kelvin),
Francis Ng, Ray Liu,
Kenneth Low.

A private jet suddenly explodes over the skies of Singapore. The Singapore Defence suspects sabotage. When they are informed by a CIA agent, Kelvin, that a Chinese American in Hong Kong is responsible for the disaster, they secretly send one of their top investigators, Eric Ong, to search for him. A few interesting action scenes were shot in Singapore, showing the city in a rather unusual way.

DA YING JIA

(a.k.a. Winner Takes All)
91 min – colour – Cantonese
Directed by Clifton Ko Chi Sum [Hong Kong].
Produced by Mandarin Films Ltd [Hong Kong].
With Sam Hui, Nicholas Tse,
Alec Su Yu-peng, Ruby Lam,
Joey Yung.

A young woman whose father has been cheated by a thief decides to take revenge. She follows him to Singapore, where she teams up with two men who also hold grudges against the cheat.

2004

RICE RHAPSODY

(a.k.a. Hainan Ji Fan,
also known under its working title, Hainanese Chicken Rice)
108 min – colour – Mandarin, English
Directed by Kenneth Bi [Hong Kong].
Produced by JCE Movies Ltd and
Kenbiroli [Hong Kong].
With Sylvia Chang (Jen),
Martin Yan (Kim),
Maggie Q (Gigi),
Melanie Laurent (Sabine),
Steph Song (Jennifer),
Craig Toh (Harry),
Alvin Chiang.

A single mother, Jen, looks after her three sons while she tries to run her restaurant business. But as if running a chicken rice restaurant and taking care of three boys were not enough work, Jen, at the urging of her rival chef cum secret admirer, Kim Chui, brings in a female French exchange student when she notices that her 17-year-old son is not showing any interest in the opposite sex.

ACCESSIBILITY

How to access the movies

SHAW'S MALAY FILM PRODUCTIONS (1947—1967)

Prints

Many of Shaw Brothers' Malay movies produced under Malay Film Productions have been transferred to digital betacam (commonly referred to as digibeta, a tape format for professional use) and are available at Shaw Organisation's office in Singapore. The exact condition of most of the original prints is not known.

Videos

Some of the Shaw Brothers' Malay movies made between 1947 and 1967 are available on VCD, mostly under Music Valley's label. They are rarely presented with English subtitles, except for the P. Ramlee ones.

SHAW'S HONG KONG MOVIES (AFTER 1958)

Made-in-Hong Kong movies by the Shaw Brothers since 1958 (*Come Drink with Me*, *The Super Inframan*, *Farewell My Love*, *Return to the 36th Chamber*) are mostly available on VCD or DVD. These are through Celestial Pictures. They are part of Hong Kong film history, even though there were strong links between Shaw Singapore and Shaw Hong Kong. This was especially so in the late 1950s and early 1960s, when Shaw Run Run moved from Singapore to Hong Kong. For more information on these titles: www.celestialpictures.com

Nasib Si Labu Labi by P. Ramlee, 1963.

CATHAY-KERIS (1953—1972)

Prints

A large number of Cathay-Keris' Malay movies were transferred onto beta tapes by Cathay Organisation in the late 1990s. These tapes are accessible at Cathay's office in Singapore. As for the prints, if some still exist, their exact condition is not known.

The prints of 18 Cathay-Keris movies are known to be lost since the early 1960s, following the split between Ho Ah Loke and Loke Wan Tho. The lost titles were taken by Ho Ah Loke when he left. They include important movies:

- The first two features of the pontianak genre, the seminal *Pontianak* and *Dendam Pontianak*, both made in 1957 by B. N. Rao.
- *Orang Lichin* by L. Krishnan.
- *Adam*, the first movie directed by S. Roomai Noor in 1956.
- *Saudaraku* and *Irama Kaseh*, the first two movies directed by Lourey Friedman in 1955.
- *Buloh Perindu*, the first Cathay-Keris movie directed by B. S. Rajhans in 1953.

Chinta Gadis Rimba (a.k.a. *The Virgin of Borneo*) was also one of the lost treasures. Fortunately, a video transfer could be made from a negative long left in a laboratory in England, where the film was initially sent for colour processing.

Videos

Most of the Malay movies produced by Cathay-Keris between 1953 and 1972 are available on VCD through two main video publishers, Music Valley (based in Malaysia), and Comstar Home Entertainment (based in Singapore).

Music Valley's movies are not always subtitled in English, and, hence, are available only in their original Malay versions.

Comstar's titles (presented with English subtitles) include *Dang Anom*, *Tun Fatimah*, *Lanchang Kuning*, *Satay*, *Sri Mersing*, *Raden Mas*, *Korban Fitnah*, and *Selendang Delima*. For more information: www.comstarhe.com

CATHAY'S MP&GI, HONG KONG (1955—1970)

A number of the Hong Kong movies produced by Cathay Organisation under its sister company MP&GI, from 1956 till 1970, are available on VCD or DVD. They are published by Panorama Entertainment, a video publisher based in Hong Kong, in their original version with English subtitles. Some of the titles are: *Mambo Girl*, which made Ge Lan, a.k.a. Grace Chang, famous throughout Asia; *Our Sister Hedy*; *My Kingdom for a Husband*; *Air Hostess*, also with Grace Chang, plus creatures with beautiful legs, and eye-catching aerial views of Singapore in the late 1950s; *Her Tender Heart*; *The Wild Wild Rose*; *Bachelors Beware*; also *The First Sword*, with which Cathay / MP&GI ventured into action and wu xia style movies in the mid-1960s; *Mission to Die*; and *The Homemaker*. These movies belong more to Hong Kong's history than to Singapore's, even though Singapore's driving force in them cannot be overlooked. For more information on these video catalogues: www.panorama.com.hk

POST-STUDIO ERA (1973 ONWARDS)

Prints

Prints of movies of the post-studio era, those made since 1973, are generally available directly from their independent producers.

Videos

Non-studio movies from the 1970s are not available on video. Most of the movies made after 1995 are available on VCD or DVD:

Jack Neo's *That One No Enough*, *I Not Stupid*, *Homerun* and *The Best Bet*, as well as Teng Bee Lian's *Liang Po Po — The Movie*, and Cheek's *Chicken Rice War* are published by Videovan Entertainment, with Chinese, English and, occasionally, Malay subtitles.

Jack Neo's *I Do I Do*, Kelvin Tong's *The Maid* and Eric Khoo's *12 Storeys*, *Mee Pok Man* and *Be with Me* are published by Scorpio East Entertainment (www.scorpioeast.com.sg).

Royston Tan's *15* is published in the US by Picture This! Home Video (www.picturethishomevideo.com).

Eating Air by Kelvin Tong and Jasmine Ng, *Forever Fever* by Glen Goei, *One Leg Kicking* by Khookoh, and *Return to Pontianak* by Djinn, *Army Daze* by Ong Keng Sen, *The Teenage Textbook Movie* by Phillip Lim, and *Tiger's Whip* by Victor Khoo are distributed by Alliance Entertainment Singapore.

Twilight Kitchen and other Gerald Lee titles are available on VCD, with English subtitles, from Gateway Entertainment (www.gateway-e.com).

A selection of award-winning Singapore short films can be found in the inaugural *Singapore Shorts DVD Compilation*: *3 Feet Apart* by Jason Lai, *Autograph Book* by Wee Li Lin, *Birthday* by Bertrand Lee, *Locust* by Victric Thng, *Mother* by Royston Tan, *Moving House* by Tan Pin Pin, *The Call Home* by Han Yew Kwang, *The Secret Heaven* by Sun Koh and *While You Sleep* by Eva Tang. The DVD is published by the Asian Film Archive (www.asianfilmarchive.org).

The famously infamous *Saint Jack* by Peter Bogdanovich is available on DVD from New Concorde Home Video. Other Western movies shot on location are apparently not available on video, so far.

Although not a movie but a pedagogical DVD, *Born in Singapore* is useful as it offers a quick history of Singapore from 1960 to 1979. It includes about 120 clips from audiovisual archives, showing different aspects of Singapore, including a number of movie premieres in the 1960s, Jurong's first drive-in in 1971, and movie theatre halls in the late 1970s. This DVD was produced and published in 2000 by the Ministry of Information and the Arts (MITA), a body which has since been renamed Ministry of Information, Communications and the Arts (MICA).

REFERENCES

Bibliography

ALJUNIED Syed Muhd Khairudin, "Films as Social History — P. Ramlee's 'Seniman Bujang Lapok' and Malays in Singapore (1950s-1960s)", in *The Heritage Journal*, vol. 2 no. 1, 2005, pp. 1-21.

ARMES Roy, *Third World Film Making and the West*, Berkeley / Los Angeles / London, University of California Press, 1987, 381 p.

An important book in its time, although a bit dated now, with only a few lines about Singapore (but written when Singapore's film industry had reached ground zero).

BERNSTEIN Matthew and STUDLAR Gaylyn (editors), *Visions of the East. Orientalism in Film*, London / New York, I.B. Tauris Publishers, 1997, 330 p.

BIRCH David, "Film and Cinema in Singapore: Cultural Policy as Control", in MORAN Albert (editor), *Film Policy: International, National, and Regional Perspectives*, New York, Routledge, 1996, pp. 185-211.

CHANG Agnes Shook Cheong, GOPINATHAN S., HO Wah Kam (editors), *Growing Up in Singapore. Research Perspectives on Adolescents*, Singapore, Pearson / Prentice Hall, 1999, 254 p.

An excellent book to gain a better understanding of Singaporean teenagers. Very useful for the general backdrop of a movie such as *15*, and certain short movies, though a bit academic.

CHEAH Philip, "Singapore Rediscovered", *Cinemaya*, 1997, n°35, pp. 54-56.

CHEAH Philip, "Film in Singapore from 1972. The Reconstruction of a Film Industry", in SEAPAVAA, *Films in Southeast Asia. Views from the Region*, 2000, pp. 195-209. A useful contribution from Philip Cheah, the only one to decently and actively represent Singapore in the world of film critics.

CHEAH Philip, "Starting over", in VASUDEV Aruna, PAGAONKAR Latika, DORAISWAMY Rashmi (editors), *Being and Becoming. The Cinemas of Asia*, New Delhi, MacMillan India Limited, 2002, pp. 380-391.

The best essay on Singapore cinema written in the last few years. By, without a doubt, the best local film critic and programmer. However, the text is a bit too short and allusive to be really comprehensive. Philip Cheah would have so much more to say, if he were given the space, or if he were taking it.

CHEW Phyllis, KRAMER-DAHL Anneliese (editors), *Reading Culture: Textual Practices in Singapore*, Singapore, Times Academic Press, 1999.

A serious book with useful information about cultural practices.

CHUA Beng Huat, "Between Economy and Race: the Asianization of Singapore", in ONCU Asye, WEYLAND Petra (editors), *Space, Culture and Power: New Identities in Globalizing Cities*, New Jersey, Zed Books, 1997, pp. 23-41. For a better grasp of Singapore's geopolitics.

CHUA Beng Huat, "Culture, Multiracialism and National Identity in Singapore", in CHEN Kuan Hsing (editor), *Trajectories: Inter-Asia Cultural Studies*, London, Routledge, 1998, pp.186-205.

By one of the best researchers in Singapore. Academic, but with strong views very clearly expressed.

CHUA Beng Huat, "Taiwan's Future / Singapore's Past: Hokkien Films in Between", in CHUA Beng Huat, *Life is Not Complete Without Shopping*, Singapore, Singapore University Press, 2003, pp. 156-173.

CHUA Beng Huat and YOW Wei Wei, "Cinematic Critique from the Margins and the Mainstream", in CHUA Beng Huat, *Life is Not Complete Without Shopping*, Singapore, Singapore University Press, 2003, pp. 177-189.

CROFTS Stephen, "Concepts of National Cinema", in HILL John, CHURCH GIBSON Pamela (editors), *World Cinema: Critical Approaches*, Oxford, Oxford University Press, 2000, pp. 1-10.

A very useful book, especially in its introduction, for someone who wants to investigate the concept of national cinema. Nothing really on Singapore, though (which is not surprising).

CURRAN James, PAK Myung-Jin, "Beyond Globalization Theory", in CURRAN James, PAK Myung-Jin (editors), *De-Westernizing Media Studies*, London, Routledge, 2000, pp. 3-18.

To get a larger picture of the issues at stake when Singapore tries positioning itself as a "global city of the arts".

DESSER David, FU Poshek (editors), *The Cinema of Hong-kong. History, Arts, Identity*, Cambridge, Cambridge University Press, 2000, 333 p.

A good comparison point, just to know how the sister film industry of Hong Kong has been doing. Nothing much about Singapore, hence proving once more that the Singapore legacy in Hong Kong has long been forgotten.

DISSANAYAKE Wimal, "Cinema, Nation and Culture in Southeast Asia: Enframing a Relationship", in *East-West Film Journal*, vol. 6, n°2, July 1992, pp. 1-22.
Classically academic.

DISSANAYAKE Wimal, "Introduction: Nationhood, History and Cinema: Reflections on the Asian Scene", in DISSANAYAKE Wimal (editor), *Colonialism and Nationalism in Asian Cinema*, Indianapolis, Indianapolis University Press, 1994, pp. IX-XXIX.
Very stimulating in the way it addresses colonial and postcolonial issues, which are of course of significance to early Singapore cinema.

EF Yusnor, *P. Ramlee Yang Saya Kenal*, Subang Jaya, Pelanduk Publications, 2000, 149 p.
A personal and well-documented account of the life of P. Ramlee by someone who knew him closely.

ELLEY Derek, "12 Storeys", *Variety*, 9-15 June 1997, p. 71.
Just to show that the movie *12 Storeys* was not overlooked by major film journals.

GEORGE Cherian, *Singapore the Air-conditioned Nation: Essays on the Politics of Comfort and Control, 1990-2000*, Singapore, Landmark Books, 2000.
An excellent introduction to the politics of Singapore, with a very precise historical perspective.

GHANI Salleh, *Sejarah Filem Melayu*, Kuala Lumpur, Variapop Group, 1989, ix-134 p.

GOPINATHAN S., PAKIR Anne, HO Wah Kam, SARAVANAN Vanithamani (editors), *Language, Society and Education in Singapore. Issues and Trends*, Singapore, Eastern Universities Press (Times Publishing Ltd), 2003, 406 p.
A heavily academic collection of essays, giving a clear view of the multilingual issues that Singapore has had, and still has, to cope with.

HARDING James and SARJI Ahmad, *P. Ramlee. The Bright Star*, Kuala Lumpur, Pelanduk Publications M. Sdn Bhd, 2002, 294 p.
Everything on P. Ramlee. A highly detailed work with rare and interesting iconography.

HEIDT Erhard U., *Mass Media, Cultural Tradition, and National Identity: The Case of Singapore and its Television Programmes*, Saarbrucken, Breitenbach, 1987, 268 p.

HO Tzu Nyen, "The Afterimage — Traces of Otherness in Recent Singaporean Cinema ", to be published, 29 p.
A heavily academic study of *Mee Pok Man*, *12 Storeys*, *15* and *Zombie Dogs*, by one of the most stimulating of Singapore's experimental artists and filmmakers.

HUKILL Mark A., "Structures of Television in Singapore", in FRENCH David and RICHARDS Michael (editors), *Contemporary Television: Eastern Perspectives*, New Delhi, Sage, 1996, pp. 132-156.

KAHN Joel S. (editor), *Southeast Asian Identities: Culture and the Politics of Representation in Indonesia, Malaysia, Singapore and Thailand*, Singapore, Institute of Southeast Asian Studies, 1998.

KOH Siong Ling (editor), *Arts, Cultural and Media Scenes in Singapore*, Singapore, Ministry of Information and the Arts, 1998, 122 p.

KRISHNAN Pillay P., *Press and Film Censorship in Colonial Singapore 1915-1959*, Department of History, National University of Singapore, 1990, 88 p.

KUO Eddie, "Confucianism as Political Discourse in Singapore: The Case of an Incomplete Revitalisation Movement", in TU Wei-Ming (editor), *Confucian Traditions in East Asian Modernity: Moral Education and Economic Culture in Japan and the Four Mini Dragons*, Cambridge, Harvard University Press, 1996, pp. 108-132.
A good comparative analysis.

KWA Chong Guan, "Relating to the World: Images, Metaphors and Analogies", in DA CUNHA Derek (editor), *Singapore in the New Millenium: Challenges Facing the City-State*, Singapore, Institute of Southeast Asian Studies, 2002, pp. 108-132.

LACABA Jose F. (editor), *The Films of ASEAN*, ASEAN Committee of Culture and Information, 2000, 218 p.

LAI Chee Kien, "Singapore as Pictures", in LIM Jen Erh, NG Siang Ping (editors), *Eye é City — A Visual Account of the Last 24 Hours of 2002*, Singapore, Firstfruits Publications, 2003.
Singapore seen through movies from all over the world, including Wong Kar-wai's.

LENT John A., *The Asian Film Industry*, Austin, University of Texas Press, 1990, 309 p.
It has an interesting chapter titled "Malaysia and Singapore: The Asian Film Industry" at a time when nothing much was written about Singapore (perhaps because there was nothing much to write about).

LIM Kay Tong, *Cathay: 55 Years of Cinema*, Singapore, Landmark Books, 1991, 223 p.

A corporate book commissioned by Cathay Organisation on its very own stories. Slightly biased, but full of very rare pictures, and very precise corporate information and trivia.

LIM Poh Huat, *Confessions of a Struggling Actor*, Singapore, ChikuBooks, 2002, 160 p.

A very funny fantasy, through which one comes across local celebrities.

LOKE Wan Tho, *A Company of Birds*, London, M. Joseph Publ., 1958, 174 p.

The personal memoirs of Loke Wan Tho, including rare information about the time he had to flee from Singapore during the Japanese invasion.

MILLET Raphaël, *Le Cinéma de Singapour. Paradis perdu, doute existentiel, crise identitaire et mélancolie contemporaine*, Paris, L'Harmattan, 2003, 144 p.

MILLET Raphaël, "Royston Tan, le vrai faux doux rebelle", *Black Movie - Festival de films des autres mondes*, catalogue, February 2005, p.14-15.

MILLET Raphaël, "Singapour - Génération 65", *Cahiers du cinéma*, numéro hors-série *Atlas du cinéma*, April 2005, p.89-90.

MOHAMAD HATTA AZAD KHAN, *Malay Cinema (1948-1989): Early History and Development in the Making of a National Cinema*, Thesis (Ph.D) - School of Theatre and Film Studies, University of New South Wales, 1994, 359 p.

MUTALIB Hussain, "Singapore's Quest for a National Identity: The Triumphs and Trials of Government Policies ", in BAN Kah Choon, PAKIR Anne, CHEE Chee Kiong (editors), *Imagining Singapore*, Singapore, Times Academic Press, 1992, pp. 69-96.

ONG Terry, "Eat My Shorts", *I-S Magazine*, April 5-18, 2002, pp. 10-16.

Very good insight on short films produced from 2000 to 2002 in Singapore.

OOI Giok Ling, SHAW Brian J., *Beyond the Port City. Development and Identity in 21st Century* Singapore, Singapore, Pearson / Prentice Hall, 2004, 176 p.

Draws interesting perspectives on what Singapore will be in the coming years, and what role culture may play then.

OON Clarissa, "Cathay Goes Regional", *The Straits Times*, November 21, 2002.

How an old local major is trying to revive its strategies.

PAKIR Anne and TONG Chee Kiong, "The Making of National Culture in Singapore", in THUMBOO Edwin (editor), *Cultures in ASEAN and the 21st Century*, Singapore, UniPress for ASEAN-COCI , 1996. pp. 174-188.

PASHA Prem K., *The Krishnan Odyssey*, Kuala Lumpur, Nasarre, 2004, 155 p.

This vanity publication is an in-house production of the Krishnan family, the author being the son of L. Krishnan. It is rich in information about the long gone and forgotten early days of the Studio Era. It also contains many interesting, previously unreleased pictures of L. Krishnan.

PEDROLETTI Brice, "Lettre de Singapour ", *Les Cahiers du Cinéma*, November 2003, 47 p.

A rare French article on today's Singaporean film industry.

SARJI Ahmad, *P. Ramlee, Erti Yang Sakti*, Subang Jaya, Pelanduk Publications, 1999, 400 p.

This very useful encyclopaedia about the life of P. Ramlee and the people he has met and worked during his career is certainly one of the most important sources of information available on the golden age of Malay cinema.

SIDDIQUE Sophia, *Images of the City-Nation. Singapore Cinema in the 1990s*, Ph.D thesis, University of Southern California, 2001, 260 p.

Certainly one the most thorough studies ever conducted on recent Singapore cinema. Very academic, but written in a very accessible style. The author expresses strong articulated views, and opens new avenues to the understanding of Singapore-made movies.

SLATER Ben, *Kinda Hot. The Making of Saint Jack in Singapore*, Marshall Cavendish, Singapore, 2006, 240 p.

SULONG Jamil, *Kaca Permata. Memoir Seorang Pengarah*, Kuala Lumpur, Dewan Bahasa dan Pustaka, 1990, xi-345 p.

In this "Memoir of a Filmmaker", Jamil Sulong gives a detailed account of his days in the movie industry, from the early 1950s until the 1980s. One of the most useful and comprehensive sources of information. Direct from the horse's mouth, thus making it rather rare.

TAMAKI Matsuoka Kanda, *Ajia: Eiga No Miyako; Honkon - Indo Mubirodo*, Tokyo, Mekon, 1997.

Available only in Japanese, it focuses partly on the Malay movies made by Indian filmmakers.

TAN Hui Leng, *Picturing Singapore. Globalisation, National Identity, Film*, unpublished M.A in Cultural Studies, London, Goldsmiths College / University of London, 68 p.

TAN Sandi, "Singapore", in LACABA José F., *The Films of ASEAN*, Singapore, ASEAN Committee on Culture and Information, 2000, pp. 166-173.

A very opinionated essay by a film critic who is also a very opinionated short film director.

TAN Y.S. and SOH Y.P., *The Development of Singapore's Modern Media Industry*, Singapore, Times Academic Press, 1994.
Obsolete, but a useful source when it comes to researching development strategies Singapore was considering for its growing media industry in the early 1990s.

TAN Y.S. et al. (editors), *Arts, Cultural and Media Scenes*, Singapore, Ministry of Information and the Arts, 1998.

UHDE Jan and UHDE NG Yvonne, *Latent Images. Film in Singapore*, Singapore, Oxford University Press in collaboration with Ngee Ann Polytechnic, 2000, 249 p.
A pioneering work which many of us are indebted to. This is the first real book in English on Singapore cinema. It explores both the past and the present, and offers many useful facts and figures, thus paving the way for further research.

VAN DER HEIDE William, *Malaysian Cinema, Asian Film. Border Crossings and National Cultures*, Amsterdam, Amsterdam University Press, 2002, 301 p.
An unexpected college essay on Malaysian cinema, with extensive cross-cultural analysis. Very useful to aspiring film critics in the region.

WEE Brandon, "Severed Ties. Forgotten Singaporean Cinema Remembered", *Cinema Scope*, n°25, Winter 2006, pp.17-19.

WHITE Timothy, "Historical Poetics, Malaysian Cinema, and the Japanese Occupation", *KINEMA*, Fall 1996, pp. 5-23.
An academic essay by a researcher once based in Singapore, who took the time to dig into the long forgotten past.

WHITE Timothy, "Pontianaks, P. Ramlee and Islam: the Cinema of Malaysia", *The Arts*, Centre for the Arts, National University of Singapore, June 1997, n°4, p. 18.
A very good cross-genre study focusing on the foundations of Malay cinema.

WHITE Timothy, "When Singapore was Southeast Asia's Hollywood", *The Arts 5*, December 1997, pp. 21-24.

WONG Ain-ling, *The Cathay Story*, Hong Kong, Hong Kong Film Archive, 2002, 416 p.
This huge collection of articles is more focused on the Chinese movies made by Cathay's Hong Kong branch, MP&GI, than on Malay movies made by Cathay-Keris, which is addressed in only one essay.

WONG Ain-ling, *The Shaw Screen*, Hong Kong, Hong Kong Film Archive, 2003, 444 p.

The Malaysian Kinema Review, International Publishing Bureau, Singapore, vol. II, 9, August-September 1920.
A shortlived specialised magazine on film, focusing mostly on Western productions, since there was nothing else at that time anyway.

Cathay Classics Film Library. A Catalogue of Digitally Restored Titles as of 2002, Singapore, 52 p.
It is only about Cathay's films produced by its Hong Kong branch, MP&GI. But it just makes you want to watch more and more movies ...

Webography

Asian Film Archive
www.asianfilmarchive.org

Filem Malaysia
www.filemkita.com

Hong Kong Film Archive
www.lcsd.gov.hk/ce/culturalservice/hkfa/

Media Development Authority of Singapore
www.mda.gov.sg

P. Ramlee Cyber Museum
www.p-ramlee.com

Screen Singapore
www.screensingapore.com

Singapore Film Commission
www.sfc.org.sg

Singapore Film Society
www.sfs.org.sg

Singapore International Film Festival
www.filmfest.org.sg

Southeast Asian Cinematheque
www.theseac.com

Index

Note: Numbers in italic denote illustrations

Picture Credits

A description has been provided within brackets where there are multiple pictures from different organisations or individuals on the same page.

Alliance Entertainment Singapore Pte Ltd:
96 (*The Teenage Textbook Movie*)

Alliance Entertainment Singapore Pte Ltd
and Glen Goei:
96 (*Forever Fever*)

Boku Films Pte Ltd:
97, 98

Cages Pte Ltd:
113

Cathay-Keris Films Pte Ltd:
11 (*Hang Jebat, Sumpah Pontianak*), 22, 23, 26, 32, 33, 34, 35 (Cameraman, Cathay-Keris studio), 36 (Noordin Ahmad), 37 (S. Roomai Noor, Siput Sarawak), 41, 43, 44, 45 (*Dendam Pontianak, Pontianak Gua Musang, Sumpah Pontianak*), 51 (*Dang Anom*), 52, 53, 54, 55, 56 (Choo Kok Leong and Lee Kuan Yew, *Air Hostess*), 63, 66, 67, 93 (Sheikh Haikel and Choo Meileen), 122, 123, 124, 125, 129, 130, 131, 132, 133, 135, 137, 138, 146

Concorde-New Horizons:
77

Ho Tzu Nyen:
108 (*Utama — Every Name in History is I*)

Joseph Lee:
115

June Chua:
107 (*The Usher*)

Martyn See:
113 (*Zahari's 17 Years*)

MediaCorp Raintree Pictures:
8, 88, 90 (*I Not Stupid*), 92
and Applause Pictures: 95
and Film Unlimited: 101, 149
and Media Asia Films: 102
and Presto Films: 12, 90 (*Homerun*), 91, 141
and Scorpio East Pictures: 142
and Singapore Film Commission: 94, 140
and Media Development Authority,
One Last Dance Productions: 99

National Archives of Singapore:
16, 19, 25

National Museum of Singapore,
National Heritage Board:
14, 50 (*Pendekar Bujang Lapok*)

Overseas Movie Pte Ltd:
89 (*Lucky Number*)

Purrfect Nine:
108 (*Locust*)

School of Film & Media Studies, Ngee Ann Polytechnic:
107 (*G-23*)

Sandi Tan:
104

Shaw Organisation, Singapore:
jacket back, 11 (*Tiga Abdul*), 17, 18, 29 (Screenlogo of Shaw's Malay Film Productions), 30, 35 (Shaw studio, Lab processing), 36 (*Hang Tuah*), 37 (Jins Shamsudin), 38, 39 (*Ali Baba Bujang Lapok*), 40, 42, 47, 48 (*Anak-ku Sazali, Seniman Bujang Lapok*), 49, 61, 62, 65, 126, 127, 128, 134, 136, 150

Singapore International Film Festival:
80, 81

Wee Li Lin:
105, 106

Working Man Films Pte Ltd:
jacket front, 13, 109, 110

Zhao Wei Films:
78, 82, 83, 84, 85, 86, 87, 89 (*Liang Po Po*), 111, 112

Private collections

Clarence Anthony:
31 Copyright Shaw Organisation, Singapore

Doris Young:
9, 68, 73, 74, 75, 139

Joo Lan Berry:
56 (*Yi Sui*)

Ow Yung Mun:
57 (Kong Ngee logo), 59 (*Romance of a Nyonya*), 148

Peter Chong:
10, 70, 71

Ramanathan family:
39 (S. Ramanathan)

Wong Han Min:
29 (*Hua Jiao Shue Liu*), 58, 59 (*Peranakan Nonya*), 60, 144;
56 and 57 (*Shi Zi Cheng*) Copyright Cathay-Keris Films Pte Ltd;
72 (*The Two Sides of the Bridge*) Copyright Overseas Movie Pte Ltd;
45 (*Anak Pontianak*) and 46 Copyright Shaw Organisation, Singapore.

Every effort has been made to trace the copyright holders and we apologise for any unintentional omissions. We would be pleased to insert the appropriate acknowledgements in any subsequent edition of this publication.